THE HILLS OF HOME

INSIGHT
GUIDES

SCOTLAND

Edited and Produced by Brian Bell

APA
PUBLICATIONS

SCOTLAND

Second Edition (Reprint)
© 1990 APA PUBLICATIONS (HK) LTD
All Rights Reserved
Printed in Singapore by Höfer Press Pte. Ltd

ABOUT THIS BOOK

Robert Louis Stevenson, the Edinburgh author of *Treasure Island* and *Dr. Jekyll and Mr. Hyde*, would not have been popular with the Scottish Tourist Board. "For all who love shelter and the blessings of the sun," he wrote, "who hate dark weather and perpetual tilting against squalls, there could scarcely be found a more unhomely and harassing place of residence." Still, Edingburgh and Scotland continue to enchant millions of visitors. Emulating Stevenson's honesty, *Insight Guide: Scotland* paints a realistic portrait of Scotland today.

The award-winning *Insight Guides* series began in 1970 with a colourful book on Bali, put together by **Hans Höfer**, a West German photographer and disciple of the Bauhaus tradition. The success of his novel design, combining top-quality photography with "insightful" text, soon blossomed into the Singapore-based Apa Publications, whose guides now cover countries and cities on every continent.

Brian Bell, the project editor for *Insight Guide: Scotland*, first became involved with Apa through writing a chapter of *Insight Guide: Great Britain* and went on to edit Apa guides to the Channel Islands and to his native Ireland. A London-based journalist with wide experience in newspapers and magazines, he believes a country's wants should not be omitted from a guide book; they can be as interesting as its beauty spots and make it more enticing to the adventurous traveller.

This view is endorsed by **George Rosie**, one of the guide's leading contributors, who began his career in Dundee with D.C. Thomson, a company that turns out newspapers and children's comics. Rosie moved to London and joined the *Sunday Times* in 1974, he returned to Scotland to write about it for the *Sunday Times*.

"In many ways," says Rosie, "Scotland is the most infuriating place in Europe–a slightly dotty 'nearly country' with its own system of law, education, established church and civil service unsupervised by any elected assembly and with no politics of its own. There are times when its very core seems to consist of a mush of bad history and sentimental song. But then I find myself on a snow-battered ridge on the Cairngorm Mountains, or helicoptering out to a North Sea oil platform, or lurching across the Minch in a fishing boat, or being dazzled by some benign and subtle point of Scots law, and I suddenly realise that no other part of the UK–not even London itself–has so much to offer."

Julie Davidson, who wrote five of the 'Places' chapters, is another Scottish journalist who has made her mark in Britain's national media. She thinks it's ideal to be able to earn part of her income in London without having to live there and cannot imagine living anywhere else other than Scotland.

One man who has done far than most to fight the myths is the author of the "Highlanders and Lowlanders" chapter, **Christopher Smout**, whose masterly two-volume *History of the Scottish People* appealed equally to both academic and general readers. Although English by birth, he has lived in Scotland since 1959 and is Professor of Scottish History at the University of St. Andrews. "All my working life," he says, "has been a investigation of the social and economic aspects of the Scottish past while living through three decades of the Scottish present. Scotland still seems to me the most beautiful country in Europe, and the Scots among the kindest people I have met. In 30

Bell

Rosie

Davidson

Smout

May

years the country has become rather more prosperous, much more unified by good roads, gained a flashy Glasgow and lost a certain amount of solid distinctiveness."

Yet, many Scots choose to live elsewhere. **Naomi May**, who wrote the chapter on Presbyterianism, was born in Glasgow, grew up in the southwest county of Renfrewshire and now lives in London. A novelist and artist, she recalls that her favourite subject at school, Scottish history, had all the right ingredients: feuds, murder, revenge, intrigue and fierce defiance of the Sassenachs (English).

Marcus Brooke, who contributed several chapters and a selection of photographs, exiled himself even further away from his native Scotland in Singapore. Since 1964, armed with typewriter and cameras, he has travelled the world pursuing his interest in archaeology and anthropology and contributing to a wide variety of newspapers and magazines.

There's a less dour side to that character, of course, brought out in the "Song and Dance" chapter by **Alastair Clark**. Not only has he written a regular music column for *The Scotsman* for the past 20 years, but he has also been deeply involved in the country's musical life as a musician.

Conrad Wilson, author of the Food chapter, writes about food and wine for *The Scotsman,* and is also the paper's music critic.

Stuart Ridsdale, who explored the Borders for this guide, could be called a near-Scot; although recent generations of his family have hailed from Yorkshire in England, earlier antecedents can be found in the tiny Northumberland village of Ridsdale. Ridsdale is a writer for a London public relations firm.

Roland Collins, another contributor to the 'Places' section, did the next best thing to being born north of the border: he married a Scot. After a long career in advertising, he now devotes time to his painting and photography. Seen through his eyes, "watering from peat smoke," Scotland's rugged individuality is the natural child of the largely inhospitable Highlands and a punishing climate.

Dymphna Bryne, a travel journalist who has written books on camping and on Israel, became interested in the Hebridean islands during camping holidays on mainland Scotland with her husband and three sons.

Cowan Ervine, who assembled the Travel Tips section and wrote the panel on Scottish law, is a Northern Irishman who has lived in Scotland for 16 years and teaches law at the University of Perth.

The photographs for *Insight Guide: Scotland* came from many sources, and were ably assembled by **Judy Lehane**, a London-based Scot and the author of a book on the Hebridean island of Eigg. But one name dominates the credit list: **Douglas Corrance**, an Edinburgh-based photographer now in demand internationally. His career began on an Inverness newspaper. He spent 11 years as the Scottish Tourist Board's principal photographer, building a library of 80,000 pictures, and has produced books on Glasgow and Edinburgh.

Should auld acquaintance be forgot, Apa Publications would like to raise a glass to the many people who helped in the compilation of this guide. Especially valuable assistance came from **Caledonian MacBrayne, Eddie Holmes** of the Scottish Tourist Board, **Libby Weir Breen** of the Shetland Tourist Organisation, **Jane Johnson** of the Oban, Mull and District Tourist Board, and **Peter Northfield** of British Rail.

—Apa Publications

Brooke

Wilson

Collins

Bryne

Ervine

CONTENTS

FEATURES

MAPS

TRAVEL TIPS

MEN
WORKING
OVERHEAD

THE SCOTTISH CHARACTER

A native of Scotland, it has been said, considers himself a Scot before he thinks of himself as a human being, thus establishing a clear order of excellence. This attitude, naturally enough, wins him few popularity points from the rest of the human race and none at all from his nearest neighbour, England. Indeed, English literature is so peppered with anti-Scots aphorisms that the cumulative impression given amounts to national defamation.

"I have been trying all my life to like Scotchmen," wrote the essayist Charles Lamb, "and am obliged to desist from the experiment in despair." P.G. Wodehouse was no kinder: "It is never difficult," he wrote, "to distinguish between a Scotsman with a grievance and a ray of sunshine." And Dr. Samuel Johnson, whose tour of the Hebrides in 1773 was immortalised by his Scottish biographer James Boswell, produced the most enduring maxim: "The noblest prospect that a Scotchman ever sees is the high road that leads him to England."

Shotgun marriage: It is a road that many have taken: an estimated 20 million Scots, one of the most inventive peoples on earth, are scattered throughout every continent—four times as many as live in Scotland itself. Yet an unease towards the English, a suspicion that they are his social superiors, has blighted the Scots psyche for centuries. The union of the two countries in 1707, after centuries of sporadic hostility, was regarded by most Scots as a shotgun marriage and more than 280 years have scarcely diluted the differences in outlook and attitude between the ill-matched partners.

In 1987, for instance, Margaret Thatcher led Britain's Conservative Party to a third successive election victory, winning a commanding number of constituencies in the south of England particularly; yet in Scotland, where she was seen as an unsympa-

thetic English figure, she won fewer than one in four of the votes cast and held only 10 of the 72 Scottish seats in the House of Commons. It was a devastating rejection and talk began once again of giving Scotland back its separate parliament. Yet, as so often before, the alienation failed to find a political focus. People recalled the frustratingly indecisive result of a 1979 referendum which asked the Scots whether they really wanted a devolved government: a third said yes, a

third said no, and the remaining third didn't bother to vote.

Although they couldn't agree on a solution, the Scots were unanimous in identifying who had caused the problem: England. It was an old tune, often played. When the future Pope Pius II visited the country in the 15th century, he concluded: "Nothing pleases the Scots more than abuse of the English."

In that respect, the Scots resemble England's other close neighbours, the French, with whom they have intimate historical connections. Both share an outspokenness, which the English mistake for

Preceding pages: Jazz at the Edinburgh Festival; Edinburgh Castle from Princes Street Gardens; road-mending squad in Lanark; Orkney airport; a Lanark glen. Left, Blackness Castle. Right, farmer at Dunbar.

rudeness. Both are proud peoples, a characteristic which, in the case of the Scots, the English translate into ingratitude. "You Scots," the playwright J.M. Barrie once had one of his characters say, "are such a mixture of the practical and the emotional that you escape out of an Englishman's hand like a trout." Barrie, the creator of Peter Pan, was a Scot himself and often cast a cynical eye over his fellow countrymen. "There are few more impressive sights in the world," he declared, "than a Scotsman on the make."

It is noticeable that the butt of most of these waspish epigrams is the Scots *man*. Until recently, women, though no less strong in character, played a subsidiary role in the

man was deemed inherently better than the next—and that included the clergy, who were made directly answerable to their congregations. This democratic tradition, allied with a taste for argument born of theological wrangling, runs deep and has led more than one English politician to brand troublesome Glasgow shipyard workers, for example, as Communists. Some might have been; but most were simply exercising their right to be individualists. It was an attitude that would allow a riveter to regard himself as being every bit as good as the shipyard boss and, whenever necessary, to remind the boss of that fact. Deference? What's that?

In many other ways, too, the Scots charac-

country's public affairs. It was very much a man's world. Therefore, although Scottish law introduced desertion as grounds for divorce in 1573 (364 years before England got around to doing so), it retained a robust, Calvinistic view about what wives ought to put up with.

Certainly, the Calvinist tradition is central to the Scots character. While England absorbed the Reformation with a series of cunning compromises, Scotland underwent a revolution, replacing the panoply of Roman Catholicism with an austere Presbyterianism designed to put the ordinary people directly in touch with their God. No

ter is a confusing one. It combines dourness and humour, meanness and generosity, arrogance and tolerance, cantankerousness and chivalry, sentimentality and hard-headedness. One aspect of these contradictions is caught by a *Punch* cartoon showing a hitchhiker trying to entice passing motorists with a sign reading "Glasgow—or else!" On the positive side, a bad climate and a poor soil forged an immensely practical people. But there was a price to be paid: these disadvantages also encouraged frugality and a deepseated pessimism. "It could be worse" comes easily to the lips of the most underprivileged.

The situation is redeemed by laughter. Scottish humour is subtle and sardonic and, in the hands of someone as verbally inventive as Billy Connolly, today's best-known comedian, can leave reality far behind with a series of outrageously surreal non-sequiturs. It has also been used, over the years, to cement many a Scottish stereotype. "My father was an Aberdonian," the veteran comedian Chic Murray would say, "and a more generous man you couldn't wish to meet. I have a gold watch that belonged to my father, he sold it to me on his death bed...so I wrote him a cheque."

Alcohol features prominently in Scottish jokes, as it does in many aspects of the pubs. Experience suggests that the worst of them could be taken by the Red Army in three days, a day-and-a-half if tactical nuclear weapons were used."

Like the Irish, the Scots have realised that there's money to be made from conforming to a stereotyped image, however bogus it may be. Although few in Scotland ever eat haggis (once described as looking like a castrated bagpipe), it is offered to tourists as the national dish. Heads of ancient Scottish clans, living in houses large enough to generate cashflow problems, have opened their houses to tour groups of affluent Americans. Others have opened "clan shops" retailing a variety of tartan artefacts, including Hairy

country's life. Until recently the single-minded aim of Scottish pubs was to enable their clientele to get drunk as fast as possible, a purpose reflected in their decor. "Some of them," wrote the journalist Hugh McIlvanney, "are so bare that anyone who wants to drink in sophisticated surroundings takes his glass into the lavatory." Matters have improved, though some hostelries should still be approached with caution. "There is," wrote McIlvanney, "a relentless inclination to exaggerate the toughness of Glasgow

Left, a pub in Jedburgh. Above, comedian Billy Connolly.

Haggisburger soft toys. Still others have taken to appearing in Japanese TV commercials extolling their "family brand" of whisky. The cult of the kilt—based, someone mused, on the self-deception that male knees are an erogenous zone—is a huge commercial success.

But the image obscures the real Scotland. It's worth lingering long enough to draw back the tartan curtain and get to know one of Europe's most complex peoples. There's no guarantee that the more innocent tourists won't have the wool pulled over their eyes; but, if it's any consolation to them, it's sure to be best-quality Scottish wool.

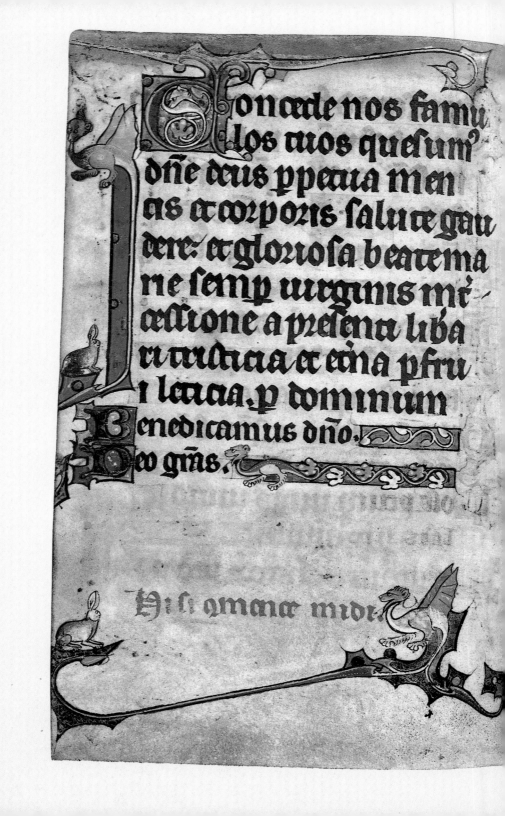

Concede nos famulos tuos quesumus dñe deus perpetua mentis et corporis salute gaudere: et gloriosa beate marie semp virginis intercessione a presenti liberari tristicia et eterna perfrui leticia. p dominum

Benedicamus dño.
Deo grãs.

Hic omnes nichil

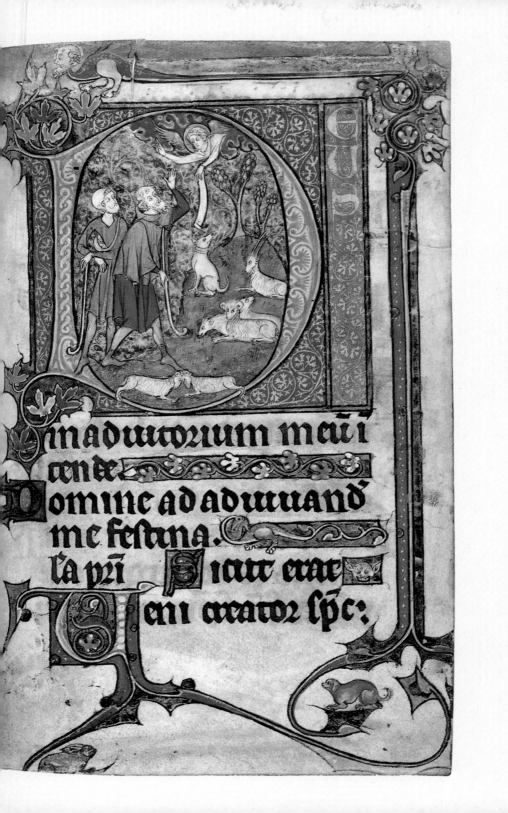

madiutozium meū i
tende.
Domine ad adiuuand
me festina.
ta pīī Sicut erat
eni creatoz spc:

On a bleak, windswept moor three witches crouch round a bubbling cauldron, muttering oaths and prophesying doom. A king is brutally stabbed to death and his killer, consumed by vaulting ambition, takes the throne, only to be murdered himself soon afterwards. "Fair is foul, and foul is fair."

To many people, these images from Shakespeare's Macbeth are their first introduction to early Scottish history. But of course, the Scots will tell you, Shakespeare was English and, as usual, the English got it wrong. There is perhaps some truth to the tale, they admit—Macbeth, who reckoned he had a better hereditary claim to the throne than its occupant, did kill Duncan in 1040—but thereafter he ruled well for 17 years and kept the country relatively prosperous.

Power games: Where Shakespeare undeniably showed his genius, however, was in managing to heighten the narrative of a history that was already (and remained) melodramatic beyond belief. Scotland's story was for centuries little more than the biographies of ruthlessly ambitious families jostling for power, gaining it and losing it through accidents of royal marriages, unexpected deaths and lack of fertility. A successful king needed cunning as well as determination, an ability to judge just how far he could push powerful barons without being toppled from his throne in the process. Future marriage contracts were routinely made between royal infants and, when premature death brought a succession of kings to the throne as children, the land's leading families fought for advancement by trying to gain control over the young rulers, occasionally by kidnapping them.

Summarise some of the stories and they seem more histrionic than historical. A sexy young widow returns from the French court to occupy the throne of Scotland, lays claim to the throne of England, conducts a series of

Preceding pages: an Arinacrinachd weaver; "_The Annunciation to the Shepherds_" from the early 14th-century Murthly Book of Hours. Left, Romans building Hadrian's Wall.

passionate affairs, marries her lover a few weeks after he has allegedly murdered her second husband, loses the throne, is incarcerated for 19 years by her cousin, the Queen of England, and is then, on a pretext, beheaded. No soap-opera scriptwriter today would dare to invent as outrageous a plot as the true-life story of Mary Queen of Scots.

Nameless peoples: Our earliest knowledge of Scotland dates back 6,000 years, when the cold, wet climate and the barren landscape would seem familiar enough to a time-traveller from the present day. Then, the region was inhabited by nameless hunters and fishermen. Later, the mysterious Beaker People from Holland and the Rhine-

Grampian Mountains and the dense forests of central Scotland united the tribes in opposition. To their surprise, the Romans, who called the natives "painted men", encountered fearsome opposition. An early Scots leader, called Calgacus by the Romans, rallied 30,000 men—a remarkable force but no match for the Roman war machine. Even so, the Romans respected their enemy's ability enough for the historian Tacitus to feel able to attribute to Calgacus the anti-Roman sentiment: "They make a wilderness and call it peace."

Soon, however, the "barbarians" began to perfect guerrilla tactics. In the year 118, for instance, the Ninth Legion marched north to

land settled here, as they did in Ireland, leaving as a memorial only a few tantalising pots. Were the eerie Standing Stones of Callanish, on the island of Lewis, built by them as a primitive observatory? Nobody can be certain. Celtic tribes, driven by their enemies to the outer fringes of Europe, settled in Scotland, as they did in Ireland, Cornwall, Wales and Brittany, and mastered iron implements. The blueprint for a tribal society was in place.

It was the Romans who gave it coherence. The desire of Emperor Vespasian in AD 80 to forge northwards from an already subjugated southern Britain towards the

quell yet another rebellion and was never seen again. Was it really worth all this trouble, the Romans wondered, to subdue such barbarians? Hadrian's answer, as emperor, was no. He built a fortified wall for 73 miles across the north of England, isolating the savages. A successor, Antoninus, tried to push back the boundaries in 142 by erecting a fortified wall on the Forth and the Clyde. But it was never an effective exercise. The Roman Empire fell without ever conquering these troublesome natives and Scottish life carried on without the benefits of Roman civilisation, such as good roads. A complex clan system evolved, consisting of large families bound by blood ties.

Europe's Dark Ages enveloped the region. What records remain portray raiders riding south to plunder and pillage. True Scots were born in the 6th century as Gaels migrated from the north of Ireland, inaugurating an epoch in which beautifully drawn manuscripts and brilliant metalwork illuminated the cultural darkness. As with much of Western Europe, Scotland's history at this time was a catalogue of invasions. The most relentless aggressors were the Vikings, who arrived in the 9th century in their Scandinavian longships to loot the monasteries founded by early Christian missionaries such as St. Ninian and St. Columba.

and was eventually killed in turn by Duncan's son.

Norman conquest: The collapse of England to William the Conqueror in 1066 drove many English lords northwards, turning the Lowlands of Scotland into an aristocratic refugee camp. Scotland's king, Malcolm, married one of the refugees, Margaret, a Hungarian-born Christian reformer. She drew her standards from England and, some believe, gave Scots their eternal inferiority complex by forcing them to measure themselves constantly against the English. Partly to please her, Malcolm invaded England twice. During the second incursion, he lost his life. This gave William Rufus, the

Eventually, in 843, the warring Picts, a fierce Celtic race who dominated the southwest, and the Scots united under Kenneth MacAlpin, the astute ruler of the west coast Kingdom of Dalriada. But Edinburgh wasn't brought under the king's influence until 962 and the Angles, a Teutonic people who controlled the south of the country, were not subjugated until 1018. Feuding for power was continuous. It was in this period that Macbeth murdered his rival, Duncan,

Left, Roman panel from Glasgow's Hunterian Museum. Above, William Wallace rallies the Scots against the English.

Conqueror's son and successor, an opportunity to involve himself in Scottish affairs by securing the northern throne for Malcolm's eldest son, Edgar, the first of a series of weak kings. A successor, David I, having been brought up in England, gave many estates to his Norman friends. Also, he did nothing to stop English replacing Gaelic and he introduced feudalism into the Lowlands.

But true feudalism never really took root. French knights, accustomed to deference, were surprised to find, when they rode through a field of crops, that the impertinent peasants would demand compensation. Although the Normans greatly influenced architecture and language, they in no sense conquered the country. Instead, they helped create a social division that was to dominate Scotland's history: the Lowlands were controlled by noblemen who spoke the same Norman French and subscribed to the same values as England's ruling class, while the Highlands remained untamed, under the influence of independent-minded Gaelic speakers, and the islands were vaguely loyal to Norway. The Highland clans, indeed, were virtually independent kingdoms, whose chiefs, under the old patriarchal system, had the power of life and death over their people. Feuds between clans were frequent and bloody, provoking one visiting

scholar to pronounce: "The Scots are not industrious and the people are poor. They spend all their time in wars and, when there is no war, they fight one another."

Over the next three centuries the border with England was to be constantly redefined. The seaport of Berwick upon Tweed, now the most northerly town in England, was to change hands 13 times. In the 1160s the Scots turned to French sympathisers for help, concluding what came to be known as the Auld Alliance. In later years the pact would have a profound influence on Scottish life, but on this occasion it was no match for England's might.

After a comparatively peaceful interlude, England's insidious interference provoked a serious backlash in 1297. William Wallace, a violent youth from Paisley, became an outlaw after a scuffle with English soldiers in which a girl (some think she was his wife) who helped him escape was killed by the Sheriff of Lanark. Wallace returned to kill the Sheriff, but didn't stop there; soon he had raised enough of an army to drive back the English forces, making him for some months master of southern Scotland. But he wasn't supported by the nobles, who considered him low-born, and, after being defeated at Falkirk by England's Edward I (the "Hammer of the Scots"), he met his expected fate by being hanged, drawn and quartered.

Bruce's victory: The next challenger, Robert the Bruce, who was descended from the Norman de Brus family, got further as a freedom fighter—as far as the throne itself, in fact, though he didn't sit on it long. During a year's exile on Rathlin Island, off the coast of Ireland, he is said to have been inspired by the persistence of a spider in a cave and he returned to Scotland to win a series of victories. Soon the French recognised him as King of Scotland and the Roman Catholic Church gave him its backing. England's new king, Edward II, although he had little stomach for Scottish affairs, could not ignore the challenge and, in 1314, the two forces collided at Bannockburn, south of Stirling. Bruce's chances looked slim: he was pitching only 6,000 men against 20,000 English. But he was shrewd enough to hold the high ground, forcing the English into the wet marshes, and he won.

Because the Pope did not recognise the new monarch, Bruce's subjects successfully petitioned Rome, and the Declaration of Arbroath in 1320 confirmed him as King.

Like the Romans, England's Edward III decided that Scotland was more trouble than it was worth and in 1328 granted it independence. He recognised Bruce as king and, cementing the treaty in the customary manner, married his young sister to Bruce's baby son. Peace had been achieved at last between two of the most rancorous of neighbours. It seemed too good to be true—and it was.

Left, Robert the Bruce's statue in Stirling. Right, Bruce kills Sir Henry de Bohun in single combat at Bannockburn.

Bruce brought his axe crashing down upon the head of Bohun

Robert Bruce sends a defiance to Edward III.

BATTLE FOR THE THRONE

The outbreak in 1339 of the intermittent Hundred Years War between England and France kept Edward III's mind off Scotland. He failed, therefore, to appreciate the significance of a pact concluded in 1326 between France and Scotland by Robert the Bruce. Yet the Auld Alliance, as the pact came to be known, was to keep English ambitions at bay for centuries and at one point almost resulted in Scotland becoming a province of France.

Principal beneficiaries of the deal were the kings of the Stewart (or Stuart) family. Taking their name from their function as High Stewarts to the king, they were descended from the Fitzalans, Normans who came to England with William the Conqueror in 1066. When the Bruce family failed to produce a male heir, the crown passed in 1371 to the Stewarts because Marjorie, Robert the Bruce's daughter, had married Walter Fitzalan. The first of the Stewarts, Robert II, immediately encountered a problem that was to plague his successors: he had constantly to look over his shoulder at England, yet he could never ignore another threat to his power—his own dissident barons and warring chieftains.

Stabbed to death: His son, as Robert III, trusted these ambitious men so little that he sent his oldest son, James, to France for safety. But the ship carrying him was waylaid and young James fell into the hands of England's Henry IV. He grew up in the English court and didn't return to Scotland (as James I) until 1422, at the age of 29. His friendliness with the English was soon strained to breaking point, however, and he renewed the Auld Alliance, siding with France's Charles VII and Joan of Arc against the English. But soon James was murdered, stabbed to death before his wife by his uncle, a cousin and another noble. His son, James II, succeeded at the age of six, setting another Stewart pattern: monarchs who came to the throne as minors, creating what has

Left, Edward III is defied by Robert the Bruce. Right, Edward III takes Berwick in 1333.

been called an infantile paralysis of the power structure. In 1460 James, fighting to recapture Roxburgh from the English, died when one of his own siege guns exploded. James III, another boy king, succeeded. He had time to marry a Danish princess (in the process bringing the Norse islands of Orkney and Shetland into the realm) before he was locked in Edinburgh Castle by the scheming barons and replaced by his more malleable younger brother. The arrange-

ment didn't last and soon James's son, James IV, was crowned king, aged 15.

This latest James cemented relations with England in 1503 by marrying Margaret Tudor, the 12-year-old daughter of Henry VII, the Welsh warrior who had usurped the English throne 18 years before. The harmony was short-lived: the French talked James into attacking England and he was killed at the battle of Flodden Hill. It was Scotland's worst-ever defeat at English hands, wiping out the cream of a generation, and some argue that the country never recovered from the blow. James's heir, predictably, was also called James and was just over a year old. The power-brokers could continue plotting.

James V entered legend by posing as a commoner to find out how his people really lived. He also carried on the unceasing battle against the cattle rustlers who controlled the border areas. Torn between the French connection and the ambitions of England's Henry VIII who tried to enrol him in his anti-Catholic campaign, James declared his loyalties by marrying two Frenchwomen in succession. Life expectation was short, however, for kings as well as for peasants, and James V died in 1542 just as his queen, Marie de Guise, gave birth to a daughter. At less than a week old, the infant was pro-

turely, and Mary made a will bequeathing Scotland to France if she died childless.

When the King of France died in 1558, Mary, still only 16, ascended the throne with her husband. Her ambitions, though, didn't end there: she later declared herself Queen of England as well, basing her claim on the Catholic assumption that England's new queen, Elizabeth I, was illegitimate because her father, the much married Henry VIII, had been a heretic.

Forged in fire: This bid for power set alarm bells ringing among Protestants. Their faith had been forged in fire, with early preachers such as George Wishart burned at the stake, and it contained little room for compromise.

claimed Mary Queen of Scots.

Ever an opportunist, Henry VIII despatched an invasion force which reduced Edinburgh, apart from its castle, to rubble. It was known as a "Rough Wooing" and left hatred that would last for centuries. The immediate question was: should Scotland ally itself with Catholic France or Protestant England? In the ensuing tug-of-war between the English and the French, the infant Mary was taken to France for safety and, when 15, married the French Dauphin. The Auld Alliance seemed to have taken on a new life. "France and Scotland are now one country," declared Henry II of France, rather prema-

The Protestants' visionary was John Knox, a magnetic speaker and former priest whose aim, inspired by Calvinism, was to drive Catholicism out of Scotland completely. His followers had burgeoned into a popular movement, pledging themselves by signing the First Covenant to "forsake and renounce the congregation of Satan", and carrying Calvin's doctrines to extremes by outlawing the Latin Mass completely throughout Scotland.

Mary Queen of Scots (who preferred the "Stuart" spelling of her dynastic name) shared none of the austere values of Knox's brethren. When her husband died in 1560, she returned to Scotland, a vivacious, wilful and sexy woman. It was hard to remember that she was still a teenager—except when it came to her judgement in choosing men. She married a Catholic, Henry Darnley, who was by contemporary accounts an arrogant, pompous and effeminate idler, and soon she began spending more and more time with her secretary David Rizzio, an Italian. When Rizzio was stabbed to death in front of her, Darnley was presumed to be responsible, but who could prove it? Mary appeared to turn back to Darnley and, a few months later, gave birth to a son. Immediately afterwards, however, Darnley himself was murdered, his strangled remains found in a building

queen, still only 24, to abdicate, locking her in an island castle on Loch Leven. Bothwell fled to Norway, where he died in exile. And so, in 1567, another infant king came to the throne: Mary's son, James VI.

Still fact rivalled fiction. Mary escaped from Loch Leven, tried unsuccessfully to reach France, then threw herself on the mercy of her cousin, Elizabeth I, in London. Her previous claim to the English throne, however, had not been forgotten. Elizabeth, adopting the motto "strike or be sticken", offered her the bleak hospitality of the Tower of London, where she remained a prisoner for the next 20 years. In 1587 she was convicted, on somewhat flimsy evi-

reduced to rubble by an explosion. Mary and her current favourite, James Hepburn, Earl of Bothwell, were presumed responsible—but again, who could prove it?

Bothwell, a Protestant, quickly divorced his wife and, with few fanfares, became Mary's third husband, three months after Darnley's death. Few writers of fiction would have dared concoct such an audacious scenario, but even Mary had gone too far this time. Protestant Scotland forced its Catholic

Left, Robert Herdman's portrait of the execution of Mary Queen of Scots. Above, Scottish border raiders; and James I.

dence, of plotting Elizabeth's death and was beheaded.

Her son, by this time secure on the Scottish throne, made little more than a token protest. Because Elizabeth, the Virgin Queen, had no heir, James had his sights set on a far greater prize than Scotland could offer: the throne of England. On March 27, 1603, he learned that the prize was his. On hearing of Elizabeth's death, he set out for London, and was to set foot in Scotland only once more in his life.

Final slight: Scots have speculated ever since about how differently history would have turned out had James VI of Scotland made Edinburgh rather than London his base when he became James I of England. But he was more in sympathy with the divine right of kings than with the notions of the ultra-democratic Presbyterians, who were demanding a strong say in civil affairs. Also, James was no John Knox: London was a warmer, drier, more comfortable place and offered a rather wider selection of civilised entertainment. And, as he wrote, ruling from a distance of 400 miles was so much easier.

His son Charles succeeded to the throne in 1625, not knowing Scotland at all. Without, therefore, realising the consequences, the absentee king tried to harmonise the forms of church service between the two countries.

swiftly to civil war. At first the Scottish Covenanters (so named because of their support for the National Covenant of 1638) backed Parliament and the Roundhead forces of Oliver Cromwell; their hope was that a victorious Parliament would introduce compulsory Presbyterianism in English and Irish churches as well as in Scotland. Soon the Roundheads began to outpace the Cavalier supporters of the king. Charles, becoming desperate, tried to gain the Scots' support by promising a three-year trial for Presbyterianism in England. But his time had run out: he was beheaded on Jan. 30, 1649.

Charles's execution came as a terrible shock north of the border. How dare England

The Scots would have none of it: religious riots broke out and one bishop is said to have conducted his service with two loaded pistols placed in front of him. A National Covenant was organised, pledging faith to "the true religion" and affirming the unassailable authority in spiritual matters of the powerful General Assembly of the Church of Scotland. Armed conflict soon followed: in 1639 the Scots invaded northern England, forcing Charles to negotiate.

Soon the king's luck ran out in England too. Needing money, he unwisely called together his parliament for the first time in 10 years. A power struggle ensued, leading

kill the king of Scotland without consulting the Scots! Many turned to Charles's 18-year-old son, who had undertaken not to oppose Presbyterianism, and he was proclaimed Charles II in Edinburgh. But Cromwell won a decisive victory at the Battle of Dunbar and turned Scotland into an occupied country, abolishing its separate parliament.

Rotten judgement: By the time the monarchy was restored in 1660, Charles II had lost interest in Scotland's religious aspirations and removed much of the Presbyterian church's power. Violent intolerance stalked the land during his reign and the 1680s became known as the Killing Time. Secret groups of Covenanters began holding services in the open air. Their risk increased when, on Charles's death in 1685, his brother James, a Catholic, became king. With the rotten judgement that dogged the Stewart line, James II imposed the death penalty for worshipping as a Covenanter. His power base in London soon crumbled, however, and in 1689 he was deposed in favour of his Protestant nephew and son-in-law, William of Orange.

Determined to exert his authority over the Scots, William demanded that every clan leader swear an oath of loyalty to him. Partly because of bad weather, partly through a

bells were only too pleased to carry out their commission and the Massacre of Glencoe in 1692 remains one of the bloodiest dates in Scotland's bloodstained history.

Queen Anne (the second daughter of James II) succeeded William in 1702. Although she had given birth to 17 children, none had survived and the English establishment was determined to keep both thrones out of Stewart hands. They turned to Sophie of Hanover, a granddaughter of James VI/James I. If the Scots would agree to accept a Hanoverian line of succession, much needed trade concessions would be granted. There was just one other condition: England and Scotland should unite under one parliament.

misunderstanding of where the swearing would take place, one chieftain, the head of the Clan MacDonald, took his oath several days after the king's deadline. Here was a chance to make an example of a prominent leader. Members of the Campbell clan, old enemies of the MacDonalds, were ordered to lodge with the MacDonalds at their home in Glencoe, get to know them and then, having won their confidence, put every MacDonald younger than 70 to the sword. The Camp-

Left, Scottish Covenanters meet in Edinburgh. Above, grief after the Massacre of Glencoe.

As so often before, riots broke out in Edinburgh and Scotland. But the opposition was fragmented and, in 1707, a Treaty of Union incorporated the Scottish parliament into the Westminster parliament to create the United Kingdom. Unknown to the signatories, the foundation of the British Empire was being laid. To the politicians in London, the fact that Scotland had ceased to exist forever as a separate nation would have seemed a small price to pay for such future glory. But many Scots took a different view: "We are bought and sold for English gold," they sang. Like so many Scottish songs, it was a lament.

THE AGE OF REBELLION

The ink was hardly dry on the Treaty of Union of 1707 when the Scots began to smart under the new constitutional arrangements. The idea of an incorporating union with England had never been popular with the working classes, most of whom saw it (rightly) as a sell-out by the aristocracy to the "Auld Enemy". Scotland's businessmen were outraged by the imposition of hefty, English-style excise duties on many goods and the high-handed Government bureaucracy that went with them. The aristocracy who had supported the Union resented Westminster's peremptory abolition of Scotland's privy council. And everybody hated the new tax on French claret, then the Scotsman's favourite tipple. Even the hardline Cameronians—the fiercest of Protestants—roundly disliked the Union in the early years of the 18th century.

All of which was compounded by the Jacobitism (support for the Stuarts) which haunted many parts of Scotland, particularly among the Episcopalians of Aberdeenshire, Angus and Perthshire, and among the Catholic clans (such as the Macdonalds) of the Western Highlands. And many Whigs who loathed the Stuart dynasty were hedging their bets. No one in Scotland (or in England, for that matter) had forgotten the Restoration of 1660 when the Stuart kings had come back from the dead. It had happened once; it could happen again.

And, given that one of the main planks of Jacobitism was the repeal of the Union, it was hardly surprising that the Stuart kings cast a long shadow over Scotland in the first half of the 18th century. In fact, within a year of the Treaty of Union being signed, the first Jacobite insurgency was under way, helped by a French regime ever anxious to discomfit the power of the English.

In January 1708 a flotilla of French privateers commanded by Comte Claude de Forbin battered its way through the North Sea gales carrying the 19-year-old James Stuart, the self-styled James VIII and III. After a brief sojourn in the Firth of Forth near the coast of Fife the French privateers were chased round the top of Scotland and out into the Atlantic by English warships. Many of the French vessels foundered on their way back to France, although James survived to go on plotting. On dry land, the uprising of 1708 was confined to a few East Stirling-

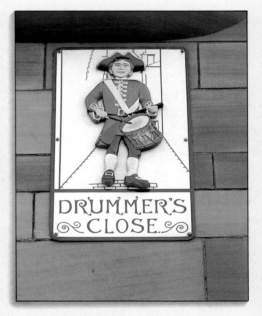

shire lairds who marched up and down with a handful of men. They were quickly rounded up, and in November 1708 five of the ringleaders were tried in Edinburgh for treason. The verdict on all five was "not proven" and they were set free.

Shocked by this display of Scottish leniency, the British Parliament passed the Treason Act of 1708 which brought Scotland into line with England. Until 1708 Scottish traitors could expect to be executed and have their estates forfeited, although their families continued to have a claim on their goods. After the Treason Act of 1708 traitors could expect to be hanged, taken

Preceding pages, David Morier's portrayal of Culloden, painted in 1746. Left, The Young Chevalier, Prince Charles Edward Stuart. Right, history recalled today in Greenock.

down alive, disembowelled while still conscious, and then "quartered" into four pieces.

The next Jacobite uprising, in 1715, was a much more serious affair, if only because it found some support in the North of England. Many historians take the view that the '15 was the only insurgency which the Jacobites *might* have won. Disaffection in Scotland with the Union was widespread, the Hanoverians had not totally secured their grip on Britain, there were loud pro-Stuart mutterings in England, and much of Britain had been stripped of its military.

An odd outcome: But the insurrection was led by the Earl of Mar, a military incompetent known as "Bobbing John", whose support came mainly from the clans of the Central and Eastern Highlands. Clan Campbell—the staunchest of Whigs—were the spearhead of the Hanoverian forces. When the two sides clashed at Sheriffmuir near Stirling on November 13, Mar's Jacobite army had a four-to-one advantage over the tiny Hanoverian force commanded by "Red John of the Battles" (as the Duke of Argyll was known). But, instead of pressing his huge advantage, Mar withdrew his Highland army after an inconclusive clash, leaving the field to a puzzled but delighted Duke of Argyll. "By this Battle," one contempo-

rary wrote, "the Heart of the Rebellion was broke."

Which was a slight exaggeration, but not much. The insurrection of 1715 quickly ran out of steam. The Pretender himself did not arrive in Scotland until the end of December, and the forces he brought with him were too little, and too late. He then did his cause no good by stealing away at night (along with Bobbing John and a few others), leaving his followers to the wrath of the Whigs. The Duke of Argyll was sacked as commander of the government forces for fear he would be too lenient. Dozens of rebels (especially the English ones) were hanged, drawn and quartered, and hundreds were deported.

Not that the débâcle of 1715 stopped the Stuarts trying again. In 1719 it was the Spaniards who decided to try to queer the Hanoverian pitch by backing the Jacobites. Again it was a fiasco. In March 1719 a little force of 307 Spanish soldiers sailed into Loch Alsh where they joined up with a few hundred Murrays, Mackenzies and Mackintoshes. This Spanish-Jacobite stage army was easily routed in the steep pass of Glenshiel by a British unit which swooped down from Inverness to pound the Jacobite positions with their mortars. The Highlanders (as was their wont) simply vanished into the mist and snow of Kintail, leaving the wretched Spaniards in their gold-on-white uniforms to wander about the sub-arctic landscape before surrendering to the British troops. (There is a still a niche high up in the Kintail mountains called Bealach-na-Spainnteach—The Pass of the Spaniards).

But it was the insurrection of 1745, "so glorious an enterprise", led by Charles Edward Stuart (Bonnie Prince Charlie), which shook Britain, despite the fact that by then the Hanoverian regime was well dug in. The Government's grip on the turbulent parts of Scotland had never seemed firmer. There were military depots at Fort William, Fort Augustus and Fort George and an effective Highland militia (later known as the

Companies (the Black Watch) had been shunted out to the West Indies, there were fewer than 4,000 (mostly green) troops in the whole of Scotland, hardly any cavalry or artillery, and Clan Campbell were no longer an effective fighting force. The result was that Bonnie Prince Charlie and his rag-tag army of Macdonalds, Camerons, Mackintoshes, Robertsons, McGregors, Macphersons and Gordons, plus some lowland Cavalry and a stiffening of Franco-Irish mercenaries, were able to walk into Edinburgh and set up a "royal court" in Holyrood Palace.

In September the Young Pretender sailed out of Edinburgh and wrecked General John Cope's panicky Hanoverian army near

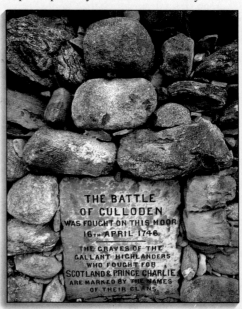

Black Watch) had been raised. General Wade had thrown a network of military roads and bridges across the Highlands. Logically Charles, the Young Pretender, should never have been allowed to set foot out of the Highlands after he raised his standard at Glenfinnan in August 1745.

But having set up a military "infrastructure" in the Highlands, the British Government had neglected it. The Independent

Left, Culloden's victor, the Duke of Cumberland. Above left, Prince Charlie's farewell in 1746 to Flora Macdonald; right, Culloden remembered.

Prestonpans, and then marched across the border into England, causing much fluttering among Whigdom's fainter hearts. But Stuart's success was an illusion. There was precious little support for his cause in the Lowlands of Scotland. Few Jacobite troops had been raised in Edinburgh, and Glasgow and the southwest were openly hostile. Some men had been drummed up in Manchester, but there was no serious support from the Roman Catholic families of northern England. Charles got as far as Derby and then fled back to Scotland with two powerful Hanoverian armies hot on his heels.

After winning a rearguard action at

Clifton, near Penrith, and what has been described as a "lucky victory" at Falkirk in January 1746, the Jacobite army was cut to pieces by the Duke of Cumberland's artillery on Drummossie Moor, Culloden, near Inverness on April 16, 1746. It was the last great pitched battle on the soil of mainland Britain. It was also the end of the Gaelic clan system which had survived in the mountains of Scotland long after it had disappeared from Ireland. The day when an upland chieftain could drum up a "tail" of trained swordsmen for cattle raids into the Lowlands were over.

Following his post-Culloden "flight across the heather", Charles, disguised as a woman servant, was sheltered on the Isle of Skye by Flora MacDonald, thus giving birth to one of Scotland's abiding romantic tales. He was then plucked off the Scottish coast by a French privateer and taken into exile, drunkenness and despair in France and Italy. A few dozen of the more prominent Jacobites were hauled off to Carlisle and Newcastle where they were tried, and some of them hanged. The estates of the gentry who had "come out" in the '45 were confiscated by the Crown. And for some time the Highlands were harried mercilessly by the Duke of Cumberland's troopers (the fiercest of whom were probably Lowland Scots).

In an effort to subdue the Highlands, the government in London passed the Disarming Act of 1746 which not only banned the carrying of claymores, targes, dirks and muskets, but also the wearing of tartans and the playing of bagpipes. It was a nasty piece of legislation, but never much of a success. The British Government also took the opportunity to abolish Scotland's inefficient and often corrupt system of "Courts of Regality" by which the aristocracy (and not just the Highland variety) dispensed justice, collected fines, and wielded powers of life and wealth.

Age of enlightenment: It is one of the minor paradoxes of 18th-century European history that, while Scotland was being racked by dynastic convulsions which were 17th-century in origin, the country was transforming itself into one of the most forward-looking societies in the world. Scotland began to wake up in the first half of the 18th century. By about 1740 the intellectual, scientific and mercantile phenomenon

which became known as the Scottish Enlightenment was well under way, although it didn't reach its peak until the end of the century.

Whatever created it, the Scottish Enlightenment was an extraordinary explosion of creativity and energy. And while, in retrospect at least, the period was dominated by David Hume the philosopher and Adam Smith the economist, there were many others such as William Robertson, Adam Ferguson, William Cullen, the Adam brothers. Through the multi-faceted talents of its "literati", Scotland in general and Edinburgh in particular became one of the intellectual power-houses of Western Eu-

rope. "I may truly say that it is not easy to conceive a university where industry was more general," wrote Sir James Mackintosh about Edinburgh University in 1780s, "where reading was more fashionable, where indolence and ignorance were more disreputable."

Not that the Enlightenment was confined to the salons of Edinburgh. Commerce and industry also thrived. "The same age, which produces great philosophers and politicians, renowned generals and poets, usually abounds with skilled weavers and ship-carpenters," David Hume wrote in 1752. "We cannot reasonably expect that a piece of woollen cloth will be brought to perfection in a nation which is ignorant of astronomy, or where ethics are neglected. The spirit of the age affects all the arts."

In the late 18th century Scotland was in the throes of industrialisation. By 1760 the famous Carron Ironworks in Falkirk was churning out high-grade ordnance for the British military. By 1780 hundreds of tons of goods were being shuttled between Edinburgh and Glasgow along the Forth-Clyde canal. The Turnpike Act of 1751 improved the road system dramatically and created a brisk demand for carriages and stage coaches. In 1738 Scotland's share of the tobacco trade (based on Glasgow) was 10

money generated within Scotland increased by a factor of more than 50, while the population stayed more or less static (at around 1.5 million).

The Clearances: But the Enlightenment and all that went with it had some woeful side-effects. The Highland "Clearances" of the late 18th and early 19th century probably owed more to the "improving" attitudes triggered by the Enlightenment than to the greed of the lairds (although that played its part). By the end of the century every Scottish landowner worth his salt was determined to improve his estate. Agricultural improvement was not only profitable, it was extremely fashionable. And the idea quickly

A View of Glasgow.

percent; by 1769 it was more than 52 percent. There was a huge upsurge of activity in many trades: carpet weaving, upholstery, glass making, china and pottery manufacture, glass, linen, soap, distilling and brewing.

The 18th century changed Scotland from one of the poorest countries in Europe to a state of middling affluence. The urban bourgeoisie grew in power and prosperity, especially in Edinburgh and Glasgow. It has been calculated that between 1700 and 1800 the

Left, a Skye crofter. Above, Glasgow in the 18th century.

spread from the landowners to their tenant farmers.

Nor was the enthusiasm confined to the plump farms of the Lowlands. The gentry of the Highlands—the clan chiefs—were also caught up in the drive to improve their lands. The enterprising Sir John Sinclair, for example, pointed out that, while the Highlands were capable of producing from £200,000 to £300,000 worth of black cattle every year, "the same ground will produce twice as much mutton and there is wool into the bargain."

The argument proved irresistible. Sheep—particularly Cheviots—and their

Lowland shepherds began to flood into the glens and straths of the Highlands, displacing the Highland "tacksmen" and their families. The worst of the Clearances—or at least the most notorious—took place on the huge estates of the Countess of Sutherland and her rich, English-born husband, the Marquis of Stafford. Although Stafford spent huge sums of money building roads, harbours and fish-curing sheds (for very little profit) his estate managers evicted tenants with real ruthlessness. It was a pattern which was repeated all over Highland Scotland at the beginning of the 19th century, and then again later when people were displaced by the red deer of the "sporting" estates. The

And for almost 40 years Scotland was dominated by the powerful machine politician Henry Melville, the First Viscount Dundas, universally known as "King Harry the Ninth". As Solicitor General, Lord Advocate, Home Secretary, Secretary for War and then First Lord of the Admiralty, Dundas wielded awesome power. And his grip on Scotland was relentless. According to the 19th-century judge Lord Cockburn, "Who steered upon him (*Dundas*) was safe; who disregarded his light was wrecked."

But nothing could stop the spread of libertarian ideas in an increasingly industrialised workforce. The ideas contained in Tom Paine's "Rights of Man" spread like wildfire

Highland Clearances remain a painful memory in Scotland.

Radicals and reactionaries: As the industrial economy of Lowland Scotland burgeoned at the end of the 18th century, it sucked in thousands of immigrant workers from all over Scotland and Ireland. The clamour for democracy grew. Some of it was fuelled by the ideas of the American and French revolutions, but much of the unrest was a reaction to Scotland's hopelessly inadequate electoral system. At the end of the 18th century there were only 4,500 voters in the whole of Scotland and only 2,600 voters in the 33 rural countries.

in the Scotland of the 1790s. The cobblers, weavers and spinners proved the most vociferous democrats, but there was also unrest among farmworkers, and among seamen and soldiers in the Highland regiments. Throughout the 1790s a number of radical "one man, one vote" organisations sprang up, such as the Scottish Friends of the People and the United Scotsmen (a quasi-nationalist group which modelled itself on the United Irishmen of Wolfe Tone).

But the brooding figure of Dundas was

Festive fun: 19th-century poster, now in Glasgow's People's Palace.

more than a match for the radicals. Every organisation which raised its head was swiftly infiltated by police spies and *agents provocateurs*. Ringleaders (such as the advocate Thomas Muir) were framed, arrested, tried and deported. Some, such as Robert Watt who led the "Pike Plot" of 1794, were hanged. Meetings were broken up by dragoons, riots were put down by musket-fire, the Scottish universities were racked by witchhunts.

Although Dundas himself was discredited in 1806 (after being impeached for embezzlement) and died in 1811, the anti-Radical paranoia of the Scottish ruling class lingered. Establishment panic reached a peak in 1820 when the so-called Scottish Insurrection ended in the legally-corrupt trial of weavers James Wilson, John Baird, Andrew Hardie and 21 other workmen. A special (English) Court of Oyer and Terminer was set up in Glasgow to hear the case, and Wilson, Baird and Hardie were sentenced to be hanged, beheaded and quartered. They were spared the latter part of the sentence.

Reform and disruption: By the 1820s most of Scotland (and indeed Britain) was weary of the political and constitutional corruption under which the country laboured. In 1823 Lord Archibald Hamilton pointed out the electoral absurdity of rural Scotland. "I have the right to vote in five counties in Scotland, in not one of which do I possess an acre of land," he said "and I have no doubt that if I took the trouble I might have a vote for every county in that kingdom." Hamilton's motion calling for parliamentary reform was defeated by only 35 votes.

But nine years later, in 1832, the Reform Bill passed into law, giving Scotland 30 rural constituencies, 23 burgh constituencies and a voting population of 65,000 (compared to 4,500). Even this limited extension of the franchise—to male householders whose property had a rentable value of £10 or more—generated much wailing and gnashing of teeth among Scottish Tories.

No sooner had the controversy over electoral reform subsided than it was replaced by the row between the "moderates" and the "evangelicals" within the Church of Scotland. "Scotland," Lord Palmerston noted at the time, "is aflame about the church question." But this was no genteel falling-out among theologians. It was a brutal and bruising affair which dominated political life in Scotland for 10 years and raised all kinds of constitutional questions.

At the heart of the argument was the Patronage Act of 1712 which gave Scots lairds the same right English squires had to appoint, or "intrude" clergy on local congregations. Ever since it was passed the Church of Scotland had argued (rightly) that the Patronage Act was a flagrant and illegal violation of the Revolution Settlement of 1690 and the Treaty of Union of 1707, both of which guaranteed the independence of the Church of Scotland.

But the pleas fell on deaf ears. The English-dominated parliament could see no fault in a system which enabled Anglicised landowners to appoint like-minded clergymen. Patronage was seen by the Anglo-Scottish establishment as a useful instrument of political control and social progress. The issue came to a head in May 1843 when the evangelicals, led by Dr. Thomas Chalmers, marched out of the annual General Assembly of the Church of Scotland in Edinburgh to form the Free Church of Scotland.

Chalmers, theologian, astronomer and brilliant organiser, defended the Free Church against bitter enemies. His final triumph, in 1847, was to persuade the London parliament that it was folly to allow the aristocracy to refuse the Free Church land on which to build churches and schools. A few days after giving evidence, Chalmers died in Edinburgh.

The rebellion of the evangelicals was brilliantly planned, well funded and took the British establishment completely by surprise. Within 10 years of the Disruption the Free Church had built more than 800 churches, 700 manses, three large theological colleges, and 600 schools, And, although it ran into some vicious opposition from landowners—especially in the Highlands—the Free Church prevailed.

In fact, it can be argued that the Disruption was the only rebellion in 18th- or 19th-century British history that actually succeeded. Chalmers and his supporters had challenged both the pervasive influence of the Anglo-Scottish aristocracy and the power of the British Parliament, and won. The Patronage Act of 1712 was finally repealed in 1874, and the Free Church remerged with the establishment in 1929.

THE MAKING OF MODERN SCOTLAND

During the Victorian and Edwardian eras, Scotland, like most of Europe, became urbanised and industrialised. Steelworks, ironworks, shipyards, coal mines, shale-oil refineries, textile factories, engineering shops, canals and of course railways proliferated all over 19th-century Scotland. The process was concentrated in Scotland's "central belt" (the stretch of low-lying land between Edinburgh and Glasgow) but there were important "outliers" like Aberdeen, Dundee, Ayrshire and the mill-towns of the Scottish borders. A few (very small) industrial ventures found their way deep into the Highlands or onto a few small islands.

It was a process which dragged in its wake profound social, cultural and demographic change. The booming industries brought thousands of work-seeking immigrants flocking into lowland Scotland. Most came from the Highlands and Ireland, and many nursed an ancient distaste for the British establishment which translated itself into left-wing radicalism. Scots of Irish descent are still the main prop of the Labour Party in Scotland. The immigrants were also largely Roman Catholic, which did something to loosen the grip of the Presbyterian churches on Scottish life.

Huge metropolis: Industry transformed the city of Glasgow and the River Clyde. From being an amiable 18th-century backwater (the name is corrupt Gaelic for "the dear green place"),Glasgow became the Second City of the Empire, the Victorian city *par excellence*. Between 1740 and 1840 its population leapt from 17,000 to 200,000 and then doubled to 400,000 by 1870. The small Georgian city became a huge industrial metropolis built on the kind of rectangular grid common in the United States, with industrial princes living in splendour while Highland, Irish, Italian and Jewish immigrants swarmed in the noisome slums.

In many ways 19th-century Glasgow had

Preceding pages, the Edinburgh residence of Scotland's Secretary of State. Left, industrial Glasgow in the 19th century. Right, slum dwellers in Glasgow's Gorbals.

more in common with Chicago or New York than any city in Britain. Working-class conditions were appalling. Rickets, cholera, smallpox, tuberculosis, diptheria and alcoholism were rampant. The streets were unclean and distinctly unsafe. Violence was endemic as Highlanders and Irishmen clashed in the stews and whisky dens, while Orangemen from Ulster were used as violent and murderous strike-breakers. The city hangman was never short of work.

But there was no denying Glasgow's enormous industrial vitality. By the middle of the century the city was peppered with more than 100 textile mills (an industry which by that time employed more than 400,000 Scots). There were ironworks at Tollcross, Coatbridge and Monklands, productive coal mines all over Lanarkshire and the River Clyde was lined with boiler makers, marine-engineering shops, and world-class shipyards. For generations the label "Clyde built" was synonymous with industrial quality.

According to the historian T.C. Smout, by 1913 Glasgow and the surrounding area was making "one-fifth of the steel, one-third of the shipping tonnage, one-half of the marine-engine horsepower, one-third of the railway locomotives and rolling stock, and most of the sewing machines in the United Kingdom".

Nor was industry confined to Glasgow and its environs. The Tayside city of Dundee forged close links with India and became the biggest jute-manufacturing centre in Britain. The Carron Ironworks at Falkirk was Europe's largest producer of artillery by the year 1800. In West Lothian a thriving industry was built up to extract oil from shale (a process discovered by James "Paraffin" Young). Scotland's east-coast fisheries

of cash. Both Edinburgh and Dundee became centres for the investment trusts which sunk large quantities of cash into ventures all over the world, and particularly the U.S.A. In 1873 the Dundee jute man Robert Fleming set up the Scottish American Investment Trust to channel money into American cattle ranches, fruit farms, mining companies, and railways, mainly in Arizona, Nevada and Texas. The biggest cattle ranch in the U.S.A.—the Matador Land & Cattle Company—was run from Dundee until 1951. The outlaw Butch Cassidy once worked for a cattle company operated from the fastidious New Town of Edinburgh.

But investment was a two-way process.

flourished, and by the end of the century the town of Wick in Caithness became Europe's biggest herring port.

As well as producing large quantities of books, biscuits and bureaucrats, Edinburgh was a centre of the British brewing industry; at one stage there were over 40 breweries within the city boundaries. And in the latter part of the 19th century the Scotch whisky industry boomed, thanks to the devastation of the French vineyards in the 1880s by phyllexora which almost wrecked the cognac industry.

Cowboy connection: Inevitably, this growth of industry generated huge amounts

By the end of the 19th century Scotland, with its educated workforce and promiximity to the markets of Europe, was attracting inward investment. The American-funded North British Rubber Company moved into Edinburgh in 1857. In 1884 the Singer Company built one of the biggest factories in the world at Clydebank to manufacture mass-produced sewing machines. It was the beginning of a 100-year trend which has done much to undermine the independence of the Scottish economy.

Despite the enthusiasm of Queen Victoria and the British gentry for the Highlands, the direst poverty stalked upland Scotland.

Land reform was desperately needed. Following an outburst of rioting in Skye in 1882 and the formation of the Highland Land League in 1884, Gladstone's Liberal government passed the Crofters Holdings Act of 1886 which gave crofters fair rents, security of tenure, and the right to pass their croft on to their families. But it was Lord Salisbury's Conservative government who put the Scottish Secretary in the British cabinet, and set up the Scottish Office in Edinburgh and London in 1886.

By the end of the 19th century the huge majority of the Scottish population was urban, industrialised, and concentrated in the towns and cities of the Lowlands. And

The Great War: When World War I broke out in 1914 the Scots flocked to the British colours with an extraordinary enthusiasm. Like Ireland, Scotland provided the British Army with a disproportionate number of soldiers. Like the Irish, the Scots suspended their radicalism and trooped into the forces to fight for King and Empire, to the despair of left-wing leaders like Keir Hardie and John Maclean. With less than 10 percent of the British population, the Scots made up almost 15 percent of the British Army. And when the butcher's bill was added up after the war it was found that more than 20 percent of all the Britons killed were Scots.

They came from every corner of Scotland.

urban Scotland proved a fertile breeding ground for the British Left. The Scottish Labour Party (SLP) was founded in 1888, although it soon merged with the Independent Labour Party (ILP), which in turn played a big part in the formation of the (British) Labour Party. Britain's first Labour MP, Keir Hardie, was a Scot, as was Ramsay Macdonald, Britain's first Labour prime minister.

Left, herring drifters near Peterhead. Above, Labour Party leader Ramsay Macdonald with his son and daughter in 1929.

The Royal Scots—which recruits in and around Edinburgh—raised no fewer than 35 battalions. Enough Glaswegians joined the Highland Light Infantry (HLI) to form 26 battalions. The Cameronians—the descendents of the Protestant zealots of the 17th century—raised 27 battalions. The Gordon Highlanders raised 21 from the area around Aberdeen. The sparsely populated Highlands produced 19 battalions of Seaforth Highlanders and 13 of Cameron Highlanders. The Hebrides, Orkney and Shetland proved rich recruiting ground for the Royal Navy and the Merchant Marine.

In addition to which, the shipyards of the

LAYING DOWN
THE LAW

"Not Proven: that bastard verdict", as Sir Walter Scott called it, is a curious feature of the Scottish legal system. At the end of a criminal trial the verdict can be "guilty" or "not guilty", as in England, *or* the jury may find the charge "not proven". It's an option that reflects Scots logic and refusal to compromise by assuming a person innocent until proved guilty; but it does confer a permanent stigma on the accused.

The jargon of Scots lawyers is distinctive, too. If you embark on litigation you are known as a "pursuer". You sue a "defender". "Law Burrows" (nothing to do with rabbits) is a way of asking the courts to prevent someone harassing you. If you disagree too outspokenly with a judge's decision, you may be accused of "murmuring the judge".

Though few outsiders realise it, the Scots have maintained a distinctive legal system despite almost four centuries of political union with the rest of the U.K. It is unique in being a legal system without a legislature of its own. Since the Act of Union in 1707 abolished the Scottish parliament the UK parliament in London has made laws for the country.

Scottish law is quite different in origin from that of England and those countries (such as the US and many Commonwealth nations) to which the English system has been exported, and is closer to the legal systems of South Africa, Sri Lanka, Louisiana and Quebec. It was developed from Roman Law and owes much more to continental legal systems than does that of England—thanks partly to the custom of Scottish lawyers, during the 17th and 18th centuries, of studying in France, Holland or Germany.

Solicitors, the general practitioners of the law, regard themselves as men of affairs, with a wider role than lawyers in some countries have adopted. Advocates, who are based in Parliament House in Edinburgh and to whom a solicitor will turn for expert advice, also refuse to become too narrowly specialised. This is important if they wish to become either Sheriffs, as the judges of the local courts are called, or Senators of the College of Justice, the judges of Scotland's highest courts,

the Court of Session and the High Court of Justiciary. Both the Sheriff and the Senator of the College of Justice have to hear both criminal and civil cases.

Some practitioners have demonstrated outstanding talents beyond the confines of the law. Sir Walter Scott was, for most of his life, a practising lawyer. In Selkirk, near the palatial house he built at Abbotsford, can be seen the courtroom where he presided as Sheriff. Robert Louis Stevenson qualified as an advocate, the equivalent of the English barrister, though he quickly deserted the law for literature. In an earlier generation James Boswell, Dr. Johnson's biographer, had been a successful advocate in Edinburgh.

Inevitably, English law has had its influence. Much modern legislation, especially commercial law, has tended to be copied from England. The traffic, however, hasn't been all one-way. In Scottish criminal trials the jury of 15 has always been allowed to reach a majority verdict, a procedure adopted by England a few years ago. The English have recently introduced a prosecution service, independent of the police, similar to that which operates in Scotland. Some would also like to import the "110-day rule": this requires a prisoner on remand to be released if his trial doesn't take place within 110 days of his imprisonment. More controversially, Scottish judges have power in criminal cases to create new crimes—a power they use sparingly.

Many in England envy the Scottish system of house purchase. Most of the legal and estate agency work is done by solicitors and it seems to be completed a great deal more speedily than in England. The Scottish laws on Sunday trading are more liberal than those in England, and divorce was available in Scotland several centuries before it was south of the border.

Along with the kirk, the separateness of the Scottish legal system plays a vital part in establishing a sense of national identity. That's why many Scots lawyers resent the failure of Westminster to have proper regard to the fact that the law is different in Scotland. Whether it's *better* is a separate question; the best verdict in this case may be "not proven".

Clyde and the engineering shops of West Central Scotland were producing more tanks, shells, warships, explosives and fieldguns than any comparable part of Britain. That explains why the British Government took such a dim view of the strikes and industrial disputes which hit the Clyde between 1915 and 1919 and led to the area being dubbed "Red Clydeside". When Glasgow workers struck for a 40-hour week in January 1919 the Secretary of State for Scotland panicked and called in the military.

Glaswegians watched open-mouthed as thousands of armed troops backed by tanks poured onto the streets of Glasgow to nip the Red Revolution in the bud. And at a huge

engineering industries—cars, electrics and machine tools—stayed stubbornly south of the border. Unemployment soared to almost three in 10 of the workforce and Scots took the emigrant ships in droves. An estimated 400,000 Scots (10 percent of the population) emigrated between 1921 and 1931.

In 1937 Walter Elliot, the Secretary of State for Scotland, wrote a memo to the Cabinet pointing out that "the social condition of Scotland is indicated by the fact that 23 percent of its population live in conditions of gross overcrowding, compared with 4 percent in England…Maternal mortality is half as high again as in England. In proportion to the population twice as many cases of

rally in George Square on January 31, 1919, the police baton-charge the crowd.

The hungry years: The 1920s and 1930s were sour years for Scotland. The great "traditional" industries of ship-building, steel-making, coal-mining and heavy engineering which towered over the Scottish economy went into a decline from which they have never recovered. The Scotch whisky industry reeled from the body-blow of American prohibition. The new light

Left, James Boswell, lawyer and biographer. Above, the Hungry Thirties: Glasgow kids keep smiling despite the poverty.

pneumonia and scarlet fever were notified…while the diptheria figure was higher by a third."

Most of urban Scotland saw its salvation in the newly-formed Labour Party, which not only promised a better life but also a measure of Home Rule. Support for the Labour Party had showed early. At the General Election of 1922 an electoral pattern was set which has remained (with one exception) ever since; England went Conservative while Scotland went Labour.

But the 1920s and 1930s also saw revival of a kind of left-wing cultural nationalism, which owed a lot to the poetry of Hugh

MacDiarmid, the writing of Lewis Grassic Gibbon and the enthusiasms of upper-crust nationalists like Ruaridh Erskine of Marr and R.B. Cunninghame-Graham. From the Scottish literary renaissance of the inter-war years the nationalist movement grew increasingly more political. In 1934 the small (but right-wing) Scottish Party merged with the National Party of Scotland to form the Scottish National Party (SNP).

The world at war: It wasn't until World War II loomed that the Scottish economy began to climb out of the doldrums. And when war broke out in September 1939 the Clydeside shipyards moved into high gear to build warships like the "Duke of York", "Howe", "Indefatigible" and "Vanguard", while the engineering firms began pumping out small arms, bayonets, explosives and ammunition. The Rolls-Royce factory at Hillington near Glasgow produced Merlin engines for the RAF's Spitfires. One way or another, Clydeside became one of Britain's most important war-time regions.

The point wasn't missed by the Germans. On March 13 and 14, 1941, hundreds of German bombers, operating at the limit of their range, devastated Clydeside. More than 1,000 people were killed (528 in the town of Clydebank) and another 1,500 or so injured. It was a fearsome raid and shocked many people who had thought Scotland out of the firing line. But it was nothing compared to the pounding inflicted on London and the cities of southern Britain, and did no permanent damage to Clydeside's contribution to the war effort.

The postwar period: War killed more than 58,000 Scots (compared to the 148,000 who had lost their lives in World War I) but had the effect of galvanising the Scottish economy for a couple of decades. And there's no doubt that the Labour Government which came to power in 1945 worked major improvements on Scottish life.

The National Health Service proved an effective instrument against such plagues as infant mortality, tuberculosis, rickets, and scarlet fever. Housing conditions improved in leaps and bounds as the worst of the city slums were pulled down and replaced by roomy (but often badly-built) council houses. Semi-rural new towns like East Kilbride, Glenrothes, Cumbernauld, Irvine and Livingston were started in key locations around central Scotland.

What went largely unnoticed in the post-war euphoria was that the Labour Government's policy of nationalising the coal mines and the railways was stripping Scotland of much of its decision-making powers, and therefore management jobs. The process continued through the 1960s and into the 1970s when the steel, shipbuilding and aerospace industries were also "taken into public ownership".

This haemhorrage of economic power and influence has been compounded by Scottish companies being sold to English and foreign predators. In 1988 British Caledonian, originally a Scotland-based airline, was swallowed up by British Airways. To an alarming extent, Scotland's economy now has a "branch factory" status.

English enthusiasm for Labour's experiment flagged and in 1951 Sir Winston Churchill was returned to power. Scotland, of course, continued to vote Labour (although in the general election of 1955 the Conservatives won 36 of Scotland's 71 seats, the only time they have had a majority north of the border). And, while Home Rule for Scotland was off the political agenda, Scottish nationalism refused to go away.

In the late 1940s two-thirds of the Scottish electorate signed a "national covenant" demanding home rule. In 1951 a squad of young nationalists outraged the British establishment by whisking the Stone of Destiny out of Westminster Abbey, and hiding it in Scotland. And in 1953 the British establishment outraged Scottish sentiment by insisting on the title of Queen Elizabeth II for the new queen, despite the fact that the Scots had never had a Queen Elizabeth I.

But while Scotland did reasonably well out of the Conservative-led "New Elizabethan Age" of the 1950s and early 1960s, the old structural faults soon began to reappear. By the late 1950s the well-equipped Japanese and German shipyards were snatching orders from under the noses of the Clyde, the Scottish coalfields were proving woefully inefficient and Scotland's steel works and heavy engineering firms were losing their grip on their markets.

And, although the Conservative government did fund a new steel mill at Ravenscraig near Motherwell and entice Rootes to set up a car plant at Linwood and the British

Motor Corporation to start making trucks at Bathgate, it was all done under duress. Scotland's distance from the market-place continued to a crippling disadvantage. The midlands and south of England remained the engine-room of the British economy. The drift of Scots to the south continued.

The impact of oil: Although the Scots voted heavily for the Labour Party in the general elections of 1964 and 1966, Labour's complacency was jolted in November 1967 when Mrs Winnie Ewing of the Scottish National Party (SNP) snatched the Hamilton by-election from the Labour Party. Although Ewing lost her seat at the general election of 1970, her success marked

Scotland engineering firms and land speculators began snapping up sites on which to build platform yards, rig repair bases, airports, oil refineries and petrochemical works. Nothing like it had been seen since the industrial revolution. A new sense of optimism pervaded Scotland.

The SNP were quick to take advantage of the mood. Running on a campaign slogan of "It's Scotland's Oil", the SNP won seven seats in the general election of February 1974 and took more than 20 percent of the Scottish vote. In October 1974 they did even better, cutting a swathe through both parties to take 11 seats and more than 30 percent of the Scottish vote. It looked as if one more

the start of an upsurge in Scottish nationalism that preoccupied Scottish (and to some extent British) politics for a decade.

When Harold Wilson's Labour government ran out of steam in 1970 it was replaced by the Conservative regime of Edward Heath (although, once again, the Scots voted overwhelmingly Labour). But in the early 1970s Scotland got lucky. The oil companies struck big quantities of oil. All round

Contrasts of modern Scotland: a Hebridean weaver using a traditional handloom to make Harris tweed; and youths in East Kilbride, soaking in the sun.

push by the SNP could see the United Kingdom dissolved, and the hard-pressed British economy cut off from the oil revenues it so badly needed. The 1970s also saw a flurry of bomb attacks on oil pipelines and electricity pylons by nationalist extremists (some of whom had links with Ireland's IRA).

The Labour government responded to the political threat posed by the nationalists with a constitutional defence. It offered Scotland a directly-elected assembly with substantial (if strictly limited) powers. The government went so far as buying a building—the old Royal High School in Edinburgh. The whole package was to go ahead if the Scottish people voted "yes" in a national referendum.

At which point Westminster changed the rules. At the instigation of Labour MP George Cunningham, Parliament decided that a simple majority was not good enough, and that devolution would go ahead only if more than 40 percent of the Scottish electorate voted in favour. It was an impossible condition. Predictably the Scots failed to vote yes by a big majority in the referendum of March 1979 (although they *did* vote yes) and the Scotland Bill lapsed. A few months later the 11 SNP members joined the vote of censure against the Labour government—which fell, ironically, by one vote. In the ensuing general election Margaret Thatcher

was voted in to power and promptly made it plain that any form of Home Rule for Scotland was out of the question.

The Thatcher years: The Devolution débâcle produced a genuine crisis of confidence among Scotland's political classes. Support for the SNP slumped, the Alliance could do nothing. And the Labour Party, armed with the majority of the Scottish vote, could only watch helplessly as the aluminium smelter at Invergordon, the steel mill at Gartcosh, the car works at Linwood, the pulp mill at Fort William, the truck plant at Bathgate and much of the Scottish coalfield perished in the economic blizzard of the

1980s. Even the energetic and well-founded Scottish Development Agency could do little to protect the Scottish economy. Unemployment climbed to more than 300,000, and the much vaunted "Silicon Glen" (the electronics industry) proved far too small to take up the slack.

So the political triumph of Thatcherism in Britain found no echoes in Scotland. At the general election of June 1987 the pattern which first emerged in 1922 repeated itself; England voted Tory and Scotland voted Labour. Out of 72 Scottish MPs 50 were Labour and only 10 were Conservative. This immediately raised the argument that the Scottish Secretary, Malcolm Rifkind, was an English governor-general with "no mandate" to govern Scotland. Rifkind's response was that the 85 percent of the Scottish electorate who voted for "British" parties were voting for the sovereignty of Westminster and therefore had to accept Westminster's rules.

But within months of the general election senior Scottish Tories began to mutter that, Mrs. Thatcher notwithstanding, the time had come to reconsider Home Rule for Scotland. At the end of 1987 the Labour Party tabled yet another Devolution Bill which was promptly thrown out by English MPs to the jeers of the SNP who claimed that Labour's "Feeble Fifty" could do nothing if they were prepared to play the Westminster game. The SNP resurrected the old quip that "a shiver ran along the Scottish Labour benches looking for a spine to run up".

Nationalism remains the question mark which hangs over the future of Scotland. Scots have now been members of the United Kingdom for 280 years, and Scottish history is deeply enmeshed with that of Britain. Yet a powerful undertow of resentment keeps breaking the surface: the Jacobite insurgencies of 1708, 1715 and 1745; the radical "rebellion" of 1820; the Disruption in the Church of Scotland in 1843; the formation of the SNP in the 1930s; the startling upsurge of nationalism in the 1970s. Whether it will ever surge strongly enough to threaten the Treaty of Union of 1707 remains to be seen.

Left, Mrs. Thatcher compaigning in Scotland during the 1987 election. Right, the Rev. Alan Cameron busking outside the Scottish National Gallery.

HIGHLANDERS AND LOWLANDERS

The division between the Highlander and the Lowlander was one of the most ancient and fundamental in Scotland's history. "The people of the coast," said John of Fordun, the Lowland Aberdeenshire chronicler, writing in 1380, "are of domestic and civilised habits, trusty, patient and urbane, decent in their attire, affable and peaceful…The Highlanders and people of the islands, on the other hand, are a savage and untamed nation, rude and independent, given to rapine, easy-living, of a docile and warm disposition, comely in person but unsightly in dress, hostile to the English people and language and, owing to diversity of speech, even to their own nation, and exceedingly cruel."

The division was seen to be based on what Fordun called "the diversity of their speech": the Lowlanders spoke Scots, a version of Middle English, the Highlanders spoke Gaelic. The line between the two languages broadly coincided with the line of the hills. North of the Highland fault running from just above Dumbarton to just above Stonehaven, and west of the plains of Aberdeenshire and the Moray Firth, Gaelic was spoken. Outside that area, Scots was spoken, except in the northern isles of Orkney and Shetland (which spoke a kind of Norse), and perhaps in a few pockets of the southwest where another form of Gaelic may have lingered until late in the Middle Ages.

Four hundred years later things hadn't changed that much. When Dorothy and William Wordsworth made a brief trip into the Highlands, they encountered Gaelic speech on Loch Lomondside within 20 miles of Glasgow, and when Patrick Sellar, the Lowland sheep-farmer, wrote to his employer, the Countess of Sutherland, about the nature of the people over whom he was appointed as estate manager, John of Fordun would have recognised the tone. Sellar spoke of "the absence of every principle of truth and candour from a population of sev-

eral hundred thousand souls." He compared these "aborigines of Britain" with the "aborigines of America", the Red Indians: "both live in turf cabins in common with the brutes: both are singular for patience, courage, cunning and address. Both are most virtuous where least in contact with men in civilized State, and both are fast sinking under the baneful effects of ardent spirits."

Then, in the 19th century, a startling turnabout occurred. The Scots, as a people,

began to adopt as their national symbols the very trappings of the despised Highland minority—the kilt and the tartan, the bagpipe and the bonnet, the eagle's feather and the dried sprig of heather: it blended into a kitsch everyone across the world can recognise. In 1987, when the American broadcasting networks wished to spend a minute of national news on why Scotland felt unsympathetic to the policies of Britain's prime minister, Margaret Thatcher, they needed to use 30 seconds setting the scene with men with hairy knees throwing pine trees about at a Highland gathering: how else could the great American people identify a Scot?

Preceding pages: Rannoch Moor; and Blackrock Cottage, Glencoe. Left, bagpipers at Glencoe. Right, starting young at Glenfinnan.

SCOTS IDIOMS

There are moments in the lives of all Scots—however educated, however discouraged by school or station from expressing themselves in the vernacular—when they will reach into some race memory of language and produce the only word for the occasion.

The Scots idiom tends to operate at two ends of a spectrum: from abusive to affectionate. So the word for the occasion might well be *nyaff*. There are few Scots alive who don't know the meaning of the insult *nyaff*—invariably "*wee nyaff*"—and there are few Scots alive who don't have difficulty telling you. Like all the best words in the Scots tongue, there is no single English word which serves as translation. The most that can be done for *nyaff* is to say it describes a person who is irritating rather than infuriating, whose capacity to annoy and inspire contempt is just about in scale with his diminutive size, and the cockiness that goes with it.

The long historical partnership between Scotland and France has certainly left its mark on the Scots tongue. Scottish cooks use "ashets" as ovenware—a word which derives from *assiette*, meaning plate—while the adjective "douce", meaning gentle and sweet-natured, is a direct import of the French *douce*, meaning much the same thing. But the most satisfying Scots words—resounding epithets like *bauchle* (a small, usually old and often misshapen person) and evocative adjectives like *shilpit* (sickly-looking) and *wabbit* (weak and fatigued)—belong to that tongue which came under threat in the early 17th century when King James VI moved to London to become James I of England.

Until then, the Lowland Scots (as opposed to Gaelic-speaking Highlanders) whose racial inheritance was part-Celtic and part-Teutonic spoke their own version of a northern dialect of English, and "Scots" was the language of the nobility, the bourgeoisie and the peasants. But when king and court departed south, educated and aristocratic Scots adopted the English of the "élite", and the Scots tongue received a blow from which it has never recovered.

Yet what could be more expressive than a mother saying of her child, "The bairn's a wee bit wabbit today"? What could be more colourful than the remark that the newspaper vendor on the corner is "a shilpit wee bauchle"? The words themselves almost speak their meaning, even to non-Scots, and they are beginning to creep back into the vocabulary of the middle-class.

At one time the vernacular was actively discouraged in Scottish schools—except, of course, when studying the work of Robert Burns, who used it for most of his poems (the *sleekit* of "wee, sleekit, cowerin', timerous beastie" means sly or cunning). But it received a transfusion of respectability when Scotland's greatest contemporary poet Hugh MacDiarmid—believed by many to be a world genius—devised his own poetic language called Lallans, which plundered the vocabulary of local dialects from all over Scotland. To MacDiarmid is owed the resurrection of wonderful words like *clamjamphrie* (or *clanjamfrie*, according to his spelling) which can either mean a rabble or a load of rubbish, and *farfochen*, which means exhausted. What better way of saying, "I'm really tired out" than "Ah'm fair farfochen?" Perhaps only by elaborating, "There's been such a stramash ben the hoose Ah'm sore trauchled." (There's been such a rumpus in our house that I'm quite tired and bothered.)

The dialects of Glasgow and the urban west of Scotland have been very much influenced by the mass infusions of Gaelic and Irish from their immigrant populations from the Highlands and Ireland, but Glasgow's legendary "patter" has an idiom all its own, still evolving and still vitally conscious of every subtle shift in the city's mores and preoccupations.

Glasgow slang specialises in abuse which can be affectionate or aggressive. A *bampot* is a harmless idiot; a *heidbanger* is a dangerous idiot, while some apparently innocuous expressions have meanings hidden from all but those who know the argot. To "go right ahead" means to come to blows with someone, although the more sinister-sounding "going on the batter" simply means to go on a drinking spree.

A drop to drink: Predictably, there is a rich seam of Glasgow vernacular connected with drink. If you are drunk you might be *steamin'*, *stotious*, *wellied*, *miraculous* or *paralytic*. If you are drinking you might be consuming a *wee goldie* (whisky) or a *nippy sweetie* (any form of spirits). And if you are penniless you might have to resort to *electric soup*, the hazardous mixture of meths and cheap wine drunk by down-and-outs. An alternative to going on the batter is *going on the randan* and if you overdo the *bevvy* (alcohol of any kind) you might get *fu' as a puggy* (full, or drunk, as a monkey, although no one really knows why monkeys are supposed to be so prone to intoxication).

If a Glaswegian calls you *gallus*, you can take it as a compliment. The best translation in contemporary idiom is probably streetwise, although it covers a range of values from cocky and flashy to bold and nonchalant. The word derives from gallows, indicating that you were the kind of personality destined to end up on them. But in Glasgow that wasn't necessarily always an occasion for disapproval.

The fact that most Scots would not be seen dead in a kilt or dream of attending anything as outlandish as the Highland games is not very relevant. The adoption of these public symbols has something to do with the campaigns of Sir Walter Scott to romanticise the Highlanders, something to do with the charismatic powers of the Glasgow Police Band, which in Victorian days was largely recruited from Highlanders, and something to do with a music hall that loved a stereotype. The mask stuck.

Rich wives: At the same time, ironically, true Highland society was in a state of collapse. Ever since the 17th century its distinctive character and Gaelic culture had been as possible as quickly as possible, just as landowners elsewhere in Scotland. In the course of the next 50 years they cleared most of the land surface of peasant farms, which paid little rent, in order to accommodate the Lowlander and his sheep, which paid a good deal more. Simultaneously, Gaelic began a catastrophic decline, from being universally the language of the Highland area to being the language, as it is today, only of the Outer Hebrides and a few other communities, mainly on islands, in the extreme west.

So the Highland-Lowland division today has a rather different meaning from what it had in the past. It is certainly not any longer the most obvious or important division,

eroded by the steady spread of hostile government power, the march of commercial forces tying Scotland together as one market, and the Lowlandisation of the clan chiefs as they sought wives with better dowries than the mountains could provide. The failure of the Jacobite risings in 1715 and 1745 was important, but the transformation would have come about anyway, for other perfectly mundane reasons.

By 1800 Highland landowners obviously wanted their estates to produce as much cash

The outdoor life: Scottish sheep drovers in the 19th century.

ethnically and culturally, among the Scottish people as a whole. The Lowlanders themselves were never uniform: The folk of Aberdeenshire spoke "the Doric", a dialect of their own, very different in vocabulary and intonation from, say, the folk of Lothian or Galloway. In the 19th century this sort of regionalism was greatly compounded and complicated by the immigration of the Irish, about two-thirds of them Catholic and one-third Protestant.

The Catholic Irish, oppressed by poverty and the sectarianism that accompanied their movement, crowded into distinct areas— Glasgow and Dundee among the cities, and the small mining or iron-working towns of Lanarkshire, Lothian and Fife. Today, especially in the west, it is the Catholic-Protestant division that continues to have most meaning in people's lives. The Catholics are, overall, still a minority in Scotland, but their church now has more attenders on Sundays than any Protestant denomination—even the Church of Scotland itself. Intermarriage between the two communities has dissoved animosities in the past half-century, but even today politicians deal cautiously with anything that touches, for example, on the right of Scottish Catholics to have their own state-aided schools.

Being a "Lowlander" has less meaning estants, and enjoy a lifestyle and a culture not obviously very different from that of the citizens of Perth or Aberdeen. They may have a name with the prefix "Mac" or theoretically belong to some clan like Grant, Murray or Munro; but, apart perhaps from a greater fondness for dressing in tartan and doing Highland reels at party time, there is little that is distinctive about being a Highlander in most communities beyond the geological Highland line.

In the west, however, in the Inner and Outer Hebrides and along the extremities of the mainland coast from Argyll to Sutherland, the ancient significance and meaning of being a Highlander is very much alive.

than having a religious affiliation, or coming from Edinburgh rather than Glasgow, or even than backing a certain football team. (Sports allegiances are a subtle blend of the regional and the religious. Celtic, for example, is Glasgow Catholic and Rangers is Glasgow Protestant, but Aberdeen United has no sectarian overtone, though an obvious regional one.)

Being a "Highlander" has an uncertain and ambiguous meaning over most of the area covered today by Highland and Grampian Region. The citizens of Pitlochry or Inverness don't, for the most part, speak Gaelic, are mostly ordinary lukewarm Prot-

Not all these communities necessarily or predominantly speak Gaelic rather than English, though in the Western Isles the power of the language is much less dimmed than elsewhere. All of them are, however, historically "crofting communities": that is, they are the relics of a traditional peasantry who, thanks to a campaign of direct action in the 1880s, won from the British parliament the right to live under the same kind of privileged land-law as their brethren in Ireland. The Crofters Holding Act in 1886 conferred on the crofting inhabitants of these areas security of tenure, the right to hand on their holdings to their heirs, and a rent which was fixed not by the whim of the estate manager but by the arbitration of a Land Court sitting in Edinburgh.

Crofting is still largely the economic foundation of these communities. It can best be described as small-scale farming that involves individual use of arable land and some communal use of the grazing on the hill and moor. Very often, crofting is (or was) combined with some other activity, such as fishing or weaving, especially on Harris and Lewis.

Today, inevitably, it involves regulation and subsidy on a massive scale, and the crofter becomes an expert in milking the grants available from the European Eco-

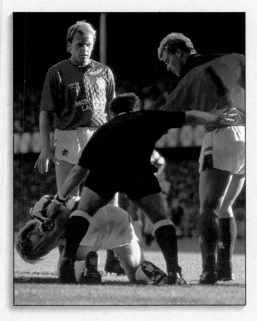

nomic Community, the Nature Conservancy, the Highland and Island Development Board, the Department of Agriculture and Fisheries, and anyone else who looks good for a touch. Old animosities are sometimes rekindled when the Lowlander considers the Highlander's expertise in living off the hand-outs of the taxpayer, and the Highlander in return considers the indifference of Edinburgh and London towards the real problems of living in remote communities.

Left, assessing the form at the Braemar Gathering. Above, aggro at a Celtic versus Rangers football game.

The real thing: But the Highland way of life in these areas goes beyond the details of economic existence, and can best be understood in Scotland by a journey to the Outer Hebrides. In Lewis the visitor encounters the Protestant version of a Gaelic culture dominated, especially on Sundays, by grim Calvinist churches known to outsiders as the "Wee Frees". In Barra and South Uist the tourist finds the Catholic version, implanted by the 17th-century Counter-Reformation and not involving such denial of life's pleasures. There are those who would argue that the Highland way of life exists in a still purer form in the Canadian Maritimes, especially in the Catholic Gaelic-speaking communities of Cape Breton Island, who trace their origins directly to the evictions and migrations that followed the 1745 Rebellion and the Clearances of the 19th century.

Wherever it survives, irrespective of religious background, the Gaelic tradition in many respects defies the dominant world outside, though the values of that world intrude even on its remotest fastnesses. In some ways, the Gaelic Highlander is indeed aboriginal, as Patrick Sellar said, though he only meant it as an insult. The Highlander is often unmodern in priorities, is materialistic yet with little sense of individual ambition, attaches little importance to clock watching. Gaelic society is supportive of its members, has an abiding sense of kinship and an unembarrassed love of a song and a story, as it has an unembarrassed love of drink.

With every passing year it appears superficially less likely that its distinctiveness can survive another generation, but its efforts to survive become more, not less, determined. The recent creation of a unified local government authority, the Western Isles Council, which conducts its business in Gaelic, has given a remarkable new confidence and ability to deal with modern political society. It is perhaps unlikely that any Ayatollah will arise in Stornoway, but the Highland way of life is far from finished on the islands.

On the other hand, elsewhere in Scotland, John of Fordun and Patrick Sellar have really had the last word. It is their Anglicised Lowland Scotland that now runs from the Mull of Galloway to John o' Groats. The tartan and the bagpipe ought not to fool the visitor: it does not fool the Scot, though he enjoys the pretence of it all.

HOW THE KIRK MOULDS MINDS

When Sunday was still solemnly observed as the Lord's Day, a young minister was asked to preach to George V at his Highland palace, Balmoral. Nervous at such an honour, the minister enquired: "What would the King like the sermon to be about?" His Majesty replied: "About five minutes."

What he was dreading, of course, was an interminable exhortation to high moral endeavour. Until recent times the Sabbath was a day when profane activity ceased. The intervals between services were spent in prayer or with improving books. The most devout drew down their window-blinds. Woe to the golfer, the wife who cooked, the child who fidgeted in the kirk (*church*), the boy who whistled on the way home! The Presbyterian ethic is strict and challenging—well-suited to promote survival in a poor country with a harsh climate. Whether the kirk has shaped the Scots or the Scots their kirk, it is impossible to understand Scottish character and attitudes without taking into account the austere religious background.

The Scots worship God, their Maker, in a plain dwelling dominated by a pulpit. There are no idolatrous statues or other Papist frumperies such as stained glass, holy pictures, gorgeous surplices or altar hangings. The clergy are attired in sober black and a (sparingly used) Communion table replaces the altar. The appeal is to conscience and the intellect, with the minister's address based on a text from the Bible, the only source of truth. To avoid "vain repetitions", there's no liturgy. Prayers, sometimes prolonged like the sermon, are *extempore*. The one concession to the senses is the singing of hymns and a psalm.

The reason for this lack of "outer show" is that ritual is thought irrelevant; what matters is the relation of the individual soul to his or her Maker. Hence the emphasis on self-

reliance and personal integrity. With honesty a prime virtue, the Roman Catholic practice of currying divine favour through bribing the saints is despised as devious. Presbyterians bow their heads in prayer, but feel no need to grovel on their knees; they talk to God direct. This directness characterises all other dealings, and strangers may be disconcerted by the forthright expression of opinion, prejudice, liking or disapproval.

Rigorously democratic, the Church of

Scotland is without bishops or hierarchy. In most other churches, the "man in the pew" has no say in the appointment of clergy, who are imposed from above. The Scots minister, however, is chosen by the congregation, whose elders, having searched far and wide for a suitable incumbent, will invite him to test his worth by a trial sermon. Where other churches' cardinals and archbishops hold office for life, the kirk's leader, the Moderator, is elected for one year only.

The kirk is also a symbol of national independence. At its General Assembly the Sassenach (English) Queen or her representative, the Lord High Commissioner, is in-

Preceding pages, Presbyterian minister. Left, Scottish Presbyterians in the 17th century worship in defiance of the law. Right, reformer John Knox.

vited as a courtesy, but may not take part in the debates. These are much publicised by the media, since, as there is no Scottish Parliament, politics and economics are discussed along with matters clerical, and a report submitted to the Government of the day. The General Assembly, which meets once a year for a week in Edinburgh, is attended by ministers and elders from every kirk in the land, its deliberations observed (sometimes critically) by laymen in the public gallery.

The belief that all are equal in the eyes of the Lord has produced a people more obedient to the dictates of conscience than to rank or worldly status. The humble shepherd,

"philosophical". At its worst this fosters a contentious pedantry, at its best moral courage and the independence of mind which, from a tiny population, has engendered an astonishing number of innovative thinkers in many diverse fields.

The academic excellence, of which the Scots are so proud, owes its merit to John Knox, who insisted that every child, however poor, must attend a school supervised by the kirk. By the beginning of the 18th century Scotland was almost unique in having universal education. Knox's concern, however, was more spiritual than scholastic: the new-born babe is not innocent but "ignorant of all godliness", his life thereafter

who roves the mountains in communion with the Almighty, will stomach no affront from his so-called "betters". This has nothing to do with modern egalitarianism: the novels of Sir Walter Scott, set long ago in feudal times, abound with scenes where servants defy their masters on points of principle. Even the Lord's anointed are not exempt: though a minister has no qualms about berating sinners from the pulpit, they in turn will take issue with him over errors in his sermon.

Cut and thrust: Unlike the English, who avoid confrontation, the average Scot has an aggressive zest for argument, preferably

being a pilgrimage (thorny and arduous) from moral ignorance at birth towards knowledge of the Lord. With the help of the *tawse* (a strap) children were brought up as slaves to the "work ethic", sober, frugal, compulsively industrious. Even today, a popular theme for sermons is the mountain climber who strains every muscle to reach the summit only to find he's not in heaven, as he'd foolishly thought, but facing a peak still higher. No respite "here below", no end to a man's striving.

A Sunday morning congregation in Stornoway in the Outer Hebrides.

Values are positive: duty, discipline, the serious pursuit of worthwhile achievement and a role of benefit to the social good. Hard-headed and purposeful, there's no time to waste on frivolous poetics. Scotland has produced philosophers like David Hume, the economist Adam Smith; Watt, Telford and Macadam, who revolutionised public transport; lawyers, doctors, scientists, engineers and radical politicians in search of Utopia—Knox's Godly Commonwealth in secular translation.

Balance sheet: With the pressure to achieve so relentless, there's short shrift for the idle. Religious imagery is businesslike: at the Last Day people go to their *reckoning* to settle *accounts* with their Maker; it's not sins or trespasses for which pardon is implored but, "Forgive us our *debts* as we forgive our *debtors*." In a land where it's a struggle to survive, the weakest, who go to the wall (and the sooner the better) have *earned* their just deserts.

"Fear of the Lord is the beginning of wisdom." Understandably so, since the Ultimate Judge, equally precise, has no truck with back-sliders. Some years ago the *Glasgow Herald* published a sermon from a minister famous for "broadsides" from the pulpit. Castigating those in kirk for false motives—the farmer praising God for a rich harvest, the vain female showing off her new bonnet—he gave an awful warning of repentance too late. "Once the account is examined and the balance found wanting, ye'll writhe in Hell, the eternal flames having a scald at your feet. Then ye'll fall on your knees and cry, 'Lord, Lord, we didna ken (*know*)'. But the Lord will look down, from His infinite mercy, and He'll say 'Well, ye ken now'."

As divine chastisement is ever-imminent, it's not surprising the Scot is canny (*cautious*) and that, when his fortunes prosper, the best he can say is, "I can't complain." There's nothing meek and mild about the masculine virtues pleasing to God the Father, the Old Testament God of Wrath, who sets the tone for those in command, especially in the family. Some of the most powerful Scottish novels, such as Stevenson's *Weir of Hermiston,* show the terrifying impact of stern fathers on weak or hyper-sensitive sons.

With one slip from the "strait and narrow"

leading to instant perdition, it's said the Scots have a split personality: Jekyll and Hyde. God's Elect are teetotal, but alcoholism is "the curse of Scotland"; while it's almost unheard of for a kirk member to go to prison, Glaswegians proudly boast the busiest criminal court in Europe. It would seem, therefore, that the unofficial influence of the kirk is defiance of all it stands for.

Its ministers have, at all times, lashed "the filthy sins of adultery and fornication" and the taboo on the flesh is so intense that, even in the nursery, mothers, fearing to "spare the rod and spoil the child", economise on caresses. Yet the poet Robert Burns, a flamboyant boozer and wencher, is a national hero, the toasting of whose "immortal memory" provides an annual excuse for unseemly revels. Visitors to puritan Scotland may be puzzled by the enthusiasm for his blasphemous exaltation of sensual delights. But perhaps, if paradoxically, Burns' anarchic *joie de vivre* also stems from the teachings of the kirk, to whose first demand, "What is the chief end of man?" the correct response is: "To glorify God and *enjoy* Him forever."

Though the kirk's faithful have declined—today fewer than one in five are regular communicants—its traditions die hard. Fire and brimstone sermons may be a thing of the past and it's only in the outer isles that the Sabbath is kept holy. Sunday is a day, as elsewhere, for sport, idle leisure or washing the car; even Christmas, once bypassed as Papist, is approved for uniting the family clan. The kirk, however, remains important both in politics, through the General Assembly, and socially as the principal dispenser of charitable aid to the poor and afflicted in this Vale of Tears.

More significant, though, than its public function is an enduring impact on the moulding of character. Scots are still brought up to be thrifty, upright and hard-working, while those who rebel put an energy into their pleasures that can often seem self-destructive. There's success or failure, no limbo in between. Nothing is done by halves and, however secularised the goal, the spur remains: a punitive drive to scale impossible heights. For the individual who fails to appease, if not his Maker, his own expectations, the jaws of Hell still gape for those found "wanting".

Scots Genuises

When the English social scientist Havelock Ellis produced his "Study of British Genius" (based on an analysis of the Dictionary of National Biography) he came up with the fact that there were far more Scots on his list than there should have been. With only 10 percent of the British population, the Scots had produced 15.4 percent of Britain's geniuses. And when he delved deeper into the "men of Science" category he discovered that the Scots made up almost 20 percent of Britain's eminent scientists and engineers.

Not only that, but the Scots-born geniuses tended to be peculiarly influential. Many of them were great original scientists like Black, Hutton, Kelvin and Clerk Maxwell whose work ramified in every direction. Others were important philosophers like the sceptic David Hume, or the economist Adam Smith whose words, according to one biographer, have been "proclaimed by the agitator, conned by the statesmen and printed in a thousand statutes".

Great Scots: Scotland, like Ireland, produced a long string of great military men such as Patrick Gordon (Tsar Peter the Great's right-hand man), James Keith, David Leslie and John Paul Jones. There are also great explorers such as David Livingstone, Mungo Park, David Bruce and John Muir, and accomplished financiers like John Law who founded the National Bank of France and William Paterson who set up the Bank of England. Andrew Carnegie, also a Scot, ruthlessly put together one of the biggest industrial empires America has ever seen, sold it when it was at its peak, then gave much of his money away on the fine Presbyterian basis that "the man who dies rich dies disgraced".

Just why a small, obscure, impoverished country on the edge of Europe should produce such a galaxy of talent is one of the conundrums of European history. As nothing in Scotland's brutal medieval history hints at the riches to come, most historians have concluded that Scotland was galvani-

Eureka! A popular version of how James Watt discovered steam power.

sed in the 16th and 17th centuries by the intellectual dynamics of the Protestant Reformation. This is a plausible theory. Not only did the Reformation produce powerful and challenging figures such as John Knox and his successor Andrew Melville, but it created a church which reformed Scotland's existing universities (Glasgow and St. Andrews), set up two new ones (Edinburgh and Aberdeen), and tried to make sure that every parish in Scotland had its own school.

When Thomas Carlyle tried to explain the proliferation of genius in 18th- and 19th-century Scotland, he found "Knox and the Reformation acting in the heart's core of every one of these persona and phenomena."

might, somehow, be related.

It was a sceptical, questioning, intellectually-charged atmosphere in which talent thrived. And, interestingly, that talent didn't fall foul of established religion: few Scots had a problem squaring their faith with their intellectual curiosity. An extraordinary number of Scotland's ablest and most radical thinkers were "sons of the manse"—that is, born into clergy homes. This meant that, in 1816, when Anglo-Catholics were squabbling over the precise date of the Creation, the Presbyterian intellectual Thomas Chalmers could ask: "Why suppose that this little spot (the planet earth) should be the exclusive abode of life and intelligence?"

This is a large claim, and overlooks the well-run network of primary schools inherited from the Roman Catholic authorities.

But, whatever the reason, 18th-century Scotland produced an astonishing number of talents. As well as David Hume and his friend Adam Smith, Scottish society was studded with able men like Adam Ferguson, who fathered sociology, William Robertson, one of the finest historians of his age, and the teacher Dugald Stewart. There were also gifted eccentrics like the high-court judge Lord Monboddo who ran into a barrage of ridicule by daring to suggest (100 years before Darwin) that men and apes

And nothing thrived more than the science of medicine. In the late 18th and early 19th centuries Edinburgh and Glasgow became two of the most important medical centres in Europe and produced physicians such as William Cullen, John and William Hunter (who revolutionised surgery and gynaecology in London), the three-generation Munro dynasty, Andrew Duncan (who set up the first "humane" lunatic asylums), Robert Liston and James Young Simpson (who discovered the blessings of chloroform). It was a Scot, Alexander Fleming, who hit on penicillin, the most effective antibiotic ever devised.

While Scotland has never produced a musician of any note, or a painter to compare with Rembrandt or Michelangelo, the reputation of 19th-century portraitists like Raeburn, Wilkie and Ramsay are now being upgraded. But in the Adam family (father William and sons Robert, John and James), Scotland threw up a dynasty of architectural genius which was highly influential. (One of the scandals of modern Scotland is the number of Adam-designed buildings which are collapsing into ruin.)

Scotland has three international class writers in Robert Burns (1759-96), Walter Scott (1771-1832) and Robert Louis Stevenson (1850-94), but the ranks of the Scottish did the same to waterproofed fabric; James Nasmyth, who dreamed up the steam hammer; James "Paraffin" Young, who first extracted oil from shale; Alexander Graham Bell, who invented the telephone. More important in world terms were Scotland's "pure" scientists such as John Napier who invented logarithms; Joseph Black, who described the formation of carbon dioxide; James Hutton, Roderick Murchison and Charles Lyell, who between them created modern geology; and Lord Kelvin (an Ulster Scot), who devised (among much else) the second law of thermodynamics and whose name is remembered (like that of Fahrenheit and Celcius) as a unit of temperature.

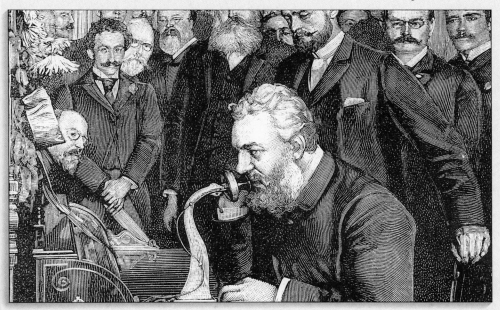

literati are modest. Certainly, they can't compare with the word-spinning talent produced by the Anglo-Irish culture of Joyce, Yeats, Synge, Shaw and O'Casey.

But the number of technologists born in Scotland is truly remarkable: James Watt, who improved the steam engine beyond measure; the civil engineer Thomas Telford; John Dunlop, who invented the pneumatic tyre; John Macadam, who gave his name to the metalled road; Charles MacIntosh, who

Left, an 1827 view of engineer John Macadam. Above, Alexander Graham Bell, inventor of the telephone.

Then there's the Scotsman who is said to have virtually invented the modern world: James Clerk Maxwell, the 19th-century physicist who uncovered the laws of electrodynamics which underlie just about everything we know of electricity, electronics and nuclear physics. Albert Einstein described Clerk Maxwell's work as a "change in the conception of reality" which was the "most fruitful that physics has experienced since the time of Newton". And Max Planck, the German physicist, said Clerk Maxwell was among the small band who are "divinely blest, and radiate an influence far beyond the borders of their land".

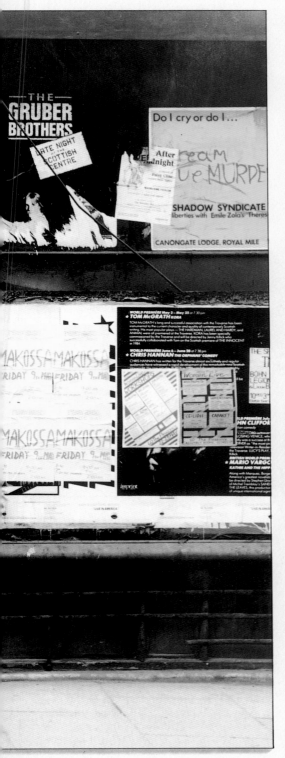

THE GREAT TARTAN MONSTER

When it comes to selling drink, the Mackinnons of Edinburgh (and formerly of Skye) are no slouches. In fact their family company, the Drambuie Liqueur Co. Ltd, is one of the most successful companies in Scotland, and demand for their sweet-tasting liqueur has boomed at a time when the sales of "conventional" whiskies have been crashing through the floor.

And it has all been done on the coat-tails of that great loser, Bonnie Prince Charlie. Not only does Drambuie claim to be based on a "secret" recipe given to the Mackinnon family by the prince himself, but the Stuart's kilted portrait adorns every bottle. And the conference room in Drambuie's Edinburgh HQ is an exact replica of the 18th-century French frigate which sailed the Prince into exile (not to mention drunkenness and despair) in France and Italy.

But, thanks to Bonnie Prince Charlie, the Mackinnons are now turning over more than £23 million a year and paying themselves huge salaries. "The drink itself may be nothing famous," says one Edinburgh expert, "but the marketing has been superb." The Jacobite rising of 1745-46 may have been a disaster for the Stuarts, but it has been good news for the Mackinnons.

The success of Drambuie—"The Prince's Dram"—is tartanry in action. The Mackinnon millions are yet another tribute to that *mélange* of chequered cloth, strident music, mawkish song and bad history which has stalked Scotland for generations and refuses to go away. Tartanry is a vigorous subculture which, by some alchemy, manages to lump together Bonnie Prince Charlie, John Knox, pipe bands, Queen Victoria, Harry Lauder, Mary Queen of Scots, Edinburgh Castle and the White Heather Club dancers. It is a cultural phenomenon which has defied every attempt by the Caledonian intelligentsia to understand it or explain it away.

Fun or frightful?: Many resent the fact that this debased and often silly version of Gaeldom has come to represent the culture of

Ancient and modern: tartan adapts itself to the punk look.

Adam Smith, David Hume, Robert Burns and James Clerk Maxwell. Others regard tartanry as a harmless effervescence which has kept alive a sense of difference in the Scottish people that may yet prove politically decisive. Even more think it is wonderful and buy Andy Stewart records.

But it certainly demands elaborate and expensive tribute. A full set of Highland "evening wear" consisting of worsted kilt, Prince Charlie Coatee, silver-mounted sporran, lace jabots and cuffs, ghillie shoes, chequered hose and *sgian dubh* can cost up to £1,000. Even a "day wear" outfit of a kilt (in "hunting" tartan), Argyle Jacket, leather sporran and civilian brogues will set the

kilts, tartans and bagpipes were hopelessly associated in the public mind with the Jacobite assaults on the Hanoverian ascendancy in 1715, 1719 and 1745. In fact, in 1746 the whole caboodle—bagpipes and all—was banned by the British Government "under pain of death" until 1782.

But, with the Jacobite menace safely out of the way, the élites of Hanoverian Britain began to wax Romantic over the Highland clans. The bogus "Ossian" sagas of James Macpherson became the toast of Europe (Napoleon loved them) while Sir Walter Scott's romantic novels became runaway best sellers. And it was Scott who orchestrated the first-ever outburst of tartan ferv-

wearer back £300.

Of course, none of this applies to the Highlanders who actually live in the Highlands. As anyone who knows the area will confirm, the day dress of the Highland crofter or shepherd consists of boiler suit, wellington boots and cloth cap. For important evening occasions he takes off his cap.

Tartanry could be regarded as Gaeldom's unwitting revenge on the country which once despised and oppressed it. Right into the 19th century there was nothing fashionable (or even respectable) about Highlanders. They were about as popular in 18th-century Britain as the IRA is now. Their

our: King George IV's state visit to Edinburgh in 1822. Determined to make the occasion high romance, Scott wheeled into Edinburgh dozens of petty Highland chieftains and their tartan-clad "tails" and gave them pride of place in the processions. The huge 20-stone (620-kgs) frame of George IV himself was draped in Royal Stewart tartan (over flesh-coloured tights).

"Sir Walter Scott has ridiculously made us appear to be a nation of Highlanders," grumbled one Edinburgh citizen at this display of tartan power, "and the bagpipe and the tartan are the order of the day." And Scott's own son-in-law, John Lockhart, pointed out that the same gentry strutting around Edinburgh in their Highland finery were the very people who were ousting their own clansfolk to make way for sheep. "It almost seems as if there was a cruel mockery in giving such prominence to their pretentions," Lockhart wrote.

But there was no stopping the tartan bandwagon. "We are like to be torn to pieces for tartan" wrote an Edinburgh merchant to the weaving firm of William Wilson and Son of Bannockburn in the wake of George IV's visit. "The demand is so great that we cannot supply our customers." Wilson took the hint and installed 40 extra looms.

The tartan business got another boost

Balmoral Castle as a summer residence and furnished it almost entirely with specially-designed (by Albert) "Balmoral" tartan. After that, the English mania for Highland Scotland knew no bounds. Every Lancashire industrialist and City of London financier had to have his shooting lodge in the mountains, while every family name in Scotland was converted into a "clan" complete with its own tartan.

All of which was helped along by the stirring performance of the Highland regiments in the Crimean War and the Indian Mutiny. In their "Government" tartans (essentially variations on the Black Watch), red coats and feathered bonnets, the Highland

when a couple of amiable English eccentrics known as the "Sobieski Stuarts" (born Charles and John Allen) popped up, claiming to be the direct descendents of Bonnie Prince Charlie and his wife Louisa of Stolberg. They also claimed to have an "ancient" (i.e. fake) manuscript which described hundreds of hitherto unknown tartans.

But the real clincher came in 1858 when Queen Victoria and Prince Albert bought

Left, Sir Walter Scott and friends, who helped create the romantic Highland image. Above, more modern manifestations of tartanry.

battalions were an awesome sight.

By 1881 the British military were so besotted with tartanry that the War Office ordered all Scotland's Lowland regiments to don tartan trousers and short Highland-style doublets. Venerable Lowland regiments like the Royal Scots and the Royal Scots Fusiliers were outraged and protested that their military tradition was both older and a lot more distinguished than that of the Highlanders. But their pleas fell on deaf ears. Only the Scots Guards, as members of the élite Brigade of Guards, were granted the right *not* to wear tartan on their uniforms.

The military victory of tartanry is now

complete. Nowadays every Scottish regiment (including the Scots Guards) has its pipes and drums, all of whom dress in full Victorian-Highland paraphernalia of dress tartan, silver-buttoned doublets, feather bonnets and horsehair sporrans. And Edinburgh Castle, which resisted every foray of Bonnie Prince Charlie's Highland raiders, is now home of the British Army's school of piping, and the centre of that triumph of Highland-military kitsch, the Edinburgh Military Tattoo.

Marauding bands: Not that the cult of the Highland bagpipe is confined to the military. Far from it. According to the Royal (*sic*) Scottish Pipe Band Association (RSPBA),

fence, the saffron-kilted pipers of Ireland have abandoned their melodic "Brian Boru" pipes for the Great Highland Bagpipe.

Another (somewhat quieter) arm of tartan imperialism is the Royal Scottish Country Dance Society (RSCDS) which is run from Edinburgh and which, at the last count, had more than 26,000 members prancing and leaping around ballrooms all over the world. This may be understandable in Scot-infested corners of the globe like the United States, Canada and New Zealand but it isn't so explicable in France, Holland, Sweden or Japan. Just why the sensible citizens of Gothenburg, Paris, The Hague, Nairobi and Tokyo should want to trick themselves out in

there are now more than 400 pipe-bands alive and wailing in the U.K. alone, with hundreds more all over the world. Every year the bands flock to the one or other of the RSPBA's five championships. The biggest prize is the World Pipe Band Championship which is normally won by a Scottish band, but which in 1987 went to the 75th Fraser Highlanders from Canada. But the world of tartanry is full of ironies. Eighty of the RSPBA's member bands are in Ulster, where the hard-line Protestants are happy to swathe themselves in the tartans of the Jacobite clans, most of whom were Catholic or Episcopalian. On the other side of the Irish

tartan to skip around in strict tempo to tunes like "The Wee Cooper O' Fife", "The Duke of Perth", "Cadgers in the Canongate" or "Deuks Dang Ower My Daddie" is a deep and abiding mystery.

It may have something to do with Scottish country dancing's Royal and aristocratic connections. The Queen herself is patron of the RSCDS, and the Royal prefix was granted by her father King George VI just before he died in 1952. Other exalted members include the Earl of Mansfield (who is President of the RSCDS) the Duke of Atholl, Lord Glenconner and Sir Donald Cameron of Lochiel.

But it seems unlikely that the Royal laying on of hands will ever extend to the crowd of kilted warblers, accordion players, comics and fiddlers who make their living entertaining Scotland (and the Scottish diaspora). Usually showbiz tartanry finds its own niche, but occasionally, as in the case of the Bay City Rollers or the fearsome Jesse Rae (half-Highlander, half-Viking), it escapes into the mainstream of pop culture. Interestingly, none of the new breed of Gaelic-speaking folk-rock bands such as Runrig or Ossian are ever seen near a scrap of tartan.

Olympic efforts: Yet another manifestation of tartanry is the Highland games circuit. Every year between May and September

attract crowds of up to 5,000, although the Braemar Gathering (with the Royal Family in attendance, can easily pull in more than 20,000.

But even Braemar cannot compete with the 40,000 or 50,000-strong crowds who flock to watch the big Highland games in the U.S.A. The event at Grandfather Mountain in North Carolina is now the biggest of its kind on earth. American tartanry buffs are very keen on "clan gatherings" in which they get togged up in a kind of "Sword of Zorro" version of Highland dress, and march up and down in front of their "chief" brandishing their broadswords.

But perhaps the daftest manifestation of

ber villages and towns the length of Scotland (plus a few in England) stage a kind of Caledonian olympics in which brawny, kilted figures toss the caber, putt the shot and throw the hammer while squads of little girls in velvets and tartans dance their hearts out to the sound of bagpipes. Andrew Rettie of the Scottish Highland Games Association (which has not yet acquired a "Royal" prefix) estimates there are about 100 such games held in Scotland every year. Most

Left, members of the Royal Family attending the Braemar Games. Above, a sheaf of tartans.

competitive tartanry is "haggis-hurling", an event dreamed up in 1977 by an Edinburgh public relations man, Robin Dunseath, as "a bit of an upmarket joke". To Dunseath's utter astonishment the "ancient" sport of haggis-hurling took off and has gone from strength to strength. Dunseath (an Irishman) now despatches his "How To Run a Haggis Hurl" kits all over the globe. The world record is held by Stewart Pettigrew of Saltcoats who hurled a 1.5lb (680-gms) "competition" haggis more than 181 ft (55 metres). It has been a golden decade for the sport's "official" haggis makers, Dalzell & McIntosh of Stockbridge in Edinburgh.

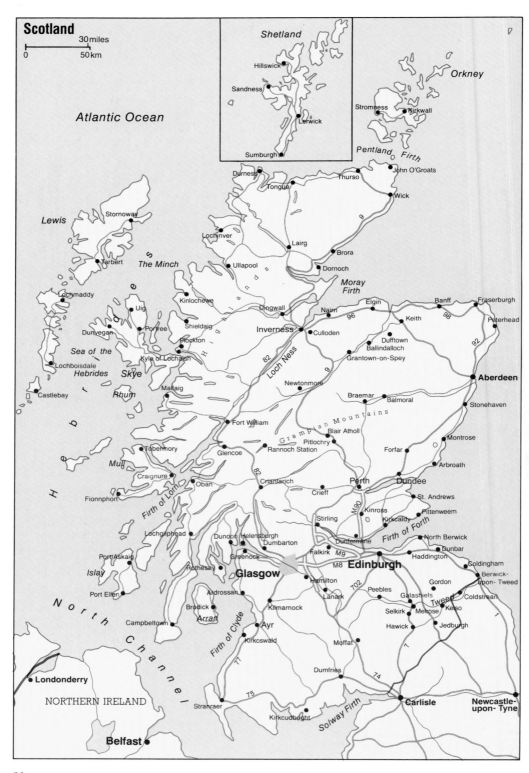

Scotland

30 miles
0   50km

Shetland

Hillswick
Sandness
Lerwick
Sumburgh

Orkney

Stromness
Kirkwall

Atlantic Ocean

Pentland Firth

Durness
Tongue
Thurso
John O'Groats
Wick

Lewis

Stornoway

Lochinver
Lairg
9
Brora

Tarbert

The Minch

Ullapool
Dornoch

Moray Firth

Lochmaddy

Kinlochewe
Dingwall
Nairn
Elgin
Banff
Fraserburgh

Uig
Shieldaig
96
Keith
96
Peterhead

Dunvegan
Portree
Plockton
Inverness
Culloden
Dufftown
92

Lochboisdale
Kyle of Lochalsh
Ballindalloch
Grantown-on-Spey

Sea of the
Hebrides

Skye

Loch Ness
82

9

Aberdeen

Castlebay

Rhum

Mallaig
Newtonmore
Braemar
Balmoral
Stonehaven

Fort William
Grampian Mountains
Blair Atholl
Montrose

Tobermory
Glencoe
Rannoch Station
Pitlochry
Forfar

Mull
Craignure
Oban
Crianlarich
Perth
Dundee
Arbroath

Fionnphort
Firth of Lorn
82
Crieff
St. Andrews

Stirling
M90
Kinross
Kirkcaldy
Pittenweem

Lochgilphead
Dunoon
Helensburgh
Dumbarton
Dunfermline
Firth of Forth
North Berwick

Port Askaig
Greenock
Falkirk
M9
Haddington
Dunbar

Islay
Rothesay
Glasgow
M8
Edinburgh
Coldingham
Berwick-upon-Tweed

Ardrossan
Hamilton
Gordon
Coldstream

Port Ellen
Brodick
Lanark
702
Peebles
Galashiels
Tweed
Kelso

Arran
Kilmarnock
Selkirk
Melrose

Campbeltown
Ayr
Hawick
Jedburgh

North Channel
Firth of Clyde
Kirkoswald
Moffat
77

Londonderry
Kirkcudbright
74

NORTHERN IRELAND
Stranraer
75
Dumfries
Solway Firth
Carlisle
Newcastle-upon-Tyne

Belfast

86

PLACES

Like Greece, Scotland is a hilly country with many small islands and a complicated history that attracts romantics. There, the similarity ends. The ethic bequeathed by Scottish Presbyterianism is a world away from Mediterranean attitudes and, at the height of summer, an umbrella is often needed as protection from the rain rather than from the sun. But few complain. The wildest Highland thunderstorm only enhances the magnificence of one of Europe's most captivating regions.

Edinburgh, a majestic capital city, enchants effortlessly, its castle towering over it on a rugged crag as a daily reminder of its turbulent history. These days, as a "court city" whose court long ago emigrated to London, Edinburgh cultivates culture and rejoices in its appellation of "the Athens of the North" (even though a character in a Tom Stoppard play suggested that a more appropriate title would be "the Reykjavik of the South").

Just 40 miles away, Glasgow, by contrast, is Britain's great unknown city, still suffering from an outdated image of industrial grime and urban decay. Yet, having had its heart ripped out by motorways in the 1960s, it has remodelled itself radically enough to have been named European City of Culture for 1990 and its Burrell Collection museum has, to Edinburgh's chagrin, soared to the top of tourism's league table.

Outside the two great cities lies an astonishingly varied landscape. To the south-west are the moorlands, lochs and hills of Dumfries and Galloway, haunt of Scotland's national poet Robert Burns; to the south-east, the castles, forests and glens of the Borders, one of Europe's unspoilt areas; to the west, the rugged splendour of the West Highlands, a fragmented wilderness of mountain and moor, heather and stag, and the jumping-off point for Skye and the Western Isles; to the north-east, the farms and fishing villages of Fife and the swing along the North Sea coast through Dundee (centre of jute, jam and journalism) towards the granite city of Aberdeen, Scotland's oil capital; and, to the north, the elusive monster of Loch Ness, the awesomely empty tracts of the Highlands, and the islands of Orkney and Shetland that are more Norse than Scottish.

Scotland's greatest appeal is to people who appreciate the open air, whether scenery or outdoor pursuits. The attractions range from pleasant rambling across moors and treks along long-distance footpaths to arduous hill walking and hair-raising rock climbs. You can ski down snow-capped mountains, fish for salmon in crystal-clear streams, or play golf in the country that invented the game.

"Scotland's For Me!" chorused a recent Scottish Tourist Board advertising campaign. There must be few visitors who could find a good reason to disagree.

EDINBURGH

Not for nothing was that great parable of the divided self, *Dr Jekyll and Mr Hyde*, written by an Edinburgh man. The author Robert Louis Stevenson may have set the story in London but he conjured it out of the bizarre life of a respectable Edinburgh tradesman called William Brodie. Brodie, who was Deacon of Wrights and Masons of Edinburgh, was a pillar of 18th-century rectitude by day and a ruthless thief by night who ended his days dancing at the end of the Edinburgh hangman's rope. Stevenson, it seems, was fascinated by Brodie and other such Edinburgh double-dealers like Major Weir, who contrived to be both a pious Presbyterian elder and a necromancing wizard, and Dr Robert Knox, the respected Edinburgh anatomist who bought about 15 freshly-murdered corpses from the Burke and Hare partnership. Burke himself was a "respectable man" apart from the fact that he was a murderer.

All of which has led more than one critic to see the Jekyll and Hyde story as a handy metaphor for the city of Edinburgh itself. Something that is at once universal and characteristically Scots. Where else, they ask, does a semi-ramshackle late medieval town glower down on such Georgian elegance? What other urban centre contains such huge chunks of sheer wilderness within its boundaries? Does any other city in Europe have so many solid Victorian suburbs surrounded by such bleak housing estates? Stevenson himself was inclined to agree. "Few places, if any," he wrote, "offer a more barbaric display of contrasts to the eye."

And not just to the eye. Edinburgh's renowned civic pride conceals some of the hardest-pressed police stations in Britain, and the worst hard drugs problem outside of London. Edinburgh may have one of Europe's most venerable medical establishments, but it also has an appalling incidence of AIDS. And, while Edinburgh's financial warlocks may juggle with billions every year, the local authorities never seem to have enough money to keep the streets clean. Behind the amiable and rational intelligence of Dr. Henry Jekyll stands the cold glare of Edward Hyde.

Raw weather: Just as Edward Hyde "gave an impression of deformity without any nameable malformation" so the meaner side of Edinburgh tends to lurk unnoticed in the beauty of the topography and the splendour of the architecture. Even the weather seems to play its part. "The weather is raw and boisterous in winter, shifty and ungenial in summer, and downright meteorological purgatory in spring," Stevenson wrote of his home town.

But the Jekyll and Hyde metaphor can be stretched too far. And for all its sly duality and shifty ways Edinburgh remains one of the most beautiful and amenable cities in Europe, a stunning confection of late medieval tenements, neo-classical terraces, tidy suburbs, rivers and wooded gardens set among a series of volcanic hills sprinkled with

Preceding pages: Shetland's capital, Lerwick; Edinburgh panorama. Left, fireworks open the Edinburgh festival. Right, participant in the Thistle Ceremony.

EDINBURGH

NORTHUMBERLAND ST

St G

YOR

GLOUCESTER LANE

Gardens

HERIOT ROW

Street

QUEEN ST

Nat. Mus
of Antiqu

MORAY
PLACE

Queen

ST ANDREW

ST ANDREW

QUEEN ST

THISTLE ST

St Andrew

SQUARE

GLENTIN HOPE ST

HILL ST

FREDERICK ST

Music Hall

CHAR-
LOTTE

CASTLE ST

GEORGE

ST

Royal Scottish
Academy

Wa

SQUARE

PRINCES ST

Scott
Monument

MARKET

Princes Street Gardens

• Fe

National
Gallery

St Giles
Cathedral

St Cuthbert

Castle

Parliament
House

KING STABLES

ESPLANADE

National
Library

LOTHIAN RD

RD

GRASSMARKET

WEST PORT

Greyfriars
Church

MORRISON ST

BREAD ST

G. Heriot's
School

College of
Art

EARL GREY ST

LAURISTON PLACE

MEADOW WALK

FOUNTAIN BRIDGE

HOME ST

NORTH MEADOW

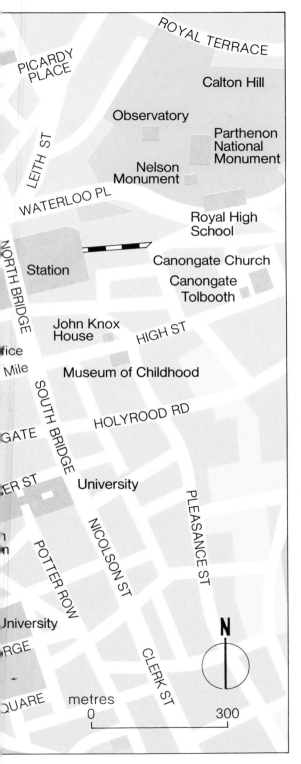

PICARDY PLACE

ROYAL TERRACE

Calton Hill

LEITH ST

Observatory

Parthenon
National
Monument

Nelson
Monument

WATERLOO PL

Royal High
School

NORTH BRIDGE

Station

Canongate Church

Canongate
Tolbooth

John Knox
House

HIGH ST

fice

Mile

Museum of Childhood

SOUTH BRIDGE

HOLYROOD RD

GATE

ER ST

University

PLEASANCE ST

Jniversity

NICOLSON ST

RGE

POTTER ROW

N

QUARE

CLERK ST

metres

0   300

small lochs. The city is hemmed to the south by the Pentland Hills—some of which are almost 2,000 ft (600 metres) high—and to north by the island-studded waters of the Firth of Forth. In 1878 Stevenson declared himself baffled that "this profusion of eccentricities, this dream in masonry and living rock is not a drop-scene in a theatre, but a city in the world of everyday reality".

Which, of course, it is. At the last count Edinburgh contained almost 440,000 people rattling around in 26,000 hectares on the south bank of the Firth of Forth. While the city's traditional economy of "books, beer and biscuits" has been drastically whittled away by the ravages of recession and change, there is a powerful underpinning of banking, insurance, shipping, the professions (especially the law), the universities, a lot of hospitals, and of course government bureaucracies (local and central). By and large, the great North Sea oil boom has passed Edinburgh by, although some of the city's financiers did well enough by shuffling investment funds around, and for a while Leith Docks was used as an onshore supply base, to coat pipes, and build steel deck modules.

And, like every other decent-sized city in the western hemisphere, Edinburgh is now a fairly rich cultural mix. The "base" population remains overwhelmingly Scots with a large Irish content, but there are big communities of Poles, Italians, Ukranians, Jews, Pakistanis, Sikhs, Bengalis, Chinese and, of course, English. Within that mix there are echoes of Ulster. Although Edinburgh has been spared the kind of religious bigotry which bedevils Glasgow, it still has separate schools for Catholic and Protestant children. And every July the city stages one of the biggest "Orange Walks" outside of Northern Ireland.

To some extent Edinburgh is a city with a hole in its psyche where a Scottish legislature should have been, the mock capital of a country without sovereignty. The last attempt to claw back some power from London came to grief in 1979 when the British Government refused to set up a Scottish Assembly because the Scots did not vote in favour of one by a big enough margin, although they did vote in favour. The building which was converted to house the Assembly (the old **Royal High School** in Waterloo Place) now lies forlorn, only partly used by the lawyers of the Crown Office.

For all that, Edinburgh wields more power and influence than any British city outside of London. It is the center of the Scots legal system, home to the Court of Session (the civil court) and the High Court of Justiciar (criminal court) from which there is no appeal to the House of Lords. Edinburgh's decision is final. Edinburgh is also the base of the Church of Scotland (the established church) whose General Assembly every May floods Edinburgh with sober-suited Presbyterian ministers from all over Scotland.

And the British Government runs its policies in Scotland through the Edinburgh-based **Scottish Office**, whose boss, the Secretary of State for Scotland, is a member of the British cabinet. Anyone seeking to consult the records of Scotland (land titles, company registration, government archives, lists of bankrupts, births, marriages, deaths) has to come to Edinburgh. And *The Scotsman* newspaper, published in Edinburgh, is still arguably the most influential piece of media north of the border, a kind of notice-board of the Scottish establishment.

The early days: No-one is quite sure just how old Edinburgh is, only that people have been living in the area for more than 5,000 years. But it seems certain that the city grew from a tiny community perched on the "plug" of volcanic rock which now houses **Edinburgh Castle**. With its steep, easily-defended sides, natural springs of water, and excellent vantage points, the castle rock was squabbled over for hundreds of years by generations of Picts, Scots, British (Welsh) and Angles, with the Scots (from Ireland) finally coming out on top. But it was the Northumbrian (i.e. Angle) king Edwin

Left, the city's old quarter. Right, the interior of Edinburgh Castle.

who gave his name to the city.

It was not until the 11th century that Edinburgh settled down to be the capital of Scotland, and a royal residence was built within the walls of Edinburgh Castle. But Edinburgh proved to be a strategic liability in the medieval wars with the English. It was too close to England. And, time after time, powerful English armies came crashing across the border laying waste the plump farmlands of the southeast, and burning Edinburgh itself. It happened in 1174 (when the English held Edinburgh castle for 12 years) in 1296, in 1313 (during the Wars of Independence), in 1357, in 1573, in 1650 and as late as 1689 when the Duke of Gordon tried, and failed, to hold Edinburgh Castle against the Protestant army of William of Orange.

The hammering of Edinburgh by the English military came to an end in 1707 (along with much else) when the Scottish Parliament, many of whom had been bribed by English interests, voted to abandon the sovereignty of Scotland in favour of an incorporating union with England. "Now there's an end of an auld sang" the old Earl of Seafield was heard to mutter as he signed the Act. But in fact, power and influence had been haemhorraging out of Edinburgh ever since the Union of the Crowns in 1603 when the Scottish King James VI (the son of Mary Queen of Scots) became the first monarch of Great Britain and Ireland.

Stripped of its Royal Family, courtiers, parliament and civil service, 18th-century Edinburgh should have lapsed into a sleepy provincialism. But that didn't happen. The Treaty of Union guaranteed the position of Scots law and the role of the Presbyterian Church of Scotland. With both these powerful institutions still firmly entrenched in Edinburgh, the city was still a place where men of power and influence met to make important decisions.

In fact, for reasons which are still not clear, 18th-century Scotland became one of Europe's intellectual power-houses, producing philosophers like

Scotland's capital, like England's, thrives on ceremonial.

David Hume, Adam Smith and William Robertson, architect-builders like William Adam and his sons Robert and John, engineers like James Watt, Thomas Telford, John Rennie, surgeons like John and William Hunter, and painters like Henry Raeburn and Alan Ramsay. It was a concentration of talent that led the amiable Englishman John Amyat, the King's Chemist, to remark that he could stand at the **Mercat Cross** near St. Giles and "in a few minutes, take 50 men of genius by the hand".

That explosion of talent became known as the Scottish Enlightenment, and one of its greatest creations was the **New Town** of Edinburgh. Between 1760 and 1840 a whole new city—bright, spacious, elegant and rational—was created on the land to the north of the **Old Town**. It was one of the wonders of the world, and was very quickly filled up by the aristocracy, gentry and "middling" classes of Edinburgh who left the Old Town to the poor and to the waves of Irish and Highland immigrants who flooded into Edinburgh from the 1840s on.

Like most British (and European) cities, Edinburgh's population burgeoned in the 19th century, from 90,786 in 1801 to just over 413,000 in 1901. There was no way that the Old Town and the New Town could house that kind of population, and Victorian Edinburgh became ringed by a huge development of handsome stone-built tenements and villas in suburbs like **Bruntsfield**, **Marchmont**, **the Grange** and **Morningside**, which in turn became ringed about by the 20th-century bungalows and speculative housing. And beginning in the 1930s the Edinburgh Corporation (and later the Edinburgh District Council) outflanked the lot by throwing up an outer ring of huge council-housing estates some of which are now fraught with awful problems.

The Old Town: Although Edinburgh's Old Town—that is, the original Edinburgh—has been allowed to deteriorate in a way that is nothing short of disgraceful, it is being revived. In the past 10 years or so, a serious effort has been made to breathe new life in to the Old Town's labyrinth of medieval streets, wynds and closes. The Yuppies of Edinburgh are in the process of discovering the heady delights of city-centre living, and a handful of developers have been restoring 17th-century tenements, and covering 19th-century breweries to cater for this enthusiasm for the Old Town. As a way of rescuing Edinburgh's many down-at-heel architectural treasures, the city fathers have been literally giving away some of the buildings (along with handsome grants) to private developers.

But even after two centuries of neglect, Edinburgh's Old Town probably packs more historic buildings into a square mile or so than anywhere in Britain. Stevenson, again, provides the reason. "It (the old Town) grew, under the law that regulates the growth of walled cities in precarious situation, not in extent, but in height and density. Public buildings were forced, whenever there was room for them, into the midst of thoroughfares; thoroughfares

Left, yesterday's transport, available today: an Edinburgh coachman. Right, city planning, made evident from the air.

THE MONEY MEN OF CHARLOTTE SQUARE

One of the more remarkable facts about Edinburgh is that it is the biggest financial centre in Europe apart from the City of London. Occasionally the bankers of Frankfurt, the Gnomes of Zurich or even the upstarts of Manchester dispute Edinburgh's claim, but their protests are half-hearted and never conceded. "Of course it's very difficult to measure these things," says Professor Jack Shaw of Scottish Financial Enterprises (the Edinburgh financiers' mouthpiece). "But Edinburgh handles more fund money than anyone outside of London. We calculate that it amounts to around £50 billion. And that's a lot of money."

Not, Shaw hastens to add, that Edinburgh is resting on its laurels. His own organisation was set up in 1986 to make sure that Edinburgh's money-men kept up with the world's latest money-market technologies. "People are much more outward looking than they used to be," he says. "They're doing far more international business. And there's a whole new merchant banking sector that virtually didn't exist 10 years ago."

The gravy train: Naturally, this huge community of bankers, investment-fund managers, stockbrokers, corporate lawyers, accountants, insurance executives and unit-trust operators has to be "serviced". Which means nice business for Edinburgh's glossier advertising agencies, public relations firms, design studios and photographers—not to mention restaurants, wine bars and auction houses like Sotheby's, Phillips and Christie's.

Just as "the City" is shorthand for London's vast financial community, so Edinburgh's is known as "Charlotte Square". But the financial district it inhabits extends far beyond the elegant boundaries of the square itself. It now takes in much of George Street, St. Andrew's Square, Queen Street, Melville Street and various other large chunks of the New Town.

Edinburgh's star role in the financial world can be traced back to the enthusiasm of the Scots for making and then keeping money. The Scots have always been among the modern world's best and canniest bankers. Which is why the Scottish clearing banks have a statutory right (dating from 1845) to print their own distinctive banknotes. This is a right the Scottish banks relish, particularly as the English banks were stripped of it following a string of bank failures in the 19th century. And the Scots are remarkably attached to their Edinburgh-based banks, as the powerful Hongkong and Shanghai Bank found to its cost when it tried to take over the Royal Bank of Scotland in 1981. The men from Hongkong were stunned by the ferocity of the opposition drummed up in Scotland, and were forced to back off. But in 1987 the Clydesdale Bank (a subsidiary of England's Midland Bank) slipped into Australian hands with hardly a murmur of objection in Scotland. "Everybody felt the Clydesdale was probably better off belonging to some hard-charging Australians than the dozy English," was the opinion of one Edinburgh financier.

Probably the biggest fish in Edinburgh's financial pond are the giant Scottish insurance companies which handle funds in the region of £30 billion. The most important by far is the Standard Life Assurance Company which has offices all over Britain, Ireland and Canada and is now Europe's biggest "mutual fund". Like most of the Edinburgh insurance companies, the Standard Life is a vintage operation (1825). Some are even older, with names that have a satisfyingly old-fashioned ring, like the Scottish Widows Fund & Life Assurance Society or the Scottish Provident Institution for Mutual Life Assurance.

Although Charlotte Square has taken much stick for being slow to get in on the booming unit trust business (a complaint it is fast putting right) there's no shortage of old-fashioned "investment trusts". It was with money from these trusts that much of the American west was built up. In the 19th century Charlotte Square was heavily into cattle ranching, fruit farming and railways in the USA. Nowadays it prefers to sink its "bawbees" into the high-tech wizardry of Silicon Valley or east Texas oil wells. And while Edinburgh as a whole benefitted little from North Sea oil, parts of Charlotte Square did very nicely.

As more than one study of the Scottish economy has pointed out, Charlotte Square is operated by a few tightly-knit and interlocking groups of fund-managers, insurance executives, lawyers and accountants. A few of their number—Peter de Vink, Vikram Lall, Angus Grossart, Iain Noble—have become semi-public figures. But the real shakers and movers, men like James Gammell of Ivory and Sime and Charles Fraser of the legal firm Dundas & Wilson, remain firmly out of the public gaze.

New threat: For all its financial clout, though, Charlotte Square doesn't have a monopoly. There's a thriving little financial community in Dundee (mainly investment trusts built from old jute money), and the businessmen of Glasgow have been throwing up glitzy new office buildings in a way that's making Charlotte Square nervous. "A bit worrying," says one Edinburgh stockbroker. "If the Japanese or the Americans start to move out of London in a big way, there'll be a lot more room for them in Glasgow than there will be in Charlotte Square. The New Town is beautiful but it ain't very big. But our chances of getting permission to put up new offices in the centre of Edinburgh are zero."

were diminished into lanes; houses sprang up storey after storey, neighbour mounting upon neighbour's shoulder, as in some Black Hole in Calcutta, until the population slept 14 to 15 deep in a vertical direction."

In this late-medieval version of Manhattan, the aristocracy, gentry merchants and commons of Edinburgh lived cheek by jowl. Often they shared the same "lands" (tenements), the "quality" at the bottom and the hoi polloi at the top. They rubbed shoulders in the dark stairways and closes, and knew one another in a way that was socially impossible in England. Any Lord of Session (high court judge) whose verdict was unpopular could expect to be harangued or even pelted with mud and stones as he made his way home. Politicians, aristocracy and church leaders came under close scrutiny. When the Scottish parliament approved the Treaty of Union with England in 1707, the Edinburgh mob went on the rampage trying to track down the "traitors" who, they felt, had sold Scotland out to the "Auld Enemy" (the English).

In fact, the Edinburgh mob was a formidable political force. For much of the 18th century it was led by one "General" Joe Smith, a bow-legged cobbler who believed passionately in the inferiority of women (his wife had to walk several paces behind him) and who could drum up a crowd of thousands within a few minutes. With the mob at his back, Joe Smith could lay down the law to the Magistrates of Edinburgh, and ran a kind of rough justice against thieving landlords and dishonest traders. His career came to an end in 1780 when he fell off the top of a stagecoach, dead drunk, and was killed outright.

Not that life in the Old Town was entirely dominated by the mob rule of General Joe Smith. Far from it. Until the end of the 18th century the Old Town was the epicentre of fashionable society, a tight little metropolis of elegant drawing rooms, fashionable concert halls, dancing academies, and a

Below, old Edinburgh up for sale.

bewildering variety of taverns, "howffs", coffee-houses and social clubs. "Nothing was so common in the morning as to meet men of high rank and official dignity reeling home from a close in the High Street where they had spent the night in drinking" wrote Robert Chambers, one of Edinburgh's liveliest chroniclers.

The heady social life of the Old Town came to an end at the turn of the 19th century when it was progressively abandoned by the rich and the influential whose houses were inherited by the poor and the feckless. "The Great Flitting" it was called, and crowds used to gather to watch all fine furniture, crockery and paintings being loaded into carts for the journey down the newly-created "earthen mound" (now called **The Mound**) to the New Town.

The spine of the Old Town is the **Royal Mile**, a wide thoroughfare which runs down from the Castle to the **Palace of Holyrood House,** and comprises (from top to bottom) Castlehill, Lawnmarket, the High Street, and the Canongate. This street was described by Daniel Defoe (who lived in Edinburgh at the beginning of the 18th century) as "perhaps the largest, longest, and finest Street for Buildings, and Number of Inhabitants, not in Britain only, but in the world."

The **Castle** itself is well worth a visit, if only for the views out over the city. Many of the castle buildings are 18th- and 19th-century, although the tiny Norman chapel dedicated to the saintly Queen Margaret, dates back to the 12th century. Also worth seeking out are the **Scottish National War Memorial,** the **Great Hall** (which has a superb hammer-beam roof), and the **Crown Room** which houses the Regalia (crown jewels) of Scotland, which were lost between 1707 and 1818 when a commission set up by Sir Walter Scott traced them to a locked chest in a locked room in the castle. For years the Scottish press have been grumbling about the appalling way the castle is run by the British Government, particularly about the layout, lighting and display in the

Left, Jenners building in Princes Street. Right, the entance to Holyrood House.

museums, and the fact that there is no café, bar or tearoom.

Just below the castle esplanade, on **Castlehill**, there is an iron fountain marking the spot where Edinburgh used to burn its witches (between 1479 and 1722); **Ramsay Gardens,** the tenements designed by the 19th-century planning genius Patrick Geddes; a **Camera Obsucra** built in the 1850s; and the Pugin's huge **Tollbooth Kirk**, where Edinburgh's Gaelic-speaking community used to worship. Now closed, the Tollbooth Kirk is about to be converted into some kind of Scottish "heritage centre" along the lines of the Jorvik Viking Centre in York.

On the north side of the Lawnmarket is **Gladstone's Land**, a completely restored six-storey 17th-century tenement now owned by the National Trust for Scotland (NTS) which gives some insight into 17th-century Edinburgh life (dirty, difficult and malodorous). There is **Lady Stairs House**, now a museum dedicated to Burns, Scott and Stevenson, and **Deacon Brodie's Tav-**

ern, named after William Brodie, the model for the Jekyll & Hyde story.

The **High Street** features (among much else) **Parliament House** (now the law courts), the **High Kirk of St. Giles** (often miscalled St. Giles Cathedral), the **Mercat Cross** from which kings and queens are proclaimed, the **City Chambers** which was built as an "exchange" (i.e. office block) and one of the first buildings in the great drive to "improve" Edinburgh in the late 18th century. The lower part of the High Street contains the 15th-century **Moubray House** which is probably the oldest inhabited building in Edinburgh, **John Knox's house,** and the recently-rebuilt **Museum of Childhood** where children find it hard to get near the displays for crowds of wistful adults.

The **Canongate** is particularly rich in 16th- and 17th-century buildings. There is the **Tolbooth, Bakehouse Close, Huntly House** (Edinburgh's own museum), **Moray House** (the most lavish of the aristocracy's town houses), the Dutch-style **Canongate**

The city as seen from Holyrood Park.

Church, **White Horse Close** (once a coaching inn), and **Acheson House**, built in 1633 by Sir Archibald Acheson, Charles I's man in Scotland. Just below the Canongate Church is the "**mushroom garden**", a small walled garden laid out in the 17th-century manner, and almost completely unknown.

The **Palace of Holyrood House** began as an Abbey in the 12th century, grew into a Royal Palace in the early 16th century, and much was added in the late 17th century by Sir William Bruce for Charles II, who never set foot in the building. Holyrood's history is long and often grisly. It was here that Mary Queen of Scots witnessed the butchery of her Italian favourite, David Rizzio, in 1558, and where the severed and scattered remains of the Marquis of Montrose were reassembled prior to being given a decent burial in 1661. Bonnie Prince Charlie held court here in 1745 during his short-lived triumph.

And Holyrood Palace was used by George IV during his hilarious state visit to Edinburgh in 1822. The portly Hanoverian stalked the palace wearing flesh-coloured tights under an exceedingly brief Royal Stewart tartan kilt. "As he is to be here so short a time," remarked one waggish Edinburgh lady, "the more we see of him the better."

But he set a precedent which the British royals have been following ever since. Queen Victoria and Prince Albert favoured Holyrood as a stop-over on their way to and from Balmoral. And every June, when the Queen is in residence, the dress-hire business booms and polite Edinburgh goes into a flap over who has and who has not been invited to the Royal Garden Party in Holyrood's gardens. It usually rains.

South of the Royal Mile, on George IV Bridge, are the **National Library of Scotland** (one of the few copyright libraries in Britain) and the little bronze statue of **Greyfriars Bobby**, the Skye terrier immortalized by Walt Disney. In Chambers Street the **Royal Museum of Scotland's** dazzling collection of 19th-century machinery and scientific instruments is well worth seeing, which

Left, the circus comes to town. Right, Greyfriars Bobby's statue.

is more than can be said for its collection of badly stuffed animals. And on the corner of Chambers Street and the North Bridge lies **The Old College,** the finest of Edinburgh university's collection of buildings.

Running roughly parallel with the Royal Mile to the south are the **Grassmarket**—the site of many a riot and public execution—a long and now rather dismal street called the **Cowgate**, which in the 19th century was crammed with Irish immigrants fleeing the Great Famine. James Connolly, one of the martyrs of the Easter Rising in Dublin in 1916, was born and reared in the Cowgate. He worked as a printer on the *Edinburgh Evening News*, and did a spell of military service with the Royal Scots, the oldest regiment in the British Army.

The Irish Catholic nature of the Cowgate is testified to by the huge but inelegant bulk of **St. Patrick's Roman Catholic church.** A much more interesting Cowgate building is **St. Cecilia's Hall**, which now belongs to Edinburgh University, but was built by the Edinburgh Musical Society as a fashionable concert hall in 1762 and modelled on the Opera House at Parma.

A landmark of Europe: "A sort of schizophrenia in stone" is how the novelist Eric Linklater once described **Princes Street**, going on to contrast the "natural grandeur solemnized by memories of human pain and heroism" of the castle rock with the tawdry commercialism of the north side of the street. This "municipal anarchy," he argued, had created a street "whose resemblance to an oriental bazaar is truly startling". In Linklater's view, the kind of tourist junk on sale in Princes Street "would look equally at home on the boat of a native vendor in Port Said". Linklater wrote that in 1960, and nothing much has changed since.

If Princes Street is still one of Europe's more elegant boulevards it is no thanks to the architects, developers and retailers of the 20th century. Just about every decent building has been gouged out of the north side of the street

Sir Walter Scott stares stonily at modern Edinburgh.

and replaced by some undistinguished piece of Marks & Spencer modern. What has saved Princes Street from tragedy is the fact that the south side remains the "broad and deep ravine planted with trees and shrubbery" that so impressed the American writer Nathaniel Willis in 1834. So unless the powers-that-be are plotting to fill in **Princes Street Gardens** with car parks (it has been suggested) and level the Edinburgh Castle, Princes Street's role as one of the landmarks of Europe should be secure.

Princes Street has always been the venue for Edinburgh promenaders, out to enjoy what Thomas Carlyle called "the finest city prospect in the World and the sight of one another". Generations of Edinburgh youths and girls have ambled up and down Princes Street, eyeing one another in the hope of striking up a conversation on the return journey. The poet Edwin Muir compared an evening stroll on Princes Street to waiting on a country railway platform for a train which is late. "There

is the same intense and permitted scrutiny of one's fellow passengers, the same growing expectation..."

With the exception of the superb **Register House** by Robert Adam at the far east end of the street, and a few remaining 19th-century shops (such as Jenners and Debenhams) everything worthwhile is on the south side of the street. The most startling edifice is the huge and intricate Gothic monument to **Sir Walter Scott,** erected in 1844 and designed by a self-taught architect called George Meikle Kemp. The unfortunate Kemp drowned in an Edinburgh canal shortly before the monument was complete, and was due to be buried in the vault under the memorial until some petty-minded member of Scott's entourage persuaded the Court of Session to divert the funeral. Another blow for Edward Hyde.

Much more typical of Edinburgh are the two neo-classical art galleries at the junction of Princes Street and The Mound. Now known as the **Royal Scottish Academy** and the **National**

A timely trim for the flower clock in Princes Street Gardens.

Gallery of Scotland, both buildings were designed by William Playfair between 1822 and 1845. The space around the galleries has long been Edinburgh's version of London's Hyde Park Corner, and is heavily used by preachers, polemicists and bagpipers. During the Edinburgh Festival it becomes the greatest free show on earth, with brass bands, string quartets, magicians, fire-eaters, comic turns and rock guitarists jostling for the attention (and silver) of the festival-going crowds.

Exhibitions at the Royal Scottish Academy come and go, but the National Gallery of Scotland houses the biggest permanent collection of Old Masters outside of London. There are paintings by Raphael, Rubens, El Greco, Titian, Goya, Vermeer and a clutch of superb Rembrandts. Gaugin, Cezanne, Renoir, Degas, Monet, Van Gogh and Turner are also well represented, and the gallery's Scottish collection is unrivalled. There are important paintings by Raeburn, Ramsay, Wilkie, Paton and the astonishing (and greatly underrated) James Drummond.

At the west end of Princes Street are a brace of fine churches: **St. Johns** (episcopalian) and **St. Cuthberts** (Church of Scotland). St. Johns supports a lively congregation which is forever decking the building out with paintings in support of various Third World causes and animal rights. The church (a Gothic revival building designed by William Burn in 1816) has a fine ceiling which John Ruskin thought "simply beautiful". There is also a thriving café in the basement which specializes in Nicaraguan coffee and other politically-sound comestibles.

It is an extraordinary fact of Edinburgh life that there is not one pub the whole length of Princes Street. A few plushy clubs, certainly, but no pubs. But **Rose Street,** a narrow and once infamous thoroughfare that runs just behind it, has more than its share. The more diverting Rose Street hostelries are **The Kenilworth** (which has a lovely ceramic-clad interior), **Scotts, Paddy's Bar**, and **The Abbotsford.**

Looking down on Princes Street.

Not far away, but not strictly on Rose Street, are the **Café Royal,** and a basement howff called **Milnes Bar,** once the haunt of the 20th-century Edinburgh literati. In the 1950s and 1960s a favourite Edinburgh sport was to try to get from one end of Rose Street to the other, taking half a pint in every pub and remain standing. Few succeeded.

The New Town: But what makes Edinburgh a truly world-class city, able to stand shoulder to shoulder with Prague, Amsterdam or Vienna, is the great neo-classical New Town, built in an explosion of creativity between 1766 and 1840. The New Town is the product of the Scottish Enlightenment. And no-one has really been able to explain how, in the words of the historian Arthur Youngson, "a small, crowded, almost medieval town, the capital of a comparatively poor country, expanded in a short space of time, without foreign advice or foreign assistance, so as to become one of the enduringly beautiful cities of western Europe".

It all began in 1752 with an anony-mous pamphlet entitled "Proposals for carrying on certain Public Works in the City of Edinburgh". It was published anonymously, but was engineered by Edinburgh's all-powerful Lord Provost (Lord Mayor), George Drummond. Drummond was determined that Edinburgh should be a credit to the Hanoverian-ruled United Kingdom which he had helped create, and should rid itself of its (justifiable) reputation for overcrowding, squalor, turbulence and Jacobitism. To some extent the New Town is a political statement in stone. It is Scotland's tribute to the Hanoverian ascendancy. Many of the street names reflect the fact: **Hanover Street, Cumberland Street, George Street, Queen Street, Frederick Street** etc.

But the speed with which the New Town was built is still astonishing, particularly given the sheer quality of the building. Built mainly in calciferous sandstone from Craigleith Quarry to a prize-winning layout by a 23-year-old architect/planner called James Craig, most of the more important New

Colour-scape created for the Edinburgh Festival.

THE WORLD'S BIGGEST ARTS FESTIVAL

When the Edinburgh International Festival explodes into life every August the city, as the *Washington Post* recently pointed out, becomes "simply the best place on Earth". Certainly the display of cultural pyrotechnics is awesome. Every concert-hall, basement-theatre and church hall in the centre of Edinburgh overflows with dance groups, theatre companies, string quartets, puppeteers, opera companies and orchestras. And for three weeks the streets of Edinburgh are awash with fire eaters, jugglers, bagpipers, clowns, warblers, satirists and theatrical hopefuls of every shape, size and colour.

All of which is a distant cry from the dead and dreary days after World War II when the idea of the festival was hatched. Three men were responsible—Sir John Falconer, then Lord Provost of Edinburgh, Harry Harvey Wood of the British Council, and Rudolf Bing, the festival's first artistic director. The original notion of a festival was, the novelist Eric Linklater observed later, "the triumph of elegance over drab submission to the penalties of emerging victorious from a modern war".

In a remarkable piece of artistic wheeling and dealing in the first half of 1947, Rudolph Bing coaxed into Edinburgh the Glyndebourne Opera Company, the Hallé Orchestra, the Vienna State Orchestra, L'Orchestre des Concertes Collones, the Old Vic Theatre Company, and the Sadler's Wells Ballet Company. The great Kathleen Ferrier turned up to sing Mahler, while William Primrose and Pierre Fournier regaled Edinburgh with chamber music by Schubert and Brahms. Even the most grudging and cloth-eared of philistines (and Edinburgh had a few) were ravished by the sight of the floodlit Edinburgh Castle at night, a display which required a special dispensation from the Ministry of Power.

Although it was a huge triumph at the time, the festival of 1947 was just a modest beginning. The event has had five artistic directors since then (Ian Hunter, Robert Ponsonby, Lord Harewood, Peter Diamand, John Drummond and Frank Dunlop), each of whom left a different imprint. It is now the biggest festival of its kind in the world, bar none.

More than 180,000 people buy tickets for the main events, a figure which doesn't include the 80,000 or so who troop into the (free) art shows or the thousands who pack the "esplanade" of Edinburgh Castle every night to relish the stunning (if occasionally somewhat sinister) glamour of the Edinburgh Military Tattoo. Not that it has been all plain sailing; nothing in Scotland ever is. Over the years there has been much wrangling with the Scottish Arts Council over money, and

bickering with the Edinburgh District Council over the "elitism" of the Edinburgh Festival Society, the festival's ruling body. During the 1980s artistic director Frank Dunlop sounded off regularly about upstart arts festivals trying to "poach" Edinburgh's hard-won commercial sponsors. In fact, the Edinburgh Festival is now doing very nicely out of big business. The festival's money-grubbers are managing to squeeze more than £500,000 a year out of companies such as IBM, Shell, BP and the Bank of Scotland. Box office takings are running at over £1 million, which sounds a lot; but, as Dunlop says, "no major festival in the world has to make do with as little money as Edinburgh does. Salzburg gets ten times as much public money."

And only Edinburgh could mount the world's biggest arts festival while simultaneously refusing to build a decent opera house (although the city has been talking about one for decades). Dunlop did manage to persuade the Conservative-run council to go ahead with one in 1984, three weeks before they lost power in the local elections. The incoming Labour Group had other priorities.

Even so, Dunlop feels he has broken down the élitism that often cocoons culture. "When I go to Marks and Spencer for clean socks, the ladies at the bus stop with their shopping bags know who I am and say hello. I think they feel the Festival is theirs now. I've worked for that."

Edinburgh's "other" festival, the Festival Fringe (which also began in 1947) has become a behemoth—so big, in fact, that it is in real danger of outgrowing the city. In 1987 the 450 companies on the Festival Fringe staged more than 1,000 performances in 144 different venues all over the city. Over the years it's been quite a nursery for new talent: Tom Stoppard, Rowan Atkinson, Billy Connolly, Robbie Coltrane and a raft of others all made their entrance into the business on the Festival Fringe.

Nor is that all. On the fringe of the Fringe (as it were) there is also a Television Festival (full of heavyweight discussions about the Role Of The Media), a Film Festival (which gets many a good movie long before London), a Book Festival (staged every two years), and a Jazz Festival (staged in just about every pub in the city centre).

Vanished pulpits: It's one of the more amiable ironies of Scottish history that this huge extravaganza of pleasure and entertainment owes much to the strict Presbyterians of the 19th century. When the "Great Disruption" of 1843 split the Church of Scotland in two, the newly-created Free Church of Scotland built dozens of churches and church halls which are now, in less God-fearing times, surplus to requirements. It is these which provide many—if not most—of the venues for the Festival Fringe.

Town buildings were in place before the end of the century: **Register House** (1778), the North side of **Charlotte Square** (1791), the **Assembly Rooms and Music Hall** (1787), **St Andrew's Church** (1785), most of **George Street, Castle Street, Frederick Street** and **Princes Street.**

The stinking Nor' Loch (north loch) under the castle rock was speedily drained to make way for the "pleasure gardens" of Princes Street. Two million cart-loads of soil from the New Town excavations were used to create an "earthen mound" (now known as **The Mound**) linking Princes Street with the Old Town.

By the 1790s the New Town was the height of fashion, and the gentry of Edinburgh were abandoning their roosts in the Old Town for the Georgian elegance on the other side of the newly-built North Bridge. Some idea of how they lived can be glimpsed in the **Georgian House** at Seven Charlotte Square (on the block designed by Robert Adam). The house has been lovingly restored by the National Trust for Scotland to its original state. It is crammed with the furniture, crockery, glassware, silver and paintings of the period, and even the floorboards have been dry-scrubbed in the original manner. The basement kitchen is a masterpiece of late 18th-century domestic technology.

Also in Charlotte Square is **West Register House** (part of the Scottish Record Office) which was built by Robert Reid in 1811 and began life as St. George's Church. A few hundred metres along George Street are the Assembly Rooms and Music Hall (1787) once the focus of social life in the New Town, and still one of the best venues during the festival. On the other side of the street is **St. Andrew's and St. George's Church** (1785) whose oval-shaped interior witnessed the "Great Disruption" of 1843. The Church of Scotland was split down the middle when the "evangelicals", led by Thomas Chalmers, walked out in disgust at the complacency of the church "moderates" who were content to have their ministers foisted on them by the gentry (as was the custom in England). Chalmers and his colleagues went on to form the Free Church of Scotland, a sterner but more democratic form of Presbyterianism.

Parallel to George Street lies **Queen Street** whose only public building of any interest is an eccentric Doge's Palace housing the **Scottish National Portrait Gallery** and the **National Museum of Antiquities of Scotland.** The rather gloomy portrait gallery is well stocked with pictures of generations of Scots worthies, while the museum contains many an intriguing artefact. The Pictish and Gaelic cross stones and carvings are extraordinary. The children's favourite seems to be "the maiden", the guillotine that stood in the Old Town and was used to shorten Edinburgh's malefactors.

Although **St. Andrew's Square** at the west end of George Street has been knocked about a bit, it is still recognisable. The American multinational IBM has done an excellent job in restoring and remodelling its Scottish headquar-

A leg-up for the Festival Fringe.

ters in the square. But the most noteworthy building in the square is the one which is now the head office of the Royal Bank of Scotland. Originally built in 1774 as the Town House of Sir Laurence Dundas, it was remodelled in the 1850s when it acquired a quite astonishing domed ceiling with glazed star-shaped cofers. The 150-ft-high (45-metre) monument in the centre of the St. Andrew's Square is to Henry Dundas, 1st Viscount Melville, who was branded "King Harry the Ninth" for his autocratic (and probably corrupt) way of running Scotland.

To the north of the Charlotte Square-St. Andrew's Square axis lies a huge acreage of Georgian elegance which is probably unrivalled in Europe. Only the English city of Bath comes close. Most of it is private housing and offices. Particularly worth seeing are **Heriot Row, Northumberland Street, Royal Circus, Ainslie Place, Moray Place** and **Drummond Place. Ann Street** near the Water of Leith is beautiful but atypical, with its gardens and two- and three-storey buildings. The street is the creation of the painter Henry Raeburn who named it after his wife Ann.

But elegant appearances can deceive. Nearby **Danube Street** used to house Edinburgh's most notorious whorehouse, run by a flamboyant madame called Dora Noyes, and much frequented by foreign seamen. Mrs. Noyes is now dead, the whores are scattered, and the house has reverted to middle-class decency.

The **Stockbridge** area on the northern edge of the New Town is an engaging bazaar of antique shops, curiosity dealers, picture framers, second-hand book stores, with a sprinkling of decent restaurants and noisy pubs. The **Royal Botanic Garden** (half a mile north of Stockbridge and the only one of its kind outside London) is 70 wonderful acres (28 hectares) of woodland, green sward, exotic trees, heather garden, rockeries, rhododendron walks and exotic planthouses.

But Edward Hyde lurks in the New Town too. The designers of the New

Street art defies Scotland's rainy climate.

Town provided it with a plethora of handsome "pleasure gardens" which range in size from small patches of grass and shrubbery to the three **Queen Street Gardens** which total more than 11 acres (4.5 hectares). All of them, without exception, are locked to the public and accessible only to the "key-holders" who live nearby. One of the drearier sights of an Edinburgh summer is to see puzzled tourists shaking the gates, at a loss of understand why they are barred from ambling round the greenery. The locked pleasure gardens of the New Town is middle-class Edinburgh at its most mean spirited.

It was the east end of the New Town built on and around the **Calton Hill** which probably earned Edinburgh the title "Athens of the North" (although a comparison between the two cities had been made in 1762 by the antiquarian James Stuart). Between 1815 and 1840 another version of the New Town was developed beyond the east end of Princes Street and Waterloo Place. Regent Terrace, Royal Terrace, Blen-heim Terrace, Leopold Place were its main thoroughfares.

This eastward expansion also littered the slopes of the Calton Hill with impressive public buildings: the monuments to Robert Burns, Dugald Stewart, and Horatio Nelson (whose memorial is in the shape of a naval telescope), the **Royal High School** (called the "noblest monument of the Scottish Greek Revival"), the **City Observatory**, and the Calton Gaol, most of which was knocked down to make way for the Scottish Office, leaving only the **Governor's House** empty and semi-derelict on its rocky pinnacle. Every attempt to persuade the Government to find a better use for the building has failed miserably.

The oddest of the early 19th-century edifices on the Calton Hill is known as "Scotland's Disgrace" and was meant to be a war memorial to the Scots killed in the Napoleonic wars, and was to be modelled on the Parthenon in Athens. The foundation stone was laid with a great flourish during George IV's visit

James Mackenzie's "We Sell Anything" shop, established in 1831.

to Edinburgh in 1822, but the money ran out after 12 columns were erected.

Maritime Edinburgh: Although more ships now sail in and out of the Firth of Forth than use the Firth of Clyde, maritime Edinburgh has taken a terrible beating over the past 20 years. Edinburgh's port of **Leith** was, until very recently, one of the hardest working harbours on the east coast of Britain, and the city's coastline on the Firth of Forth is studded with fishing villages: **Granton, Newhaven, Portobello, Fisherrow,** and further east, **Cockenzie, Port Seton** and **Prestonpans**. Ships from Leith exported coal, salt fish, paper, leather and good strong ale, and returned with (among much else) grain, timber, wine, foreign foods and Italian marble. Their destinations were Hamburg, Bremen, Amsterdam, Antwerp, Copenhagen and occasionally North America and Australia.

Right up to the mid 1960s at least four fleets of deepsea trawlers plied out of Leith and the nearby harbour of **Granton**, and the half-Scottish half-Norwegian firm of Christian Salvesen were still catching thousands of whales every year into the 1950s (which is why there is a Leith Harbour in South Georgia). The two-mile stretch of shore between Leith and Granton used to be littered with shipyards, ship repair yards, a ship breaking yard, drydocks, marine engineering shops, a ropeworks, a wireworks and a network. The women of Leith and Granton used to earn extra money by making fishing nets at home. The streets of Leith itself were full of shipping agents, marine insurance firms, grain merchants, ships' chandlers, plus a burgeoning "service sector" of dockside pubs, clubs, flophouses, bookies and whores.

But most of it is gone. The trade has shifted to the container ports on the east coast of England. The maritime heart has gone out of Leith, and therefore Edinburgh. A few cruise liners still make an occasional appearance, and every now and again an oil-industry supply boat or a visiting naval vessel comes through the harbour mouth.

The Georgian look, lending style to the old city.

There have been attempts to turn Leith round. The Scottish Development Agency and the local authorities have been spending millions restoring the exteriors of some of Leith's handsome commercial buildings such as the old **Customs House** (now part of the Royal Museum of Scotland), the **Corn Exchange**, the **Assembly Building,** and **Trinity House** in the Kirkgate. At the same time private developers have been converting old warehouses, office buildings, lodging houses and at least one veteran cooperage into high-priced flats and houses.

Leith now hosts a cluster of fashionable restaurants (with vaguely maritime names like "Skippers"), at least one art gallery, and one of the dock-gate buildings has been converted into a successful wine bar. A pub which used to be known (for obvious reasons) as "The Jungle" and where the police feared to tread, is now a posh watering-hole called "The King's Wark" where customers in ties are preferred.

But the ancient port is worth a visit, if only for its powerful sense of what used to be. And many of the buildings on Bernard Street, Commercial Street, Constitution Street and The Shore are handsome and interesting. And Leith has an intriguing constitutional history, first part of Edinburgh, then a separate burgh, and then swallowed up by Edinburgh again (in 1920). Halfway up the street known as Leith Walk there is a pub called the "Boundary Bar" through which the municipal border between Edinburgh and Leith used to run. As the two towns then had different drinking hours, customers could extend their happiness by moving from one end of the bar to the other when the time came. Or so the legend goes.

And if ever a village had been killed by conservation it must be the little port of **Newhaven**, a mile west of Leith. Into the 1960s Newhaven was a brisk, if grubby little community, with a High Street and a Main Street lined with shops and little businesses through which tram-cars and later buses used to trundle. But now that the picturesque

A colourful species of Edinburgh youth.

houses have been "restored" there is hardly a shop left in the place, the once-crowded Main Street is a ghostly dead-end, and Newhaven harbour is occupied by a few pleasure yachts. There is talk of closing the Newhaven primary school. The Ancient Society of Free Fishermen, the trade guild founded in 1572, still exists but lists precious few fishermen among its members.

All of which is a great pity. New-haven is one of Edinburgh's more interesting corners. The village was founded in the late 15th century by James IV to build the "Great Michael", then the biggest warship on earth and destined to be the flagship of a new Scottish navy. But like many such grandiose schemes—particularly the grandiose schemes hatched in Scotland—the "Great Michael" was never a success. After the ruin of the Scots army (and the death of James IV) at Flodden in 1513, the great ship which was the pride of Newhaven was sold to the French who left her to rot in Brest harbour.

The villages: Like most other cities sprawling outwards, Edinburgh has enveloped a number of villages. The most striking of them is probably the **Dean Village**, a few minutes' walk from the West End of Princes Street. Now one of the more fashionable corners of Edinburgh, the Dean Village is at least 800 years old, and straddles the Water of Leith at a point which was once the main crossing on the way to Queensferry. The Incorporation of Baxters (i.e. bakers) of Edinburgh once operated 11 watermills and two flour granaries here. Its most striking building is Well Court, an unusual courtyard of flats built in the 1880s as housing for the poor by John Findlay, proprietor of *The Scotsman*. Dean Village is linked by a riverside walk to the shops, wine bars and pubs of Stockbridge.

Other villages which have been swallowed by the city are **Corstorphine** in the west of the city where Edinburgh keeps its famous **Zoological Garden**, starring a fine collection of penguins from the Antarctic. There is also **Colinton** in the south, which features an

18th-century parish church and a "dell" beside the Water of Leith, and **Cramond** on the Firth of Forth which used to sport an ironworks and which was the site of a Roman military camp.

More interesting is **Duddingston**, tucked under the eastern flank of Arthur's Seat, beside a decent-sized loch which is also a bird sanctuary. As well as being home to the current Secretary of State for Scotland, Duddingston claims that its main pub, "The Sheep's Heid", is the oldest licensed premises in Scotland. Duddingston also has a fine Norman-style church, and a 17th-century house used by Bonnie Prince Charlie in 1745.

And on the northern slopes of the Pentland Hills lies **Swanston,** a small huddle of white-painted thatched cottages, where the Stevenson family used to rent the nearby Swanston Cottage as a summer residence for the sickly RLS. For some odd reason, the gardens of Swanston are decorated with statuary and ornamental stonework taken from the High Kirk of St. Giles when it was being "improved" in the 19th century.

The hills of Edinburgh: If there is such a creature as the Urban Mountaineer, then Edinburgh must be his or her paradise. Like Rome, the city is built on and around seven hills, none of them very high but all of them offering good stiff walks and spectacular views of the city. They are, in order of altitude, **Arthur's Seat** (823 ft), **Braid Hill** (675 ft), **West Craiglockhart Hill** (575 ft), **Blackford Hill** (539 ft), **Corstorphine Hill** (531 ft), **Castle Hill** (435 ft) and **Calton Hill** (328 ft). In addition, Edinburgh is bounded to the south by the Pentland Hills, a range of amiable minimountains which almost (but not quite) climb to 2,000 ft (600 metres), and which is heavily used by Edinburgh hill walkers, fell runners, mountain bicyclists, rock scramblers and the British Army. Downhill skiers are catered for at Hillend park which has the biggest dry ski slope in Europe.

Of the "city-centre" hills, Calton Hill at the east end of Princes Street probably offers the best views of Edinburgh.

The glory that was Edinburgh; the view from Calton Hill.

But it is Arthur's Seat, that crag-girt old volcano in the Queen's Park, which must count as the most startling piece of urban mountainscape. It is one of the many places in Britain named after the shadowy (and possibly apocryphal) King Arthur. But Edinburgh has a better claim to Arthur than most. The area around Edinburgh was one of the British (Welsh) kingdoms before it was overrun by Angles and Scots.

On the flanks of Arthur's Seat, the feeling of *rus in urbe* can be downright eerie. Dorothy Wordsworth pointed this out in 1803 when she described the old hill as being "as wild and solitary as any in the heart of the Highland mountains". And its 853 ft (260 metres) high bulk provides some steep climbing, rough scrambling and dangerous (and now illegal) rock climbing on **Salisbury Craig**. But one of the choicest experiences Edinburgh has to offer is to watch the sun go down over the mountains of the west from the top of Arthur's Seat and then descend the darkened hillside into a sea of lights.

The outer darkness: Although Edinburgh may not have an "inner city" problem, it certainly has its "outer city" difficulties. It is ringed to the east, south and west with some of the most depressing, crime-ridden council-housing estates in Britain, places like **Craigmiller** and **Niddrie, Oxgangs** and **Gilmerton, Pilton, Muirhouse** and **Wester Hailes.** Most of the people who live in these sprawling schemes were "decanted" there from the High Street, the Cowgate and Leith, and many would go back at the drop of a hat if only they could find a tolerable house they could afford to live in.

Foreign visitors are often shocked that a city with the style (and affluence) of Edinburgh tolerates such conditions. But respectable Edinburgh has long since learned to contemplate the other Edinburgh with the equanimity of Henry Jekyll seeing the face of Edward Hyde in the mirror for the first time. "I was conscious of no repugnance," Dr. Jekyll says, "rather of a leap of welcome. This, too, was myself."

Compact city: the countryside is conveniently close to the centre.

THE BORDERS

"When you pass the *Welcome to Scotland* sign, just press on." That, at least, is how received wisdom goes, the accompanying assumption being that, compared with all those northerly lochs and glens, rushing rivers and barren moors, the Borders have only border-line appeal.

In reality the region suffers from little more than its bland name. The Borders (administratively, it includes the four "shires" of Peebles and Berwick in the north and Selkirk and Roxburgh in the south) comprise one of Europe's last unspoilt areas. There are castles here, barren moorland, ruined abbeys, baronial mansions, historic houses and evidence of past turbulent struggles against the English that gives the region a romance all of its own. It even has a loch. And, when it comes to rushing rivers, you can't do better than the Tweed, which has inspired romantic Borders ballads for hundreds of years and was held by the novelist Sir Walter Scott to be the most precious river in the world. The Tweed, also noted for its salmon, has its source in the Borders and cuts right through three of the most important Border towns: Peebles, Melrose and Kelso.

Quiet beginnings: Directly south of Edinburgh, **Peebles** owes much of its charm to its Tweedside location. Here the river already runs wide and fast. Peebles' central thoroughfare is equally wide but much more sedate. The town was never renowned for its hustle and bustle: an 18th-century aristocrat coined an ungenerous simile: "As quiet as the grave—or Peebles". While each June things liven up considerably with the week-long Beltane festival, during the rest of the year Peebles is still a quiet introduction to the Borders; the places usually recommended to visitors owe their origins to either religion or dictionaries.

The **Cross Kirk,** was erected in 1261 after the discovery of a large cross on this site. The remains include a large 15th-century tower and foundations of cloister and monastic buildings. St. Andrew's Collegiate Church, the forerunner to Cross Kirk, sits in a cemetery on the Glasgow road. Here too only a tower remains; the remainder was burnt by the English at the time of the sacking of the four great Border abbeys. At the bottom of Peebles High Street, the Gothic outline of Peebles Parish Church adds to the town's general air of sobriety.

The **Chambers Institute**, Peebles' civic centre and museum, was a gift to the place from William Chambers, a native of the place and the founding publisher of Chambers Encyclopedia.

Following the Tweed: Just a few minutes out of Peebles, perched high on a rocky bluff overlooking the Tweed, **Neidpath Castle**, a well preserved example of the many medieval Tower Houses in the region, offers more excitement. Wordsworth visited in 1803 and wrote a famous poem lamenting the desolation caused in 1795 when the

absentee landowner, the 4th Duke of Queensberry, cut down all the trees for money to support his extravagant London lifestyle.

Wordsworth would have been happier with the botanical gardens of **Dawyck House**. Dawyck is an outstation of Edinburgh's Royal Botanic Garden and contains a fine collection of mature specimen trees, many of them over 100 years old. In fact, the earliest record of tree planting here dates back to 1680.

In **Broughton**, close to the eastern edge of the Borders, Broughton Place is an imposing castillian house that looks as if it was built centuries ago; it was in fact designed this century. Inside, Broughton Gallery has a fine collection of work by British artists and craftsmen for sale. John Buchan, author of the best-selling *The Thirty Nine Steps*, grew up in this village. In later life he wrote that he "liked Broughton better than any place in the world". Just south of the village, the **John Buchan Centre** is a small museum that paints a detailed picture of a man who led a varied and distinguished life which eventually saw him become Governor General of Canada.

Buchan also liked the **Crook Inn**, just outside Tweedsmuir. One of the oldest Border inns, it has strong literary associations. Robert Burns was inspired to write his poem "*Willie Wastle's Wife*" in the kitchen (now the bar). Sir Walter Scott used to visit here, as did his lesser known contemporary James Hogg, the poet known by locals as "The Ettrick Shepherd". John Buchan was born nearby and took his title of first Baron of Tweedsmuir from this parish.

The source of the Tweed is just a few miles south of the village of **Tweedsmuir**. The two highest points in the Borders, Broad Law and Dollar Law rise to more than 2,750 ft (840 metres) and 2,680 ft (820 metres) respectively. If it's rugged moorland and craggy terrain you're after, you won't find much better outside the Scottish Highlands. Draw a line between Hawick and Broughton and then stay

south of it and you'll see the best the Borders has to offer. A popular route is the side-road out of Tweedsmuir up to the **Talla Reservoir** and **Megget Reservoir**. Steep slopes and rock-strewn hillsides provide a stunning panorama as you twist and turn your way down to the A708, where you reach another favourite spot: **St. Mary's Loch**, the only loch in the Borders region.

Step outside the Borders just a mile or two, towards Eskdalemuir, and you'll be greeted by a real surprise: the **Kagyu Samye Ling Tibetan Monastery**. This Tibetan Buddhist centre was founded in 1967 for study, retreat and meditation and incorporates Samye Temple, an authentic Tibetan Buddhist monastery being built in the centre's grounds. Samye Ling, which long ago threw off its "hippy" image, has received written support from David Steel, the Liberal Party leader who lives just a few miles north at Ettrickbridge. Visitors, regardless of faith, can join free conducted tours around the centre's facilities.

Traquair House is still owned by the

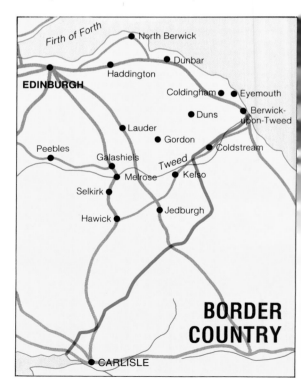

BORDER COUNTRY

118

family that acted as hosts when Mary Queen of Scots stayed there with her husband Darnley in 1566. Its history goes much further back; parts of it date from the 12th century. The wide avenue leading away from the house to the large gates by the main road has been disused for more than two centuries. After Bonnie Prince Charlie visited in 1745, the 5th Earl of Traquair closed the Bear Gates after him and swore they would not open until a Stuart king had been restored to the throne.

On the road west back towards Peebles, **Kailzie Gardens** adds to the beauty of the Tweed Valley with its formal walled garden, greenhouses and woodland walks—a combination that quickly earned it a place on the tourist map of the area.

Heart of the Borders: Though it has little to tempt today's visitor, **Galashiels** has played a pivotal role in the Borders economy as a weaving town for more than 700 years. The world-famous Scottish College of Textiles, founded in 1909, has helped to cement the reputation of the tartans, tweeds, woollens and other knitted materials sold in the mills here. Most people understandably assume, therefore, that the word "tweed" was adopted by the woollen industry because of the river; in fact, it was originally a misprint—by an English publisher, naturally—for *tweels*, the Border name for woollen fabrics. Though the industry across the region has declined, there are numerous working mills open to the public: **Peter Anderson of Scotland** in Huddersfield Street, which holds conducted tours and features a textiles museum, is one of the most popular.

It's not only Galashiels that lets you sample the Borders' textiles. Tourism has fashioned the **Borders Woollen Trail**, which includes eight other towns involved in this industry. One of them, **Selkirk**, became a textile centre in the 19th century only when the growing demand for tweed could no longer be met by the mills of Galashiels. Like Galashiels, Selkirk's manufacturing background leaves little for you to en-

A change from the kirk: the Shrine Room at Kagyu Samye Ling Tibetan Monastery.

joy other than shopping for tweeds and woollens. The one exception is 18th-century **Haliwell's House**, an old iron-mongers that is now a small museum telling the story of Selkirk in entertaining detail.

Don't leave the locality without visiting **Bowhill House**. Dating from 1812, Bowhill has for eight generations been the home of the Scotts of Buccleuch and Queensberry, once one of the largest landowners of all the Border clans. More than 300 years of discerning art collecting has resulted in a collection that includes works by Canaletto, Guardi, Leonardo, Reynolds and Gainsborough.

If the Borders have a sort of visitors' Mecca, then **Abbotsford House**, home of Sir Walter Scott from 1811 to 1832, undoubtedly lays claim to the title. Ironically, Abbotsford does lie right at the centre of the Borders; nobody can really claim to have "done" this part of Scotland unless they pay homage to the man and his home. Scott spent £50,000 and the rest of his life turning a small farm into an estate that could do justice to his position as a Border laird. Yet Abbotsford is not visited for its architecture; Ruskin said the house was "the most incongruous pile that gentlemanly modernism ever designed". People come instead to enjoy its baronial, literary and magnificently preserved interior. All of the Waverley novels were written here, though Scott didn't admit to being the author until 1827, feeling that it wasn't "decorous" of a Clerk of Session at Selkirk to be seen writing novels. This is just one detail in the long and fascinating account of Scott's rise to fame and celebrity status, his financial ruin and his final days at Abbotsford, all colourful chapters that make for a highly romantic story in themselves.

Scott was buried at **Dryburgh**, one of the four great 12th-century abbeys in the Borders. While the ruins at Jedburgh, Kelso and Melrose lie near the edge of their respective towns, Dryburgh, founded by Hugh de Morville for monks from Alnwick in Northum-

Dryburgh Castle: a brooding reminder of a bloody history.

berland, is tucked away in an idyllic location among trees by the edge of the Tweed. Until 1544, Dryburgh referred to an important town as well as the Abbey. Both suffered a violent and fiery end (as did the three other Border abbeys) on the orders of Henry VIII, who was intent on orchestrating a marriage between the infant Queen Mary and his own son Edward.

Dryburgh's setting is no match for **Scott's View**, which offers a sweeping view of the unmistakeable triple peaks of the **Eildon Hills** (reputed to be the legendary sleeping place of King Arthur and his knights) and a wide stretch of the Tweed Valley. Scott came here many times to enjoy the panorama. When his mile-long funeral cortege was on its way from Abbotsford to Dryburgh, it is said the horses stopped at this point of their own accord.

The town of **Melrose** escaped much of the industrialisation that affected Selkirk, Hawick and Galashiels and is more attractive because of it. **Melrose Abbey** seals the town's pedigree. It even accounts for the beginning of Sir Walter Scott's rise to fame, for it was eloquently described in *"The Lay of the Last Minstrel* , the great narrative poem of 1805 that made him famous. The Abbey was founded in 1136 by King David I (he founded all four of the great Border abbeys), and was the first Cistercian monastery in Scotland. Tragically it lay in the path of repeated English invasions long before Henry VIII made his presence felt in the 16th century. An attack in 1322 by Edward II prompted Robert Bruce to fund its restoration. Bruce's heart, it is said, was buried near the high altar, though subsequent excavation has failed to locate any trace of it.

Just a few miles north of Melrose on the outskirts of Lauder is **Thirlestaine Castle**, once the seat of the Earls of Lauderdale. One of Scotland's oldest and finest castles, it was built on a 12th-century foundation and today houses an impressive collection of furniture and paintings as well as some renowned 17th-century plaster ceilings. Local

Playtime in the shadow of Jedburgh Abbey.

enthusiasts were responsible for the castle's Border Country Life Museum, an exhibition on the history of Borders agriculture.

Roman reminders: Historically, **Jedburgh** is the most important of the Border towns. It was also strategically important; as the first community across the border it frequently received the full brunt of invading English armies. Earlier invaders came from even more distant lands than the English. Two miles north of Jedburgh it is possible to follow the course of Dere Street, the road the Romans built in southern Scotland more than 1,900 years ago.

The most ancient surviving building, **Jedburgh Abbey**, was founded in 1138 by Augustinian canons from northern France. Stonework in the abbey's museum dates from the first millennium AD and proves that the site had much older religious significance. Malcolm IV was crowned here and Alexander III married his second wife in the abbey in 1285. Legend tells of a ghostly figure appearing at the wedding feast nearby in Jedburgh Castle prophesying the death of the King and disaster for Scotland. Alexander died the following year and Scotland from then on suffered the centuries of strife that accompanied the struggle to find a new Scottish king.

The castle at which Alexander confronted the prophetic spectre occupied a site in Castlegate. It was demolished in 1409 to keep it out of English hands. In 1823 the **Castle Gaol** was built on the old castle's foundations; its museum of social history is well worth a visit.

Near the High Street, display panels and artefacts in **Mary Queen of Scots' House** tell a short but crucial chapter in Scotland's history. It was in this house in late 1566 that Queen Mary spent several weeks recovering from serious illness (at one point she was left for dead) after her renowned dash on horseback to Hermitage Castle to see her injured lover James Hepburn, Earl of Bothwell. Her ride resulted in scandal that was made all the worse by the

Old money: The Duke of Roxburgh at home.

murder of her husband Darnley in the following February. From there on, her downfall was steady. Years later, during her 19 years of imprisonment in London, Mary Queen of Scots regretted that her life hadn't ended in the Borders before her many misfortunes: "Would that I had died at Jedburgh."

If you decide to re-trace Mary's footsteps to Hermitage Castle, you're more than likely to pass through **Hawick** (pronounced "Hoik"). The Borders' textile industry is all around you here. World-famous knitwear and clothing brand names are emblazoned boldly above factory gates, while at **Wilton Lodge Museum** a fascinating collection of exhibits picks up older sartorial threads.

Kelso and castles: Still retaining its central cobbled streets leading into a spacious square, **Kelso** is one of the most picturesque of the Border towns. Sir Walter Scott, who was a pupil at the Grammar School in the nave of the ruined abbey, wrote and spoke fondly of it. Just a hundred yards from the town's centre, **Kelso Abbey**, once the largest and richest of the Borders abbeys, suffered the same fate as its counterparts at Melrose, Jedburgh and Dryburgh and is today the least complete of all of them.

It's ironic that, while the English destroyed Kelso's abbey, the Scottish were responsible for the much greater devastation of the town of **Roxburgh** and its castle. Roxburgh had grown up on the south bank of the Tweed (Kelso occupies the north bank) around the mighty fortress of Marchmount. An important link in the chain of border fortifications, Marchmount controlled the gateway to the north.

In the 14th century the English took Roxburgh and its castle and used it as a base for further incursions into Scottish territory. The fortress built for protection had begun to serve precisely the opposite purpose. In 1460 James II of Scotland attacked Marchmount but was killed by a bursting cannon. His widow urged the Scottish troops forward. On achieving victory they destroyed Roxburgh's castle (in order to keep it forever out of enemy hands) with a thoroughness the English would have found difficult to emulate. The town itself fell into decay. Today, on a mound between the Teviot and the Tweed about a mile to the west of Kelso (the plain village of Roxburgh a few miles on is no direct relation of the ancient town), only a few fragments of Marchmount's walls survive.

On the north bank of the Tweed, Kelso thrived, however. So far as castles go, Kelso picked itself up, brushed itself off and went one better with **Floors Castle**. The original house was designed by Robert Adam and built between 1721 and 1726. It owes its present flamboyant appearance to William Playfair who re-modelled and extended it between 1837 and 1845. An outstanding collection of German, Italian and French furniture, Chinese and Dresden porcelain, paintings by Picasso, Matisse and Augustus John, and a prized 15th-century Brussels tapestry are some of the many glittering prizes that give Floors an air of palatial elegance. Tradition has it that a holly tree in the large grounds marks the spot where James was killed by the cannon.

Outsiders could be forgiven for thinking the Borders too generously endowed with aristocratic art and architecture. They only have to drive eight miles (13 km) out of Kelso to make their point. **Mellerstain House** is one of Scotland's finest Georgian mansions, the 18th-century product of the combined genius of William Adam and his son Robert. Externally it has the dignity, symmetry and well-matched proportions characteristic of this period. Inside there's furniture by Chippendale, Sheraton and Heeplewhite as well as paintings by Gainsborough, Constable, Veronese and Van Dyck, and also exquisite examples of moulded plaster ceilings, doorheads, mantelpieces and light-fittings. As if all this weren't enough to impress, formal Italian gardens were laid out in 1909 to create a series of gently sloping terraces and the house became a popular venue for fashionable dances. If all else in the Border Country fails to whet your appetite, Mellerstain, and its neighbour Floors, are reason enough for visiting.

Border crossings: East of Kelso the Tweed marks the natural boundary between England and Scotland. **Coldstream**, one of the last towns on this river before Berwick, has little to offer the visitor other than history. The town's name was taken by the famous regiment of Coldstream Guards that was formed by General Monck in 1659 before he marched south to support the restoration of the Stuart monarchy. The regiment today loans material to the **Coldstream Museum**, set up in a house that served as Monck's headquarters.

Nearly 150 years earlier, in 1513, James IV of Scotland crossed the Tweed at Coldstream to attack the English with a much larger force. Though Henry VIII was at that time fighting in France (James IV's invasion was a diversion intended to aid the French) an English army was sent north to meet the threat. The encounter, which took place near the English vil-lage of Branxton but was known as the Battle of Flodden, was a military disaster for Scotland: the king, his son, and as many as 46 nobles and 9,000 men were slain.

Happier endings are to be had at **Kirk Yetholm**, just yards from the English border. Overlooking the village green, the part-thatched Border Hotel bills itself as the "End of the Pennine Way". A few miles away **Linton Kirk**, said to be the oldest building in continuous use for Christian worship on the Scottish border, sits proudly on a hummock of sand in a picturesque valley. Here the slopes rise steeply to join the Cheviots—a ridge of hills that forms another natural ingredient in the border between Scotland and England.

When it comes to identifying precise borderlines, **Berwick-upon-Tweed** can be forgiven for feeling a little confused. Boundaries around here lack a sense of fair play: Berwick is not part of Berwickshire. But there's worse to come. For, while the town takes its name from the river that has its source

Hallowe'en trick-or-treat for children in Berwickshire.

in the Scottish Borders, runs through the heart of the Scottish Borders (Peebles, Abbotsford and Kelso included) and even forms part of the border line itself, Berwick-upon-Tweed is not within Scotland. It's in Northumberland, England.

It wasn't always like that. Berwick made its way into Scotland many times previously. For well over 300 years it was nothing less than a strategic shuttlecock. The town changed hands no fewer than 13 times between 1147 (when it was surrendered by William the Lion after his capture at the Battle of Alnwick) and 1482 (when it was finally taken for England by Richard, Duke of Gloucester—later Richard III).

Historically Berwick is very much a part of the Borders. The town's castle, built in the late 12th century by Henry II, once towered high above the Tweed. Much of it was demolished in 1847 to make space for the station, which bears an appropriate inscription by Robert Stephenson: "The Final Act Of Union". Berwick's Town Wall, built on the orders of Edward I, has fared better and is one of the most complete of its kind in Britain. Berwick still retains its medieval street plan and there are several steep, cobbled streets that are worth exploring.

Situated in Scotland, along the coast just north of Berwick, **Eyemouth** is a small, working fishing town whose museum vividly outlines Eyemouth's long tradition as a fishing port. The museum's centrepiece is the Eyemouth Tapestry, made by local people in 1981 to commemorate the Great Disaster of 1881 when 189 local fishermen were drowned, all within sight of land, during a storm. A few miles north, **Coldingham**'s Medieval Priory and **St. Abb's Nature Reserve** are two further justifications for making this detour off the A1 to Edinburgh. You could head inland and take another route to Edinburgh: the A68. If you do, make a point of stopping at **Manderston House**, just outside Duns, to enjoy what has been dubbed "the finest Edwardian country house in Scotland".

Mellerstain, one of Scotland's most glorious Georgian houses.

THE SOUTH-WEST

It's often said that the substantial island of **Arran**, in the Firth of Clyde, represents a topographical microcosm of Scotland: "Scotland in miniature", say its publicists. It has highlands, lowlands, coast (of course), its own offshore island and a handsome castle. But Arran's character is exclusively rural, with an economy rooted in agriculture, forestry and tourism. A more appropriate scaled-down version of modern Scotland can be found on the nearby mainland, between the great estuaries of Clyde and Solway.

In the landscape and seacapes of South-west Scotland, in the pretty villages of Dumfries and Galloway and the hill farms of south Lanarkshire, in the industrial townships of Ayrshire and the ports and holiday resorts of the Clyde coast you will find something of the rest of Scotland. All that is missing, perhaps, is the intimidating grandeur of the West Highlands. The **Galloway Hills** are lonely, lovely places in their own right, but none rises to more than 2,800 ft (850 metres). The South-west is altogether a kindlier country, with a Covenanting history whose sometimes brutal nature belies the comeliness of the land, and with a dense concentration of literary associations.

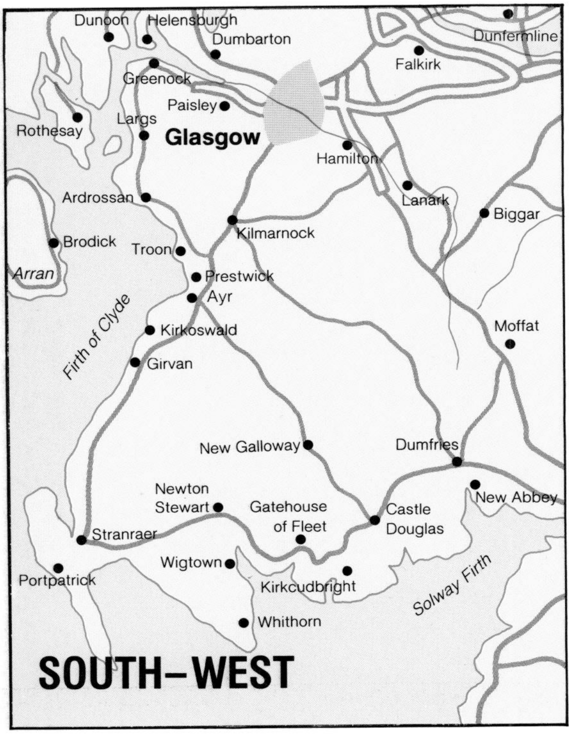

Travellers from England often bypass the rewarding littoral of the Solway with its pastoral hinterland in their scamper up the grim A74 to points north and the Highlands, hesitating only at a name which is legendary for rather trivial reasons. **Gretna Green**, just over the Border (until the boundary between England and Scotland was agreed in 1552, this area was known simply as the Debatable Land) became celebrated for celebrating marriages. It was the first available community where eloping couples from England could take advantage of Scotland's different marriage laws. Many a makeshift ceremony was performed at the **Old Smithy**, which is now a museum, and, although seldom pursued by horse-whipping fathers, many a romantic bride still chooses to be married at Gretna Green today.

The Burns legend: A few miles farther north is the village of **Ecclefechan**, where the house in which Thomas Carlyle was born is now a modest literary shrine. (The man of letters, who was soon to make a dazzling reputation for himself in London, returned to South-west Scotland for a brief, bleak period of farming at Craigenputtock, on the moors above Moniaive). But the South-west is more inescapably identified with the poet Robert Burns, whose life and legend is one of the main props of Scottish tourism.

The urban epicentres of the Burns industry are Dumfries and Ayr. **Dumfries** is also "the Queen of the South", an ancient and important Border town whose remaining character survives the unsightly housing estates and factories on its periphery, and which is within easy striking distance of the haunting, history-rich Solway

SOUTH—WEST

Map labels: Dunoon, Helensburgh, Dumbarton, Dunfermline, Falkirk, Greenock, Paisley, Largs, **Glasgow**, Rothesay, Hamilton, Lanark, Biggar, Ardrossan, Kilmarnock, Brodick, Troon, *Arran*, Prestwick, Ayr, Firth of Clyde, Kirkoswald, Moffat, Girvan, New Galloway, Dumfries, Newton Stewart, Gatehouse of Fleet, Castle Douglas, New Abbey, Stranraer, Portpatrick, Wigtown, Kirkcudbright, Solway Firth, Whithorn coast. Burns, the farmer-poet, took over Ellisland Farm some six miles (10 km) outside the town in 1788, built the farmhouse and tried to introduce new farming methods. His venture collapsed and he moved to Dumfries to become an Exciseman, but the farm where he wrote *"Tam O'Shanter"* and *"Auld Lang Syne"* is now a museum—as is the house in Mill Vennel, Dumfries (now Burns Street) where he died in 1796. His first home in the town was a three-room flat in the Wee Vennel, which Burns re-christened Stinking Vennel, but it isn't open to the public.

The handsome waterfront of the **River Nith**, with its 15th-century bridge, and the red sandstone dignity of nearby **St. Michael's Church**, in whose churchyard Burns is buried, give Dumfries its distinctive character. Its environs have just as much to offer. On opposing banks of the Nith estuary, where it debouches into the Solway, are **Caerlaverock Castle and National Nature Reserve** (winter haunt of wildfowl) and Sweetheart Abbey.

The castle, strikingly well-preserved, dates back to the 13th century and was the seat of the Maxwell family, later Earls of Nithsdale—one of the most powerful local dynasties. It was besieged by Edward I during the Wars of Independence and in 1640 fell to a 13-week siege mounted by the Covenanters. The graceful ruin of **Sweetheart Abbey**, in the pretty village of New Abbey, is a monument to the marital devotion of the noble Devorguilla Balliol, who not only founded this Cistercian abbey in 1273 but founded Balliol College, Oxford, in memory of her husband. She also carried his heart around her until her own death in 1290, when she and the heart were buried together in front of the high altar.

Good beaches: The shallow estuary of the Solway has some notoriety for the speed of its tidal race and the treachery of its sands, but the hazardous areas are well signposted and if you follow the coast from River Nith to **Loch Ryan** (on a main road which makes little

Sculptures by Rodin (left) and Henry Moore gaze from Shawhead towards nearby Dumfries.

130

detours inland to take account of the deeper bays) you will find an amiable, undemanding succession of villages, yachting harbours, attractive small towns and good beaches marred only by the ubiquitous caravan parks; not to mention many secret coves and snug, deserted little bays available to those who can use their feet.

This is the ancient territory of Galloway, whose people once fraternised with the Norse raiders who settled on the coast and whose lords preserved a degree of independence from the Scottish crown until the 13th century. Many of Scotland's great names and great causes have seen action among the hills and bays of Galloway: at **Dundrennan Abbey**, near Kirkcudbright, Mary Queen of Scots is believed to have spent her last night in Scotland, sheltering in this 12th-century Cistercian house on her final, fatal flight from the Battle of Langside to her long imprisonment in England.

At **Wigtown**, the Martyrs' Monument is one of the most eloquent and moving testaments to the Covenanters, who were heroically supported in the South-west—the site of the stake where two women, one elderly and one young, were left to drown on the estuary flats. And at **Whithorn** Christianity came to Scotland when St. Ninian built his church there around the year 400, although all that remains are early Christian memorial stones.

Kirkcudbright itself, at the mouth of the River Dee, has the reputation of being the most attractive of the Solway towns, with a colourful waterfront (much appreciated and colonised by artists) and an elegant Georgian town centre. Little remains of the Kirkcudbright which took its name from the vanished Kirk of Cuthbert (which once played host to the saint's bones) but it has a Market Cross of 1610 and a Tolbooth from the same period which entertained John Paul Jones. He was imprisoned for the manslaughter of his ship's carpenter, who had died after a flogging but he went on to take the credit for laying the foundations of the

Keeping the telephones in working order in the rural south-west.

American navy.

Not far inland from Kirkcudbright is another neat and dignified little town, **Castle Douglas**, which stands on the small loch of Carlingwark, where you will find one of the most formidable tower strongholds in Scotland. **Threave Castle** was built towards the end of the 14th century by the wonderfully named Archibald the Grim, third Earl of Douglas, and was the last Douglas castle to surrender to James II during the conflict between the king and the maverick Border family. It, too, has associations with the Covenanters, who seized it in 1640 and vandalised the interior. (Like all men of God in those days, they had their violent moments.)

Gourmet's Galloway: It's worth mentioning, for the benefit of self-caterers, that Castle Douglas has some of the best food shops in Scotland, particularly butchers' shops, as it serves as market centre to a large tract of Galloway's rural hinterland. Here you will find villages unusually pretty for a country which isn't famous for the aesthetics of its small communities. Their characteristic feature is whitewashed walls with black-bordered doors and windows— as if they have taken their colour scheme from the black and white Belted Galloway cattle.

Many of the most pleasant villages— **New Galloway**, **Balmaclellan**, **Crossmichael**—are in the region of long, skinny **Loch Ken**, which feeds the River Dee; while to the west, shrouding the hills to the very shoulders of the isolated **Rhinns of Kells**, a tableland of hills around 2,600 ft (800 metres), is the massive Galloway Forest Park, 150,000 acres (60,000 hectares) crisscrossed by dull Forestry Commission trails.

Despite the conifers, you *can* sometimes see something interesting for the trees: **Clatteringshaws Loch**, 12 miles (19 kms) north of Newton Stewart (a "planned town" built in the late 17th century by a son of the Earl of Galloway) is the site of the **Galloway Deer Museum**. It will not only improve your knowledge of the habits of the Red Deer

but alert you to a range of the area's natural history.

Nearby, **Bruce's Stone** represents the site of the Battle of Rapploch Moss, a minor affair of 1307 but one in which the energetic Robert the Bruce routed the English. There are, in fact, two Bruce's stones in Galloway Forest Park, which creeps within reach of the coast at Turnberry, where he may have been born; the second stone is poised on a bluff above Loch Trool, at the heart of the park, and recalls those hefted down the hill by the hero in another successful wrangle with the English. Below is a more sombre landmark—the **Memorial Tomb** of six Covenanters murdered at prayer. It is a simple stone which records their names and the names of their killers.

Back on the coast, the road between benign **Gatehouse of Fleet** and **Creetown**, which hugs the sea below the comely outriders of the distinctive hill **Cairnsmore of Fleet**, was said by Thomas Carlyle to be the most beautiful road in Scotland. This was very much a subjective judgement, and considered something of a Scottish slight to Queen Victoria, who posed the question hoping for a reference to her favoured Deeside. But it's certainly an agreeable road, with views across **Wigtown Bay** to the flat green shelf which was the cradle of Scottish Christianity.

Saints and sharks: The coast becomes harsher and the villages bleaker on this promontory south of the pleasant town of Wigtown, as if it indeed required the gentling influence of Christianity. There is today a priory and museum in the village of Whithorn, where St. Ninian built his little stone church, and in the museum you will find the Latinus Stone of 450, the earliest Christian memorial in Scotland, as well as a significant collection of early Christian crosses and stones. The confusingly named **Isle of Whithorn**— which is, in fact, a small port frequented by shark and tope fishers—has more connections with St. Ninian: there is the ruined **St. Ninian's Chapel**, which dates from 1300 and may have been used by pilgrims from overseas; and along the coast is **St. Ninian's Cave**, said to have been used by the saint as an oratory.

A little inland from the undistinguished shoreline of Luce Bay, playground of the Ministry of Defence, are some relics of the Iron Age and Bronze Age, including **Torhouse Stone Circle**, a ring of 19 boulders standing on a low mound. The most impressive sight in this corner, however, is **Glenluce Abbey**, a handsome vaulted ruin of the 12th century where, says legend, Michael Scott the Wizard lived in the 13th century and where he lured the plague, which was then raging, to trap it in a vault.

Resort towns: From Glenluce the traveller crosses the "handle" of that hammer of land called the **Rhinns of Galloway**, the south-west extremity of Scotland terminating in the 200 ft (60-metre) high cliffs of the Mull of Galloway, from which Ireland seems within touching distance. At the head of the deep cleft of **Loch Ryan** is the port of **Stranraer**, market centre for the rich agricultural area, modest holiday resort and Scotland's main seaway to Northern Ireland. The Rhinns' other main resort is **Portpatrick**, and among the somewhat limited attractions of this remote peninsula are two horticultural ones: the sub-tropical plants of **Logan Botanic Garden** and the great monkey puzzle trees of **Castle Kennedy Gardens**, near Stranraer.

Stranraer's trunk roads are the A75, infamous for the volume of heavy traffic disembarking from the ferries from Ireland, which strikes west to Dumfries and points south and blights Thomas Carlyle's "loveliest stretch" between Creetown and Gatehouse of Fleet; and the A77, which conducts you north past the cliffs of **Ballantrae** (*not* the Ballantrae of R.L. Stevenson's novel) to the mixed pleasures of Ayrshire and, ultimately, the edge of the Glasgow conurbation. It, too, is a busy road, giving early intimations of a return to urban life, and it takes you to the heart of Burns country.

Cattle auction at Newton Stewart, a busy market town in Wigtownshire.

En route, you will encounter the pleasant resort of **Girvan**, first of a series of resorts interspersed with ports and industrial towns which stretches to the mouth of the Clyde. Ten miles offshore is a chunky granite monolith over 1,000 ft (300 metres) high—the island of **Ailsa Craig**, sometimes called Paddy's Milestone for its central position between Belfast and Glasgow. Here, too, you begin to see more clearly the mountains of Arran and the lower line of the Kintyre peninsula, while at **Turnberry**, temple of golf and site of some fragments of castle which promotes itself as the birthplace of Robert the Bruce, there is a choice of roads to Ayr.

The coast road invites you to one of the non-Burnsian showpieces of Ayrshire—**Culzean Castle**, magnificently designed by Robert Adam, built between 1772 and 1792 for the Kennedy family, now owned by the National Trust for Scotland and, with its country park of 560 acres (226 hectares)—the first in Scotland—open to the public. Transatlantic visitors are entertained by the **Eisenhower Presentation**, which recalls the flat presented to the General for his private use for life. A few miles beyond Culzean the road entertains drivers at the **Electric Brae**, where an optical illusion suggests you are going downhill when in fact you are going up.

The inland road takes you through the village of **Kirkoswald**, where Burns went to school, and the first of the cluster of Burns shrines and museums: **Souter Johnnie's Cottage**, once the home of the cobbler who was the original of Souter Johnnie in *"Tam O' Shanter"*. A minor road then conducts you to the Mecca of Burns pilgrims, the village of **Alloway**, where he was born. Here, amid the usual tourist apparatus of visitor and "interpretation" centres, you can pick up the **Burns Heritage Trail** and visit in quick succession: Burns Cottage, Alloway Kirk (where his father is buried and which features critically in *"Tam O' Shanter"*), the pretentious Burns Monument (a neo-

Burns characters converse eternally at Souter Johnnie's Cottage. Right, Burns memorabilia.

THE PLOUGHMAN POET

Few poets command popular reverence from their own countrymen; fewer still could hope to have their birthday celebrated in the most unexpected parts of the world nearly 200 years after their death. Yet the observance of Burns Night, on 25 January, goes from strength to strength. It marks the birth in 1759 of Scotland's national poet, Robert Burns, one of seven children born to an Ayrshire farmer who barely scraped a living from the poor soil.

It was an unpromising beginning, yet today Burns's verses are familiar in every English-speaking country (with the arguable exception of England) and are especially popular in Russia, where Burns Night is toasted in vodka. He has even appeared on a postage stamp in Romania.

Millions who have never heard of Burns have, at some celebration or another, joined hands and sung his words to the tune of that international anthem of good intentions, *Auld Lang Syne* (dialect for "old long ago"):

> Should auld acquain-
> tance be forgot,
> And never brought to
> mind?
> Should auld acquain-
> tance be forgot,
> And days o' auld lang
> syne?

This was one of many traditional Scottish songs which he collected and re-wrote, in addition to his own original poetry. He could and did write easily in 18th-century English as well as in traditional Scots dialect (which, even in those days, had to be accompanied by a glossary). His subjects ranged from love songs (*Oh, my luve's like a red, red rose*) and sympathy for a startled fieldmouse (*Wee, sleekit, cowrin', tim'rous beastie*) to a stirring sense of Scottishness (*Scots, wha hae wi' Wallace bled*) and a simple celebration of the common people (*A man's a man for a' that*).

The key to Burns's high standing in Scotland is that, like Sir Walter Scott, he promoted the idea of Scottish nationhood at a time when it was in danger of being obliterated by the English. His acceptance abroad, especially in Russia, stems from his effective championing of the rights of ordinary men and women and his satirical attack on double standards in general and the unctuous hypocrisy of Church of Scotland clergy in particular. He proclaimed his love of freedom in the poem *"The Jolly Beggars"*:

> A fig for those by law protected!
> Liberty's a glorious feast!
> Courts for cowards were erected,
> Churches built to please the priest.

Romance surrounds even Burns's birth. When his father was riding to find a doctor to assist at the delivery, so the story goes, he helped an old gypsy woman across a flooded stream. In gratitude, she visited the new baby to bless him and predicted that he would be famous. Romance of a more carnal nature surrounded his adulthood. An attractive and gregarious youth, he had a long series of amorous entanglements and, once famous, took full advantage of his acceptance into Edin-

burgh's high society. Living life to excess did little for his health but seems to have been a source of poetic inspiration. Finally, however, he married Jean Armour, a girl from his own village, and settled down on a poor farm at Ellisland, near Dumfries.

No more able than his father had been to make a decent living from farming, he moved to Dumfries in 1791 to work as an Excise Officer. It was a secure job, and riding 200 miles a week on horseback around the countryside on his duties gave him time and inspiration to compose prolifically. Although his patriotism was questioned because of his strong support for the French Revolution, he was able to hang on to his job. His affairs continued: the niece of a Dumfries innkeeper became pregnant, but died during childbirth. Four years later, Burns too was dead, of rheumatic heart disease. He was 37.

Today one of the 612 copies of his first edition of poems, sold in Kilmarnock in 1786 for three shillings (15p), will fetch £10,000. Almost 100,000 people in more than 20 countries belong to Burns clubs and the poet's enduring popularity embraces the unlikeliest of locations. The story is told, for example, of a black gentleman who rose to propose a toast at a Burns Night supper in Fiji. "You may be surprised to learn that Scottish blood flows in my veins," he told the gathering. "But it is true. One of my ancestors ate a Presbyterian missionary."

Classical temple) and the 13th-century **Brig o' Doon**, whose single span permitted Tam O' Shanter to escape from the witches.

You are now on the doorstep of **Ayr**—unsurpassed, according to Burns, "for honest men and bonnie lasses"—which is the principal resort of the Clyde coast and a busy, bustling centre at any time of the year. It has associations, too, with the warrior-patriot William Wallace, who was born not very far away at **Elderslie**, near Paisley, and who was once imprisoned in Ayr. (**Paisley**, incidentally, is worth a visit for its museum and art galleries, which house a celebrated collection of Paisley shawls.)

Inland from Ayr, to the west and north is another clutch of Burns associations: the village of **Mauchline**, where he married Jean Armour and where their cottage is now yet another museum; and **Poosie Nansie's Tavern**, the ale-house (still a pub) which inspired part of his cantata *"The Jolly Beggars"*. Nearby at **Failford** is High-

land Mary's Monument, which allegedly marks the spot where Burns said farewell to the doomed Mary Campbell, who died before they could marry; while the sprawling, cheerless industrial town of **Kilmarnock** also claims intimacy with Burns, who published the first edition of his poems there in 1786. One hundred years later the town built him a monument, which contains—no prizes for guessing— yet more Burns material.

The A77 from Kilmarnock—that road which began life in Stranraer—takes you straight to the heart of Glasgow. But, if you are island or Highland bound, you should return to the coast. Between the industrial port and new town of **Irvine** and the increasingly desolate shipbuilding town of **Greenock** is a succession of ferry points for the Clyde islands and the Cowal peninsular. (South of Irvine are the two golfing resorts of **Troon** and **Prestwick**, whose airport is the entry point to Scotland for many transatlantic visitors.)

Ardrossan serves the island of **Arran**, the ferries disembarking passengers and cars at **Brodick**, the capital. Arran is popular with walkers and climbers (the sharp profile of the Arran ridge, which reaches 2,866 ft [874 metres] at the elegant summit of Goatfell, provides some challenging scrambles) and even unenthusiastic pedestrians will find the two miles from Brodick's attractive harbour to **Brodick Castle** congenial and effortless. The castle, parts of which date from the 14th century, is the ancient seat of the dukes of Hamilton and, with its country park, is open to the public. It contains various paintings and *objets d'art* from the collections of the dukes, and its woodland garden justly claims to be one of the finest rhododendron gardens in Britain.

Arran's other main villages are **Lochranza**, **Blackwaterfoot**, **Kilmory** and **Lamlash**, where a precipitous offshore island spans the mouth of Lamlash Bay. **Holy Island** owes its name to St. Molaise, who lived and meditated in a cave on its west coast.

Brodick Castle on Arran: art inside, flowers outside.

The other Clyde islands regularly serviced by ferry are **Bute**, with its attractive, ancient capital **Rothesay**, and **Great Cumrae**, with the family resort of Millport. The amiable little island of Great Cumrae is reached from **Largs**, the most handsome of the Clyde resorts and the scene, in 1263, of a famous battle which conclusively repelled persistent Viking attempts to invade Scotland when the forces of Alexander III defeated those of Hakon, King of Norway.

Rothesay was once the premier destination for day trippers on the Clyde paddle steamers which took Glaswegians "doon the watter" from the heart of their city, and is still a popular resort despite the mass exodus to the Mediterranean every Glasgow Fair holiday. It's a Royal burgh which gives the title of Duke to the Prince of Wales, and the unusual round ruin of its castle dates back to the early 13th century, when it was stormed by the Norsemen soon to be routed at Largs. Bute is a comely, undemanding island with no great

heights to scale, but provides its own spectacle at the narrow **Kyles of Bute**, where the northern end of the island almost closes the gap with the Cowal peninsula. But the ferry crossing is from **Wemyss Bay**, between Largs and Gourock—from where you reach the Cowal peninsula most directly at Dunoon.

For many people in west central Scotland, the **Cowal peninsula** represents Highland escapism. It has a new population of second home-owners from the Glasgow conurbation, which makes it busy during weekends and holidays, despite the time it takes to negotiate its long fissures of sea-lochs (**Loch Fyne** to the west and **Loch Long** to the east, with several others in between). **Dunoon** is its capital, another ancient township turned holiday resort with another 13-century castle, of which only remnants remain on **Castle Hill**, where you will again meet Highland Mary. Just round the corner is the **Holy Loch**, which plays host to an American naval base. Indeed, this part

Lochranza, one of Arran's villages.

of the Clyde is famous, or infamous, for its military installations and nuclear bases, both British and American. There are more towards Glasgow in **Gare Loch**.

Last resort: West of Gare Loch, the Clyde begins to be compressed between the once-great shipbuilding banks of **Clydeside**, with the last of its resort towns on the north bank at **Helensburgh**, these days more of a stately residential satellite of Glasgow. Industrial **Dumbarton** is even closer to the city and its name confirms it has been there since the days of the Britons. Its spectacular lump of rock was their fort, and supports a 13th-century castle which has close connections with Mary Queen of Scots.

The eastern edge of South-west Scotland is dominated—some might say intimidated—by the A74, the frenzied dual-carriageway which is Glasgow's access to the Border and England. Yet this unpleasant road is carved through some of the shapeliest hills in Scotland, with some lovely, lonely places and

unexpected treasures tucked away in their folds. The briefest of detours will bring you to **Moffat**, an elegant little town which was once a minor spa and has the broadest main street in Scotland, and on to the **Devil's Beef Tub**, a vast, steep, natural vat in the hills where Border raiders used to hide stolen cattle; while, on either side of the A74, a few miles driving on suddenly silent roads will take you to the highest villages in Scotland (**Leadhills** and **Wanlockhead**, once centres of lead, gold and silver mining), glorious Drumlanrig Castle, a home of the Dukes of Buccleuch and Queensberry, the heartland of John Buchan country at Broughton, the historic market town of Lanark and the social experiments of Robert Owen at New Lanark, and the lush orchards and dramatic falls of the River Clyde.

Drumlanrig Castle is reached by descending the gloomy, precipitous **Dalveen Pass**, a natural stairway between the uplands of South Lanarkshire and the rolling pastures and exquisite broadleaf woodland of Dumfriesshire. It is a palace of pink sandstone built in late 17th-century Renaissance style on the site of an earlier Douglas stronghold and near a Roman fort. Its rich collection of French furniture and Dutch paintings (Holbein and Rembrandt are represented) includes some interesting relics of Prince Charles Edward Stuart, and its benign parkland offers a particularly exciting adventure playground for children.

On the Buchan trail: The A74's tributary to **Lanark** skirts the perfect breast of **Tinto Hill**, the highest in Lanarkshire, much-climbed and much-loved by Lanarkshire schoolchildren who traditionally carry stones to add to the enormous cairn which now forms the hill's nipple. To the East, across the Clyde by a series of roads, is the pretty village of **Broughton** and the **John Buchan Centre**, devoted to the life and work of the Scottish statesman who was also a best-selling novelist, and whose childhood summers were spent in the nearby valley of the Upper Tweed.

Biggar is a lively and rewarding little

Largs: the Clyde resorts are magnets for Glasgow holiday-makers.

town, with an active museum life focusing on local history as if in defiance of the greater celebrity of its big neighbour, Lanark. This high, handsome old Royal burgh was already important in the 10th century, when a parliament was held there, but is more closely identified with the origins of William Wallace's rebellion against the English. Wallace is said to have lived in the Castlegate and hidden in a cave in the Cartland Craigs, just below the town, after killing an English soldier in a brawl. When he heard that his wife had been murdered he attacked the English garrison with a band of friends, who became his first army of resistance against the invaders.

Lanark was also a Covenanting centre and is still a place of great character, much of it due to its weekly livestock market and the steep fall of the Clyde below the town at **New Lanark**. There, the buildings of the cotton spinning village where Robert Owen opened a free school and operated a co-operative store in the early 18th century have been sensitively restored as modern housing and shops.

The cataracts of the **Falls of Clyde Nature Reserve** are the preface to one of the river's prettiest passages, its last Arcadian fling among the orchards and market gardens of Kirkfieldbank and Hazlebank and Rosebank before it reaches the industrial heartland of North Lanarkshire. Near one of those pastoral villages, **Crossford**, you will find one of Scotland's best-preserved and most impressive medieval castles. **Craignethan Castle**, was built between the 15th and 16th centuries on a splendid site above a wooded pass two miles from the Clyde, and was a stronghold of the Hamiltons, fierce friends of Mary Queen of Scots.

Its claim to be the original Tillietudlem in Sir Walter Scott's *Old Mortality* is pretty well authenticated. It represents a handsome and stirring farewell to the romance (and brutality) of the Middle Ages before the Reformation reached Scotland, together with a harsh new realism.

144

GLASGOW

Glasgow is a city for connoisseurs. It always has been, from the days when one of its earliest tourists, the 18th-century writer Daniel Defoe, described it as "the cleanest and beautifullest and best built city in Britain", to its recent, silver-tongued, brass-necked promotion of itself as the city "that's miles better". Yet there are few places in Europe which have been more publicly misunderstood and misrepresented than this monstrous, magnificent citadel to the worst and the best of commerce and capitalism, to the price and the prizes of Empire and the Industrial Revolution. And there can be few cities which have inspired more furious conflicts of opinion of its worth, or ignited so many conflagrations of controversy.

Invincible spirit: Glasgow accommodates no neutrality. It is either loved or loathed by native Scots (exempting Glaswegians, of course, whose chauvinism has been called "a formidable if ill-founded kind of sub-nationalism") and it is either admired or avoided by visitors who know only its two reputations: its friendly one or its fearsome one.

Yet even in the darkest days of its reputation, when Glasgow slums and Glasgow violence were the touchstone for every sociologist's worst urban nightmares, it was still a city for connoisseurs. It appealed to those who were not insensitive to the desperate consequences of its 19th-century population explosion, when the combination of cotton, coal, steel and the River Clyde transformed Glasgow from elegant little merchant city to industrial behemoth; and who were not blind to the dire effect of 20th-century economics which, from World War I onwards, have presided over the decline of its shipbuilding and heavy industries; but who were nevertheless able to uncover, behind its grime and grisliness, a city of noble character, handsome buildings and invincible spirit. Glasgow, in other words, has always appealed to the kind of tourist who responds to the very nature of cities—their sublime expression of human achievement at its most aspirational and its most problematic.

Its enthusiasts have always recognised Glasgow's qualities, and even at the height of its notoriety they have been able to give Glasgow its place in the pantheon of great Western cities. Today, it has become fashionable to describe it as European in character, for the remarkable diversity of its architecture and a certain levity of heart, or even to compare it with North America for its grid-iron street system and wisecracking street wisdom.

But these resonances have long been appreciated by experienced travellers. In 1929, at a time when social conditions were at their worst, the romantic but perceptive travel writer H.V. Morton found "a transatlantic alertness about Glasgow which no city in England possesses" and—the converse of orthodox opinion—was able to see that "Edinburgh is Scottish and Glasgow is

Preceding pages: Glaswegian football crowd; re-generated Glasgow. Left, old-style Glasgow pub. Right, new-style Glasgow coffee lounge.

GLASGOW

KELVIN BRIDGE

GREAT WESTERN RD

Western Infirmary

ST GEORGE'S CROSS

Kelvingrove Park

Kelvin Hall

Art Gallery & Museum

ARGYLE STREET

Scho

RENFREW S

SAUCHIEHALL STREET

CHARING CROSS STN.

CLYDESIDE EXPRESSWAY

Outer Basin

North Basin

South Basin

ARGYLE STREET

ST VINCENT STREET

PITT STREET

BOT

River Clyde

North Basin

Centre Basin

South Basin

GOVAN ROAD

GOVAN ROAD

KINGSTON BRI.

YORK ST

BROOMIEL

KING GE

CESSNOCK

WEST PAISLEY RD

MORRISON ST NE

KINNING PARK

M8 MOTORWAY

SHIELDS RD

WEST ST

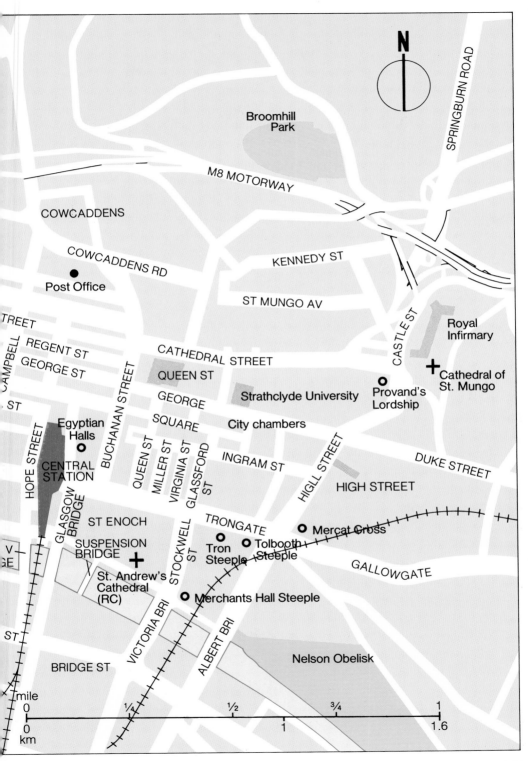

cosmopolitan". And in 1960, as the demoralised city was poised to lose many of its finest buildings to the brutal surgery of redevelopment, the "British place-taster" Ian Nairn discovered with a sense of shock that "Glasgow was without doubt the friendliest of Britain's big cities, and probably the most dignified and coherent as well".

Nairn was immediately struck by what you might call the multi-national look of the place, aware that "there is far more Continental influence in Scottish architecture (first French, then Dutch) than there ever is in English", and detecting, too, that influence which Glasgow's Victorian architects and planners shared with and sometimes exported to America: "In looks it is much more like the best parts of some American cities—Boston or Philadelphia—than anywhere in England." But above all he identified that celebrated quality (celebrated into myth, in many ways) which makes Glasgow an experience for those who care nothing for fine buildings: "Any Glasgow walk is inflected by a multitude of human contacts—in shops, under umbrellas (there *is* a good deal of rain in Glasgow), even from policemen—and each of them seems to be a person-to-person recognition, not the mutual hate of cogs in a machine who know their plight but cannot escape it."

Iron fists: Yet Glaswegians themselves will admit that their positive qualities have a negative side. Even today, although Glasgow has no more violent crime than any other British city and less than some, matiness can turn to menace in certain dismal pubs where too much whisky is chased by too much beer. (The working man's tipple in Glasgow has traditionally been "a wee hauf and hauf"—a measure of whisky pursued by a half pint of beer—although the disaffected young have turned to more lethal mixtures of vodka and cheap wine, while yuppies have discovered Piña Colada). Religious bigotry, the obverse of honest faith, still runs deep, finding its most aggressive focus in the sub-culture of football.

Close scrutiny in the city's art gallery for Sir James Guthrie's "Old Willie, a Village Worthy".

And Glasgow's legendary humour, made intelligible even to the English through the success of comedians like Billy Connolly but available less commercially on every street corner, is the humour of the ghetto. It has been nurtured on hard times. It is dry, sceptical, irreverent and often black. It's the humour of self-defence, the wit of people who know if they don't laugh they will cry. The Glasgow writer Cliff Hanley compares it to American-Jewish humour in its fast pace but places it in "the hard, subversive, proletarian tradition of the city".

Glasgow today is visibly, spectacularly a city in transformation. Unlike the English port of Liverpool, which has suffered similar problems of economic decline and urban devastation, it hasn't allowed its "hard, subversive, proletarian tradition" to lead it into brick walls of confrontation with central government. The result? A city which has massively re-arranged its own environment; which now sees its future in the service industries, in business conferences, exhibitions and indeed in tourism; which has already achieved some startling coups on its self-engineered road to becoming "Europe's first post-industrial city"; and which has probably never been more exciting to visit since, at the apogee of its Victorian vigour, it held the International Exhibition of Science and Art 100 years ago.

Glaswegians allow themselves a sly smile over their elevation to the first rank of Europe's cultural centres, and have taken to calling their home town "Culture City". But the smile becomes a little bitter for those who live in those dismal areas of the city as yet untouched by the magic of stone-cleaning, floodlighting or even modest rehabilitation. Defenders of the new Glasgow argue that their turn will come; that you can't attract investment and employment to a city, with better conditions of everyone, unless first you shine up its confidence on the inside and polish up its image on the outside.

"Instant city": Like all four Scot-

Glasgow traders: fast-talking and hard-bargaining.

tish cities, Glasgow is defined by hill and water. Its suburbs advance up the slopes of the vast bowl which contains it, and the pinnacles, towers and spires of its university, colleges and cathedral occupy their own summits within the bowl. It is, therefore, a place of sudden, sweeping vistas, with always a hint of ocean or mountain just round the corner. Look north from the heights of **Queen's Park** and you will see the cloudy humps of the Trossachs and the precipitous banks of Loch Lomond. Look west from **Gilmorehill** to the great spangled mouth of the Clyde and you will sense the sea fretting at its fragmented littoral and the islands and resorts which used to bring thousands of Glaswegians "doon the watter" for their annual Fair Fortnight.

The antiquity of this July holiday—Glasgow Fair became a fixture in the local calendar in 1190—gives some idea of the long-term stability of the town on the Clyde. But for centuries Glasgow had little prominence or significance in the history of Scotland.

Although by the 12th century it was both market town and cathedral city (with a patron saint, St. Mungo) and flourished quietly throughout the Middle Ages, it was largely by-passed by the bitter internecine conflicts of pre-Reformation Scotland and the running battles with England. Most of Scotland's trade, too, was conducted with the Low Countries from the East Coast ports. But it had a university, now five centuries old and a distinguished centre of medical and engineering studies, and it had the Clyde. When trade opened up with the Americas, Glasgow's fortune was made.

Today, the names of the streets of 18th-century Glasgow—Virginia Street, Jamaica Street and the vanished Havannah Street—tell something of the story which turned a small town into the handsome fief of tobacco barons. The tobacco trade with Virginia and Maryland brought the city new prosperity and prestige and prompted it to expand westwards from the medieval centre of the High Street. (Little of me-

Motorway city: old-timers wouldn't recognise the place.

dieval Glasgow remains.) In the late 18th century the urbanisation of the city accelerated with an influx of immigrants, mainly from the West Highlands, to work in the cotton mills with their new machines introduced by merchants who were deserting the tobacco trade. The Industrial Revolution had begun, and from then on Glasgow's destiny—grim and glorious—was fixed.

The deepening of the Clyde up to the Broomielaw, near the heart of the city, in the 1780s and the coming of the steam engine in the 19th century consolidated a process of such rapid expansion that Glasgow has been called an "instant city". In the 50 years between 1781 and 1831 the population of the city quintupled, and was soon to be further swelled by thousands of Irish immigrants crossing the Irish Sea to escape famine and seek work. The Victorians completed Glasgow's industrial history and built most of its most self-important buildings as well as the congested domestic fortifications which were soon to become infamous as slum tenements. Since World War II, its population has fallen below the million mark to about 740,000, the result of policies designed to decant citizens into "new towns". New policies are now encouraging the repopulation of the inner city.

The dear green place: There's some dispute about the origins of the name Glasgow. Scholars say it derives from the language of the British Celts, but variously interpret the genesis of its two syllables to mean anything from "dear stream" to "greyhound" (which some say was a nickname of St. Mungo, its patron saint). But there's no dispute about the version which has been adopted by the city, which was the title of a novel about Glasgow and which has now worked its way assiduously into its tourist literature and marketing lore: Glasgow means "dear green place". What else? It has, after all, over 70 parks—"more green space per head of population than any other city in Europe", as the tour bus drivers tell you.

Glasgow University: some traditions haven't changed.

CULTURE COMES IN FROM THE COLD

Glasgow's elevation to the position of European City of Culture 1990 (a title bestowed by the Ministers of Culture of the 12 member states of the European Economic Community) was received in Britain with a mixture of astonishment and amusement. Other competitors, such as Bath, Cambridge and Edinburgh, were more obvious centres of cultural activity, and none resented the success of Glasgow's submission more bitterly than Edinburgh, which has grown complacent on the annual feast of its famous international festival, and which has long perceived itself as the guardian of Scotland's most civilised values.

But Scots who take an interest in the arts have been aware that for some time Glasgow has been stealing initiatives over Edinburgh. The capital's city fathers have been trying to make up their minds to build an opera house for nearly 30 years, but Glasgow went ahead and converted one of its general-purpose theatres, the **Theatre Royal**, and in 1975 invited the highly regarded Scottish Opera to make it its home.

The city is also host to the Scottish National Orchestra, beneficiary of a new £18 million concert hall in Buchanan Street, a replacement for the St. Andrews Halls which were burnt in 1962. (Even in Glasgow the wheels of civic creativity grind slow.) The BBC Scottish Symphony Orchestra, the National Youth Orchestra for Scotland, the successful Scottish Ballet and the more fragile Scottish Theatre Company all have their headquarters in Glasgow, while the city is home to the Royal Scottish Academy of Music and Drama.

Besides its traditional theatres—the **King's** and the **Pavilion**—it has several interesting studio theatres, including the **Tron**, founded by Glasgow Theatre Club in 1979, the **Mitchell Theatre**, in an extension of Glasgow's most distinguished library (the Mitchell Library is the largest civic-owned reference library in Europe and is gloriously housed in a 1911 building in North Street, near Charing Cross) and the small theatre of the dynamic **Third Eye Centre**, a multi-media arts centre opened in Sauchiehall Street in 1975. However, Glasgow's most distinctive theatre—in concept as much as content—is the innovative **Citizens Theatre**.

Each year, or so it seems, Glasgow adds a new festival to its calendar. Mayfest, a general celebration of the arts, has been followed by international jazz, folk music and choral festivals, each held during successive months of the summer to keep the visitors coming. But the turning point in Glasgow's progress towards cultural respectability in the wider world came with the opening, in 1983, of the new building in Pollock Country Park which houses the Burrell Collection.

The great cliché about the **Burrell Museum** is that the building outshines the collection. Certainly its stunningly inventive design attracts people who have only a passing interest in the eclectic taste of Sir William Burrell, the Glasgow shipowner who bequeathed his priceless assembly of Chinese ceramics, ancient Mediterranean artefacts, Persian carpets, medieval stained glass and furniture and modern paintings and sculpture to the city in 1944.

It now claims to be Scotland's most popular tourist attraction—over 4 million people tramped through its doors in its first three and a half years—but its popularity has tended to overshadow the attractions of Glasgow's other distinguished art galleries and museums. **Kelvingrove**, at the Western end of Argyle Street, which has a strong representation of 17th-century Dutch paintings and 19th-century French paintings as well as many fine examples of the work of the late 19th-century Glasgow Boys; and the university's **Hunterian Museum and Art Gallery**.

Other museums of special interest are the **Museum of Transport**, which contains the largest range of vehicles in the U.K. and which is being rehoused in the revitalised Kelvin Hall as part of a new sports and leisure complex; **Haggs Castle**, a period museum with a focus on children's educational activities, on the South Side; and the charming, miniature repository of social history which is the **Tenement House**, a two-room-and-kitchen flat in a 1892 tenement in Garnethill which has been wonderfully preserved in its original state and is now owned by the National Trust for Scotland.

The most unexpected, idiosyncratic and oldest of its parks—in fact, the oldest public park in Britain—is **Glasgow Green**, once the common grazing ground of the medieval town and acquired by the burgh in 1662. To this day Glasgow women have the right to dry their washing on Glasgow Green, and its Arcadian sward is still spiked with clothes poles for their use, although there are few takers. Municipal Clydesdale horses, used for carting duties in the park, still avail themselves of the grazing, and the general eccentricity of the place is compounded by the bizarre proximity of Templeton's Carpet Factory, designed in 1889 by William Leiper who aspired to replicate the Doge's Palace in Venice. (The factory is now a business centre.)

Here, too, you will find the **People's Palace**, built at the turn of the century as a cultural centre for the East End community, for whom its red sandstone munificence was indeed palatial. It's now a museum dedicated to the social and industrial life of the 19th-century city, and the adjacent Winter Gardens have been turned into the cosiest and most verdant cafeteria in town.

The most distinguished of the remaining 69-odd parks include the **Botanic Gardens**, in the heart of Glasgow's stately West End, with another palace—the **Kibble Palace**—the most enchanting of its two large hothouses. It was built as a conservatory for the Clyde Coast home of a Glasgow businessman, John Kibble, and moved to its present site in 1873. The architect has never been identified, although legend associates it with Sir Joseph Paxton, who designed the Crystal Palace in London.

Kelvingrove Park, which lies between Great Western Road and Argyll Street, was laid out in the 1850s and has been the venue of Glasgow's principal Victorian and Edwardian international exhibitions, although that function has now been conceded to the new Scottish Exhibition and Conference Centre. It is a spectacular park, however, traversed by the River Kelvin and dominated on one side by the Gothic pile of **Glasgow University** (this seat of learning was unseated from its original college in the High Street and rehoused on Gilmorehill in 1870) and by the elegant Victorian precipice of **Park Circus** on the other side.

Pollock Park, on the city's South Side (those who live south of the Clyde consider themselves and are considered to be a separate race of Glaswegian) has now got a well-worn path beaten to the door of the new **Burrell Museum** but is also the home of **Pollock House**, one of the few Glasgow buildings whose construction, in the 18th century, involved that great Scottish architectural dynasty, the Adam family. It, too, is an art gallery with works by El Greco, Murillo, Goya and William Blake.

Yet more greenery can be found among the sylvan glades of **Queen's Park**, also on the South Side, and in **Victoria Park**, near the north mouth of the Clyde Tunnel, which has a glasshouse containing several large fossil trees of some 350 million years' antiquity. Back across the river is **Bella-**

Left and right, two aspects of the Burrell Collection.

houston Park, the city's main sports centre.

Dark welcome: In his book *In Search of Scotland*, H.V. Morton describes the launching of a ship on the Clyde in a passage which brings tears to the eyes: "Men may love her as men love ships…She will become wise with the experience of the sea. But no shareholder will ever share her intimacy as we who saw her so marvellously naked and so young slip smoothly from the hands that made her into the dark welcome of the Clyde."

That was written in 1929—at a time when the Clyde's shipbuilding industry was on the precipice of the great depression from which it never recovered. Soon another writer, the novelist George Blake, was calling the empty yards and silent cranes "the high, tragic pageant of the Clyde", and today that pageant is just a sideshow. At Stobcross Quay, site of the **Scottish Exhibition and Conference Centre** on the north bank, you can marvel at the industrial colossus of the Finnieston Cran (crane), preserved to remind us of the heavy locomotives once hefted on board ships which carried them all over the world.

Stobcross Quay is also a terminus of the **Clyde Walkway**, which represents Glasgow's first attempt to direct its great river towards the new industries of leisure and tourism. You can walk from the quay through the centre of the city past Glasgow Green to the suburb of **Cambuslang**, but somehow the journey isn't as cheerful as it should be, still lacking the kind of vigorous commercial, social and domestic life which has turned other derelict waterfronts into major attractions.

The central section is the most interesting, taking in the city's more distinguished bridges and many of the buildings associated with its maritime life. (The architectural historians Gomme and Walker identify only two bridges, the pedestrian Suspension Bridge and the Victoria Bridge, as worthy of notice, dismissing the others as "a sorry lot".) The Victoria Bridge was built in 1854 to replace the 14th-century Old Glasgow Bridge, and the graceful Suspension Bridge was completed in 1871 and designed by Alexander Kirkland, who later became Commissioner of Public Buildings in Chicago.

Custom House Quay, which looks across to the delicate Georgian façades of Carlton Place on the south bank, has some opulent sandstone landscaping, a bandstand, a pub and the SV Carrick, an old clipper which still holds the world sailing record for the 12,000-mile (19,000-km) voyage between Adelaide and London. The Carrick did it in 65 days, but now reposes as the headquarters of the Royal Naval Volunteer Reserve Club of Scotland.

There's much still to be done for the **Broomielaw**, which is even richer in sailing history. To the west of George IV Bridge and Central Station's railway bridge, it was once the departure point for regular services to Ireland, North America and the west coast towns of Scotland. Today, only two passenger ships make special excursions from Glasgow: the "Waverley", which is the last sea-going paddle steamer in the

Teeing off by the River Clyde.

world (and it has been some struggle to keep it paddling) and the "Balmoral", which does trips from Anderston Quay during the tourist season.

There is new life stirring, however, on the vast deserted wharfs of the Clyde. On the south bank, near Govan, over 100 acres at **Princes Dock** have become the site of a garden festival; and the two massive Rotundas at either end of the old Clyde Tunnel, designed for pedestrians and horses and carts (a new road tunnel was built in the early 1960s) have been restored as, respectively, restaurant and planetarium.

Central points: "Rough, careless, vulnerable and sentimental". That's how the writer Edwin Morgan described Glaswegians, and they are certainly qualities which Glaswegians have brought to their environment. The city has been both brutal and nostalgic about its own fabric, destroying and lamenting with equal vigour. When the city fathers built an urban motorway in the 1960s they liberated Glasgow for the motorist but cut great swathes through its domestic and commercial heart, and were only just prevented from extending the Inner Ring Road to demolish much of the Merchant City.

But the disappearance of the last tramcars in the 1960s has been regretted ever since and today there is talk of retrieving them; while Glaswegians have taken a long time to accept their updated underground transport system and grow to love the "Clockwork Orange"—the violently coloured new rolling stock which replaced the original carriages in the 1970s. (**Glasgow District Subway**, opened in 1896, was one of the earliest in Britain and the only one in the country which is called, American-style, "the Subway".)

But to Morgan's list of adjectives might have been added "pretentious" and "aspirational", two sides of the architectural coin which represents Glasgow's legacy of magnificent Victorian buildings. They aren't hard to find: the dense grid-iron of streets around George Square and westwards invites the neck to crane at any number

Glasgow's confident slogan on display in George Square.

of soaring façades, many bearing the art of the sculptor and all signifying some chapter of 19th-century history.

George Square is the heart of modern Glasgow. Like most Scottish squares, it contains a motley collection of statues, British (mainly English) prime ministers and Scottish notables. The 80-ft (24-metre) column in its centre is mounted by the novelist Sir Walter Scott, gazing southwards, so they say, to the land where he made all his money. But the square is more effectively dominated by the grandiose **City Chambers**, designed by William Young and opened in 1888. The marble-clad interior, which you can now visit on guided tours, is even more opulent and self-important than the exterior.

George Square's other monuments to Victorian prosperity are the **Head Post Office** on the south side and the noble **Merchants' House** on the northwest corner, which is now the home of Glasgow Chamber of Commerce. Its crowning glory is the gold ship on its dome, drawing the eye ever upwards—a replica of the ship on the original Merchants' House.

Just off Buchanan Street is the recently named **Nelson Mandela Place**. It used to be St. George's Place and the new name was Glasgow District Council's tribute to the imprisoned South African political leader. Here you will find **Glasgow Stock Exchange**, designed in the 1870s by John Burnet, whose reputation was to be eclipsed by his more celebrated son J.J. Burnet; and the **Royal Faculty of Procurators** (1854), which is rich in decorative stonework and influenced by Italian Renaissance style.

In nearby streets are examples of the work of another distinguished Glasgow architect, the younger James Salmon, who designed the Mercantile Buildings in **Bothwell Street** (1897-98) and the curious "Hat-rack" in **St. Vincent Street**, given its name for the extreme narrowness and the projecting cornices of its tall façade.

Farther west, J.J. Burnet's extraord-

Charing Cross: full of 19th-century confidence.

inary residence **Charing Cross Mansions** (1891), with its grandiloquent intimations of French Renaissance style, was spared the surgery of motorway development which destroyed many 19th-century buildings around Charing Cross; while in Great Western Road over the hill you will find **Great Western Terrace**, one of the best examples of the work of Glasgow's most famous Victorian architect, Alexander "Greek" Thomson, called "Greek" for the passion of his classicism.

Back towards the city centre in St. Vincent Street is Thomson's prominent **St. Vincent Street Church**, now destined to become an arts centre. Here the streets rise towards **Blythswood Square** which, with its surroundings, provides a graceful mixture of late Georgian and early Victorian domestic architecture. Blythswood Square itself has two claims to notoriety. It is stigmatised as a rendezvous for prostitutes and their clients, and it was the home of one Madeleine Smith, who poisoned her French lover there in 1858. (It must be said that this "respectable" young woman was discharged by the Edinburgh jury with the verdict of "not proven"—which generally means "We know you did it but we can't prove it, so go away and don't do it again." She took the implicit advice to heart, moved to London, entertained George Bernard Shaw and married a pupil of the designer William Morris.)

Across Buchanan Street in St. Vincent Place are the offices of Greater Glasgow Tourist Board. When you drop in to pick their brains and pick up their brochures you'll find yourself mounting the steps of another imposing mid-Victorian building, although the interiors have been reconstructed. Behind St. Vincent Place is **Royal Exchange Square**, which is pretty well consumed by one of the most visually dramatic public libraries in the country. **Stirling's Library** began life as the 17th-century mansion of a tobacco lord, has been a bank and the Royal Exchange and in 1832, to the design of David Hamilton, it was extended to

Two local entertainers: Lulu at the Pavilion, and a street musician.

include the portico and the clock tower.

Among the city centre's most distinguished Georgian buildings are, in Ingram Street, **Hutcheson's Hospital Hall**, also designed by David Hamilton and now the Glasgow home of the National Trust for Scotland with a National Trust visitor centre and shop; and, in nearby Glassford Street, **Trades House** which, despite alterations, has retained the façade designed by the great Robert Adam.

But any excursion round Glasgow's architectural treasures must be highlighted by the work of the city's most innovative genius, Charles Rennie Mackintosh, who overturned the Victorians in a series of brilliant designs between 1893 and 1911. Mackintosh's influence on 20th-century architecture, along with his leading contribution to *art nouveau* in interiors, furniture and textile design, has long been acknowledged and celebrated throughout Europe, although all his finest work was done in Glasgow.

His sometimes austere, sometimes sensuous style, much influenced by natural forms and an inspired use of space and light, can be seen in several important buildings: his greatest achievement, the **Glasgow School of Art** (designed in 1896) in Renfrew Street; **Scotland Street School**, on the South Side, opened in 1904 and now a Museum of Education; and the **Martyrs' Public School**, perched above a sliproad to the M8 motorway near Glasgow Cathedral.

In Sauchiehall Street the façade of his **Willow Tea-Room** (1903) remains, and a room on the first floor has been turned over to tea-time again, with reproduction Mackintosh furniture. But more stunning examples of his interior designs can be seen at the **Mackintosh House** at the University of Glasgow's Hunterian Art Gallery on Gilmorehill. There, rooms from the architect's own house have been reconstructed and exquisitely furnished with original pieces of furniture, watercolours and designs.

There's not much left in Glasgow which is old by British standards. The oldest building is **Glasgow Cathedral**, most of which was completed in the 13th century, but the only pre-Reformation dwelling house is **Provand's Lordship**, built in 1471 as part of a refuge for poor people and extended in 1670. It's now a museum of medieval material and, less logically, hosts an early 20th-century sweet shop.

Both old buildings stand on **Cathedral Street**, at the top of the High Street—the cathedral on a site which has been a place of Christian worship since it was blessed for burial in A.D. 397 by St. Ninian, the earliest missionary recorded in Scottish history. A severe but satisfying example of early Gothic, it contains the tomb of St. Mungo, Glasgow's patron saint. Behind the cathedral, overseeing the city from the advantage of height, are more tombs—the intimidating Victorian sepulchres of the **Western Necropolis**. This cemetery is supervised by a statue of John Knox, the 16th-century reformer, and among the ranks of Glaswegian notables buried there is one

Behind the Necropolis are the Cathedral and the Royal Infirmary.

William Miller, "the laureate of the nursery". He wrote the bedtime jingle, "Wee Willie Winkie".

Glasgow's two oldest churches, other than the cathedral, are **St. Andrew's Parish Church**, which contains some spectacular plaster-work, and the episcopal **St.-Andrew's-in-the-Green**, once known as the Whistlin' Kirk for its early organ. Both were built in the mid-18th century and both can be found to the northwest of Glasgow Green, in the Merchant City.

There you will also find two remnants of the 17th century, the **Tolbooth Steeple** and the **Tron Steeple**. The Tolbooth Steeple, at Glasgow Cross (where the Mercat Cross is a 20th-century replica of a vanished one) is a pretty substantial remnant of the old jail and courthouses, being seven storeys high with a crown tower.

The Tron Steeple was once attached to the Tron Church, at the junction of Argyle Street and the Trongate, and dates back to the late 16th and early 17th centuries. (Glasgow does have a habit of losing bits of its buildings.) The original church was burnt down in the 18th century and the replacement now accommodates the lively Tron Theatre.

Those truly dedicated to the pursuit of antiquity, however, could always proceed to the refined northwest suburb of **Bearsden**, where once rough Romans roamed. Bearsden lies on the line of the Antonine Wall, built during the 2nd century, and chunks of the Roman occupation remain to be seen.

Market forces: Heavy industry has come and gone, but Glasgow still flourishes as a city of independent enterprise—of hawkers, stallholders, street traders and marketeers. Even the dignified buildings of its old, more respectable markets—fish, fruit and cheese—have survived in a city which has often been careless with its past, and are now part of the rediscovery of that area called the Merchant City, which stretches from the **High Street** and the **Saltmarket** in the east to **Union Street** and **Jamaica Street** in the west, and which contains most of the city's re-

Left, a room in the Hunterian Museum. Right, Glasgow's Art School.

maining pre-Victorian buildings.

The old **Fishmarket** in Clyde Street is in fact Victorian, but it accommodates a perpendicular remnant of the 17th-century Merchants' House, demolished in 1817. This slender steeple, built in the Dutch style in 1659, now signals the venue of the **Briggait Centre**, which has turned the Fishmarket into a rather superior trading house for boutiques, cafés and entertainers.

In **Candleriggs**, slightly to the north, the old Fruitmarket now houses a more traditional style of weekend market selling fresh produce and inexpensive clothes, but Glasgow's market celebrity still belongs to the **Barrows**, in the Gallowgate to the east, where both repartee and bargains were once reputed to rival those of Paris's Flea Market and London's Petticoat Lane. Founding queen of "the Barras" was one Mrs. McIver, who started her career with one barrow, bought several more to hire out on the piece of ground she rented in the Gallowgate and was claimed to have retired a millionaire.

More local colour and open-air tat, useful or useless, can be found in **Paddy's Market**, in the lanes between Clyde Street and the Bridgegate, many of the stalls occupying the arches of an old railway bridge. This market has its genesis in Ireland's "Hungry Forties", when the great Potato Famine of the 1840s sent thousands of destitute Irish people to Glasgow (and elsewhere) to find a toehold or starve.

The West Highlands of Scotland were almost as badly affected by the potato famine and they, too, looked to Glasgow for salvation. Comic tradition has it that they also looked to **Argyle Street** for shelter. This famous shopping street is traversed by the railway bridge to Central Station. The bridge has always been called the Heilanman's Umbrella. The slander is that Highlanders stood under it when it rained rather than spend money on buying umbrellas; but the truth is that it has long been a favourite rendezvous of Glasgow's Highland community.

Argyle Street, **Sauchiehall Street** and the more upmarket **Buchanan Street** are Glasgow's great shopping thoroughfares, although an area round **Byres Road**, in the West End, has recently become a centre for interesting bric-à-brac and boutiques. In **West Regent Street** you will find a Victorian Village (a collection of small antique shops forming a street in old business premises) and in the old Tobacco Market in **Virginia Street**, where once the American shipments were auctioned, you will now discover the Virginia Antique and Crafts Galleries.

Glaswegians have always spent freely, even flashily, belying the slur on the open-handedness of Scots, and the city's commercial interests still seem to believe that the appetite for shopping is insatiable. The site of the demolished St. Enoch Railway Station and hotel (one of Glasgow's major acts of vandalism) is being occupied by a £62 million glass-covered complex of 50 shop units, fast-food "court", ice rink and multi-storey car park. "Edinburgh is the capital," as an old joke goes, "but Glasgow *has* the capital."

Left, pawnbroker's sign, traditionally a familiar sight in the Gorbals. Right, police transport suitable for patrolling pedestrian precincts.

FORTH AND CLYDE

The royal burgh of **Stirling,** whose name resounds down the more turbulent corridors of Scottish history, stands at the apex of a triangle which is rich in character but poor in obvious tourist appeal. Stirling is the ornamental brooch on the plain, workmanlike belt which clasps the waist of central Scotland. The lower reaches of the rivers Forth and Clyde have been the waterways of that belt since the opening of the Forth and Clyde Canal in 1790 linked the industrial towns of west central Scotland with the east coast at Grangemouth—now the epicentre of a vast petrochemical plant. The canal was closed to working navigation in 1963 but now supplies some modest recreational activity.

Natural fortress: Stirling's title of "gateway to the Highlands" is no invention of its tourist officers. Its Old Bridge

was of great strategic importance for centuries, providing access to the north across the lowest bridging point of the River Forth, while the 250-ft (75-metre) volcanic plug which supports its castle—every bit as impressive as Edinburgh Castle—was the natural fortress which made Stirling significant from the 12th century onwards.

The **castle** had its most active moments during Scotland's Wars of Independence. Surrendered to the English in 1296, it was recaptured by the warrior-patriot William Wallace after the Battle of Stirling Bridge (not the stone bridge, built around 1400, which exists today, but a wooden structure in the same place). It then became the last stronghold in Scotland to hold out against Edward I, the "Hammer of the Scots". Eventually, though, it went back to the English for 10 years, until Robert the Bruce re-took it in 1314 after the Battle of Bannockburn, which decisively secured the independence of Scotland. There remains a lot to see at the castle; the Stewarts favoured it as a Royal residence, James II was born in it and Mary Queen of Scots crowned there at the age of nine months, and its splendid collection of buildings reflects its history as palace and fortress.

The achievements of both Wallace and Bruce are conspicuously recalled in the environs of Stirling. On the rock of **Abbey Craig**, above the site where Wallace camped, is the ostentatious, overbearing Wallace Monument, built by the Victorians in one of their more vulgar moods and home of the hero's two-handed sword. From its elevation, however, you feel you can almost touch the leaping ramparts of the **Ochil Hills**, while to the south-east the Forth spreads across its flat plain to the spectacular flare-stacks of **Grangemouth**.

The site of the Battle of Bannockburn is a few miles south of Stirling and has been more or less consumed by a housing estate. No one is precisely sure where the battle was fought anyway, but the rotunda beside the heroic bronze equestrian statue of Bruce is said to mark the spot of his command post. In the usual way of these things, the **Ban-**

Stirling
Bannockburn
Grangemouth
Falkirk
Kirkcaldy
M90
Firth of Forth
Dunfermline
South Queensferry
Edinburgh
M8
Motherwell
Wishaw
M74
A702
Lanark
River Clyde
Peebles

FORTH AND CLYDE

nockburn Heritage Centre will give an audio-visual account of the matter; but, as Scotland's battlefields go, this most famous one could hardly be called atmospheric.

Stirling is almost equidistant from Edinburgh and Glasgow. If you take the motorway to Edinburgh (and the M9, incidentally, must be the emptiest motorway in the U.K.), you will find yourself keeping roughly parallel to the broadening course of the Forth. There are some rewarding diversions to be made on this route. Near the industrial town of Falkirk are four good sections of the Roman **Antonine Wall**, a turf rampart on a stone base which the Emperor Antoninus Pius caused to be built between the firths of Clyde and Forth around AD 140; while the motorway itself has opened up a distracting view of the loch and **Palace of Linlithgow**, the well-preserved ruins of Scotland's most magnificent palace.

Birthplace of Mary Queen of Scots (who was born while her father, James V, lay dying in Falkland Palace, across the Forth in Fife) Linlithgow's chapel and great hall are late 15th-century, while its handsome courtyard has an elaborate 16th-century fountain. The characterful small town is itself one of Scotland's oldest and is worth visiting, too, for the **Church of St. Michael**, the largest pre-Reformation parish church in Scotland, conspicuous for the abstract golden crown mounted on its tower in 1964.

From the M9, you can also foray down to the village of **South Queensferry** on the southern bank of one of the Forth's oldest crossings, where river becomes estuary. Until the building of the Forth Road Bridge, ferries had plied between South and North Queensferry for 900 years. Today, South Queensferry huddles between and beneath the giant bridges which provide such a spectacular contrast in engineering design—the massive humped girders of the rail bridge, opened in 1890, and the delicate, graceful span of the suspension bridge, opened in 1964. Pedestrians, incidentally, have their own footpath on the road bridge and can tramp for over a mile through the boisterous air between river and sky.

Near South Queensferry are two of Scotland's stately homes, both open to the public: **Hopetoun House**, home of the Earls of Hopetoun, magnificently situated in parkland beside the Forth and splendidly extended and rebuilt by William Adam and his son John between 1721 and 1754; and **Dalmeny House**, home of the Earls of Rosebery and a fine collection of paintings.

You can walk delightfully beside the Forth through the wooded Rosebery estate to the **River Almond**, where a funny little rowing-boat ferry transports you across this minor tributary to the red pantiles and white crowstep gables of **Cramond**. Now a suburb of Edinburgh, Cramond is still very much its own 18th-century village, with a harbour which was used by the Romans. Its **Roman Fort**, whose foundations have been exposed, was built around AD 142, and may have been used by Septimius Severus when he marched vengefully into north-east

Stirling Castle: it changed hands often between Scots and English.

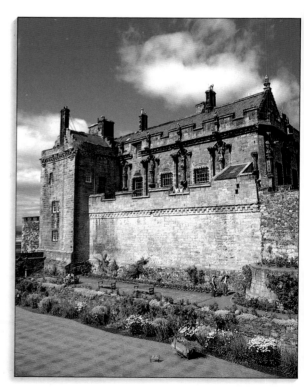

166

Scotland a century later.

Scotland's pre-eminent river, the **Clyde**, undergoes more personality changes than any other in its progress to the western seaboard. The limpid little stream which has its source in the hills of Tweedale, 80 miles south-east of Glasgow, moves prettily through the orchards and market gardens of Clydesdale before watering the industries of North Lanarkshire and welcoming the ships and shipyards of Glasgow. The lower reaches of its valley have been colonised by the city's satellites, and by a clutter of hill towns which all more or less run into each other—Wishaw, Motherwell and Hamilton.

Once drab coal and steel towns (Motherwell is still the home of the vast Ravenscraig steelworks), they are now recovering their dignity and vitality through (among other things) the creation of **Strathclyde Country Park**, a huge recreational area which includes a 200-acre (80-hectare) loch, formed by diverting the Clyde, and part of the old estate of the Dukes of Hamilton. Of the three towns, **Hamilton** has the longest history, with associations with Mary Queen of Scots, Cromwell and the Covenanters, who were defeated by Monmouth at nearby Bothwell Bridge in 1679. Many of the escaping Covenanters sheltered in the woods of the sympathetic Duchess of Hamilton, who urged the victor not to disturb her game. **Bothwell Castle,** a red ruin above the Clyde, is often called the finest 13th-century castle in Scotland.

Memories of more recent adventures can be found in the adjacent community of **Blantyre**, birthplace of the explorer and missionary David Livingstone. The **Livingstone National Memorial** imaginatively incorporates the mill tenement where he was born, and a variety of exhibits recalls his harsh early life and his great mission in Africa against the slave trade. Livingstone was eventually buried in Westminster Abbey, but only after his bearers had lovingly transported his body 1,500 miles from the interior to the coast—an episode described in sculptured wood.

Bothwell Castle: the country's finest 13th-century stronghold.

THE WEST COAST

From the long finger of Kintyre to the deep fissure of Loch Broom, the west coast is that part of Scotland which most perfectly conforms to its romantic image. Mountain and moor, heather and stag, castle and loch—and the magical seaboard of isolated villages and small ports where, on a whim, you can jump a ferry to the Western Isles—are all to be found on this gloriously intricate and spectacular littoral. Nowhere else in Scotland (outside Caithness and Sutherland) is a physical sense of travelling more thrillingly restored; and few other areas provide such opportunities for solitude and repose, as well as the slightly scary impression that this dramatic landscape of sometimes savage desolation is not to be trifled with.

It all begins gently enough at the Clyde estuary where the deep penetration of the sea at **Loch Fyne** has created Scotland's longest peninsula, which is 54 miles (87 kms) from Crinan to the Mull of Kintyre and never wider than 10. This mighty arm is nearly bisected by West Loch Tarbert into the two regions of Knapdale and Kintyre, and its isolated character makes it almost as remote as any of the islands. Here there are rolling hills rather than mountains, rough moors and forests in Knapdale, grassy tops in Kintyre, and a coast which is most interesting on its west side, with its close view of the island of Jura from **Kilberry Head** (where you can also view a fine collection of late medieval sculptured stones) and, farther south, the vast beaches of **Machrihanish** and **Tayinloan**, where you can take the 20-minute ferry ride across to the tiny island of Gigha.

Tarbert is an agreeable little port, but of the Kintyre metropolis of **Campbeltown** the writer W.H. Murray has this to say: "It would be unjust to call it ugly but certainly it is not fair. Campbeltown is no more hideous to the eye than the grunt of a pig to the ear." There, however, you are within easy reach of the tip of the peninsula, the **Mull of Kintyre** itself.

The north coast of Ireland is only 12 miles (19 km) away, and legend has it that St. Columba first set foot in Scotland at **Keil**, near the holiday village of Southend. You can see his "footprints" imprinted on a flat rock near a ruined chapel. (There is also a St. Columba's cave on the shores of **Loch Caolisport**, in Knapdale, a recess which was certainly used as a Christian chapel around the 6th century, but which archaeology has pronounced was occupied as far back as the Middle Stone Age.)

Scenic drama: From the great lighthouse of Mull, built in 1788 and remodelled by Robert Stevenson, the grandfather of Robert Louis Stevenson, there is no where else to go. You can retreat back up the secondary road of Kintyre's east coast, which has its own scenic drama in the sandy sweep of **Carradale Bay** and the view across the water to the mountainous Clyde island of Arran. On your way north you can take in the ruined walls and sculptured tombstones

Preceding pages, wild deer. Left, the nerve-centre of Glenfinnan railway station. Right, steam excursions run regularly in summer.

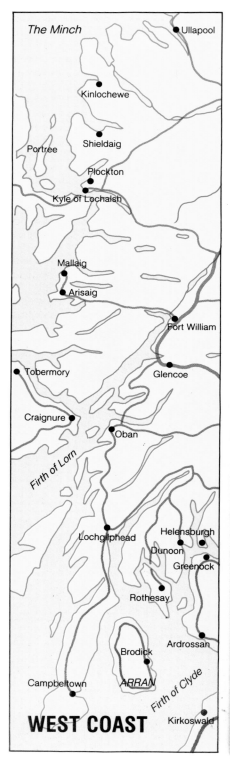

The Minch

Ullapool

Kinlochewe

Portree
Shieldaig

Plockton

Kyle of Lochalsh

Mallaig

Arisaig

Fort William

Tobermory
Glencoe

Craignure

Oban

Firth of Lorn

Lochgilphead
Helensburgh

Dunoon

Greenock

Rothesay

Ardrossan

Brodick

Campbeltown
ARRAN
Firth of Clyde

WEST COAST
Kirkoswald

of **Saddell Abbey**, a 12th-century Cistercian house, and the gardens of **Carradale House**. The hump behind them is **Beinn an Tuirc**, Kintyre's highest peak (1,490 ft; 450 metres). The name means Mountain of the Boar, from one fearsome specimen said to have been killed by an ancestor of the Campbells.

From Lochgilphead, where the Crinan Canal crosses the neck of the peninsula and connects Loch Fyne to the Atlantic Ocean, you have a choice of two main routes to the handsome port and resort of Oban (the tourist capital of the West Highlands). The longer route, up Loch Fyne by Inverary to Loch Awe (A83), is probably the more dramatic, although the shorter route (A816) takes you close to the coast and its vistas of those low-lying islands which are the floating outriders of the mountains of Jura and Mull.

Both routes are punctuated with places of interest. The most celebrated castle in this part of Scotland is **Inverary**, which has been the seat of the chiefs of the Clan Campbell, the Dukes

Music maker: craftsmen are much in demand.

of Argyll, for centuries. The present building—Gothic-revival, famous for its magnificent interiors and art collection and open to the public—was started in 1743, when the third Duke also decided to re-build the village of Inverary. The result is a dignified community with much of the orderly elegance of the 18th century; even if its snowy buildings on the shores of Loch Fyne can look like a promotion for whitewash.

There are two very different museums in the neighbourhood. One, attached to the castle, is the **Combined Operations Museum**, which recalls the passing of a quarter of a million Allied troops through this little Highland village during World War II, when Inverary was the British Combined Operations base. The other, some five miles (eight kms) south of the village, is **Auchindrain Museum of Country Life**, whose dwellings and barns of the 18th and 19th centuries were once a communal-tenancy Highland farm, paying rent to the Dukes of Argyll.

Loch Awe, where the road takes you past the fallen house of the Breadalbane family—the romantic ruins of **Kilchurn Castle**, on a promontory on the water—is the longest freshwater loch in Scotland. At its north-west extremity, where it squeezes past the mighty mountain of Ben Cruachan and drains into Loch Etive through the grim slit of Brander, it's as awesome as its name promises. The **Pass of Brander** is so steep and narrow that legend claims it was once held against an army by an old woman wielding a scythe. Almost a mile inside the mountain is Cruachan pumped storage generating station, an artificial cavern which can be visited daily in the summer.

Ancient echoes: If you approach Oban by the coast on the A816, you will pass one of the ancient capitals of Dalriada, the kingdom of the early Celts. The striking eminence of **Dunadd Fort** (c. 500 to 800) sets the mood for a spectacular range of prehistoric sites near the village of **Kilmartin**: standing stones, burial cairns and cists, all easily

Glen Tarbert: almost as remote as one of the Western Isles.

accessible. As you drive north the coast becomes ever more riven, while the natural harbours of the sea lochs and the protective islands of **Shuna** and **Luing** and **Seil** make it the playground of yachtsmen and women.

Seil and its neighbours were supported by a vigorous slate industry in the 19th century, until a great storm in 1881 flooded the quarries deep below sea level and efforts to pump them out failed. You can see some vivid evidence of those days in **Easedale Island Folk Museum**, a short ferry crossing from Seil. The island of Seil itself comes so close to the mainland that it's reached by the single stone arch of the Clachan Bridge, "the bridge over the Atlantic". Built in 1791, this hump is also a site of the rare "fairy foxglove", and on its island side is the Tigh na Truish inn, whose name—House of the Trousers—recalls the vindictive law which prohibited the wearing of the kilt after the 1745 Rising.

Oban, ringed by wooded hills and clasped within the sheltered bay which gives it the finest harbour on the Highland seaboard, still has much of the charm which turned it into a major resort in the mid-19th century. Modern tourism hasn't been so kind to the dignity of its high street, and it lost the delightful Victorian buildings of its railway station in a recent act of institutionalised vandalism. But the town still has atmosphere—most of it centred on the busy harbour which is the seaway to the Hebrides, and where even the most landlocked traveller feels the pull of the islands.

All the usual (sometimes oppressive) infrastructure of tourism can be found in Oban, whose only beach, Ganavan Sands, is two miles outside the town. There is local island-hopping to be done (the long island which lies across the bay is **Kerrera**) and there are castles to be visited: the fragment of **Dunolly** on its precipitous rock and the well-preserved 13th-century fortress of **Dunstaffnage**. There are hills to be climbed—**Pulpit Hill** is the town's best viewpoint—and there is the

Oban, dominated by the folly of MaCaig's Tower.

extraordinary folly of **McCaig's Tower** to be admired or despised. ("Its effect is damnable, if one feels in damning mood," says W.H. Murray). John Stuart McCaig was an Oban banker who financed this strange enterprise on a hill above the town centre to give work to the unemployed and provide himself with a memorial. The tower was raised between 1890 and 1900 but McCaig's grand plan was never completed. What remains looks like an austere Scottish Colosseum.

Oban is also the gateway to the lovely lands of Benderloch and Appin, and lonely Morvern, where a short ferry ride across the great sea loch of **Linnhe** and a long, tortuous car journey will take you to isolated **Ardnamurchan Point**, the most westerly headland of the Scottish mainland. **Appin** is a name which evokes romantic tragedy: there, in a historical incident made famous by Robert Louis Stevenson in *Kidnapped*, James Stewart of the Glens was wrongly hanged for the murder of Colin Campbell, "the Red Fox" and govern-

Glencoe: even the unimaginative feel their spine tingle.

ment land agent, in yet another of the internecine feuds which followed the Jacobite Rising of 1745.

Bloody massacre: To the north and west of the Ballachulish Narrows the greatest grandeur of the West Highlands now lies before you. To the east is the forbidding dark gash which is probably the most famous glen in Scotland: **Glencoe**, where, in a savage winter dawn in 1692, 40 members of the Clan MacDonald were slaughtered by the government soldiers of the Argyll regiment (Details: page 33).

Today, Glencoe seems to have trapped the gloom and grisliness of that awful event. Even the unimaginative must feel a shiver of the spine as they descend the main road between its black buttresses of mountain, which even ski development and a visitor centre have not been able to cosmeticise. These very mountains— **Buachaille Etive Mor**, **Bidean nam Bian** and the **Aonach Eagach**—are notorious for other reasons: they are one of Britain's supreme mountaineer-

ing challenges, and nearly every winter they claim lives.

Big Ben: Some 15 miles (24 km) to the north is **Fort William**. But, despite its fine position below the Mammore Mountains on Loch Linnhe, this straggling, congested town has little to recommend it beyond its proximity to **Ben Nevis** and glorious Glen Nevis. Britain's highest mountain—a mere 4,406 ft (1,340 metres)—looks a deceptively inoffensive lump from below, where you can't see its savage north face, and it can be easily enough climbed. But there are risks. The volatile nature of the Scottish climate should never be underestimated when setting out on any hill or mountain expedition.

From Fort William, you can turn east along **Loch Eil** (A830) to a splendid dead end, passing the huge, moribund pulp mill at **Corpach**. This is the "Road to the Isles" and to **Mallaig**, another seaway to the Hebrides (particularly the "small isles" of Eigg, Rhum, Canna and Muck). More importantly, Mallaig is the west coast's principal fishing port—and the most important herring and shellfish port in Britain. It is also the road to a dense concentration of associations with Charles Edward Stuart, running between the clan territories of Moidart and Morar, whose chief, MacDonald of Clanranald, raised the clans in support of the prince along with Cameron of Lochiel.

Five thousand men rallied behind the charismatic young prince's impetuous adventure, which was to cost the Highlands dear, at **Glenfinnan,** where Charles raised the white and crimson Stewart banner to the sound of their mighty cheers. A monument was erected on the spot in 1815—a grey column in baroque style with a bearded clansman on top which, says W.H. Murray, "impairs the splendid scene down the loch". The prince landed from his French brig at **Loch nan Uamh**, a bay on the Arisaig coast a few miles west. Just over a year later, after the disaster of Culloden, he left from the same place, having wandered around the Highlands with a price

The Glenfinnan Viaduct, still carrying trains from Glasgow to Mallaig.

of £30,000 on his head. It says something for the character of the Highlander—who was left to pay the prince's debts in death, persecution and attempted cultural genocide—that he was never betrayed, only helped to escape. A memorial cairn on the shore of Loch nan Uamh marks his final exit from Scotland.

Monster attraction: From **Arisaig** the road passes between the silver sands of Morar and **Loch Morar** itself (reputedly the home of Scotland's other water monster) and comes to an end at Mallaig. There you can catch a car ferry up the Sound of Sleat to Kyle of Lochalsh, hugging the great, roadless mountain wilderness of Knoydart with its two long sea lochs, Nevis and Hourn—the lochs of Heaven and Hell.

The sail also takes you past **Glenelg**, which can be reached over a giddy mountain road from Loch Duich and the A87 through Kintail. (The graceful **Five Sisters of Kintail** must be among the most photographed mountains in Scotland, while the Mackenzies' restored **Eilean Donan Castle,** on its islet over a causeway in Loch Duich, is certainly the most photographed castle.) Glenelg is worth a visit not only for its beauty but for its two Iron Age brochs—circular towers with walls which still stand over 30 ft (nine metres) high. There, too, are the remains of **Bernera Barracks**, quartered by Hanoverian troops during the 18th century, and at nearby Kyle Rhea you can cross the 500 metres of water to Skye, as Dr. Johnson and Boswell did, although the little ferry runs only in summer.

From **Kyle of Lochalsh**, the main ferry crossing for Skye, mainland travellers continue north by lovely **Loch Carron,** leaving Inverness-shire for the tremendous mountain massifs of **Wester Ross**. Here, on the isolated Applecross peninsula, among the famous peaks of **Torridon** with their views to the Cuillins of Skye and the distant, drifting shapes of the Outer Hebrides, you will find some of the most spectacular scenery in Europe—with exhilarating driving yielding to richer rewards for those who are prepared to use their feet.

Sublime loch: More gentle pursuits—amid equally wild and empty scenery—can be found at the village of **Poolewe**, where the road through the fishing port of Gairloch passes between Loch Ewe and **Loch Maree**, possibly the most sublime inland loch in Scotland, outranking Loch Lomond with no effort. (Loch Maree's particular features are the old Scots pines which line its shores and the impressive presence of the mountain Slioch above it.) The celebrated **Inverewe Gardens**, a sumptuous international collection of plants, shrubs and trees, were created last century by Osgood Mackenzie, a son of the 12th chief of the Gairloch Mackenzies. Now in the care of the National Trust for Scotland, they are open all the year round from morning until sunset.

A few miles farther north is the glittering four-mile scoop of **Gruinard Bay**, with its coves of pink sand from the red Torridon sandstone, nearly 800 million years old. Gruinard's distinction as a beauty spot has a touch of notoriety about it. On one stretch of road notice boards warn you that Gruinard Island, three-quarters of a mile offshore, is contaminated and mustn't be approached by boat. "Danger Zone," say the maps. The explanation, which isn't given, is that during World War II Gruinard Island was used as an experiment in germ warfare by the Ministry of Defence, and is still polluted with deadly anthrax bacilli.

The road then takes you round **Little Loch Broom**, below the powerful shoulders of An Teallach (3,483 ft; 1,060 metres) highest of those Torridon peaks which, says W.H. Murray, make "most Munros of the south and central Highlands seem tame by comparison". (A Munro is a Scottish mountain of over 3,000 ft, named for the man who collated them). And you are now within easy striking distance of **Loch Broom** itself, a seasonal home to fish factory ships from Russia and Eastern Europe, and the substantial northern fishing port of **Ullapool**.

THE INNER HEBRIDES

In the competition for visitors between Mull and Skye, the easiest Hebridean islands to reach, Skye wins hands down. "If Bonnie Prince Charlie had escaped over the sea to Mull, we'd been enjoying the benefits of mass tourism here," says one envious Mull hotelier.

Some scorn **Mull**'s green prettiness, dismissing it as Surrey with a tartan fringe. They might think again if they strolled on a wet day through the boggy desolation of the **Ross of Mull** or walked to the top of Mull's only mountain, **Ben More**, a respectable 3,000 ft.

The island is shaped like a gigantic teddy bear, but don't be deceived by its size, only 25 by 26 miles. A drive on the mainly single-track roads, running mostly round the perimeter, is made even slower by Scotland's most feckless and fearless sheep, which regard roads simply as grassless fields.

Mull's trump card is **Tobermory**, the prettiest port in Western Scotland, captivating and cheerful. Skye has nothing to touch it; even the impeccably renovated stable block at the Clan Donald Centre can't compete with the natural charm of Tobermory tucked in its wooded protected bay.

The tall, brightly painted houses curving round the harbour go back to the late 18th century when the British Fisheries Society planned a herring port. But the fish were fickle and today Tobermory's sparkling harbour bobs with pretty pleasure yachts. The other towns, **Craignure** on the east where the Oban ferry docks, **Salen**, in the narrow neck of the island, and **Dervaig** in the northwest, are neat serviceable little places. Visitors come to the volcanic island of Mull for the contrasting scenery, wooded and soft to bleak and bare; for fishing in the lochs; and for walking. Drive through Glen More, the ancient royal funeral route to Iona which bisects Mull from east to west, for some of the best scenery on the island.

To understand what the 19th-century Clearances meant to all Hebrideans and to grasp the harshness of a crofting life, see the tableaux, with sound commentary, at the **Old Byre Heritage Centre** at Dervaig. They help explain the islanders' fatalistic attitude to life. Some charitable outsiders think this attitude stems from the trauma of the Clearances which still trouble the collective consciousness. But cynical mainlanders say the islanders are simply idle, and get lazier. Islanders—when you can find them, for many service jobs, particularly those connected with tourism, seem to be run by incomers—say they work as hard as anyone. Crofting and fishing, they argue, just aren't understood by urbanised outsiders.

On the west of the island there's **Calgary**, the silvery sanded beach where, after the Clearances, despairing emigrant ships set sail for the New World. The beach held happy memories for one visitor: Colonel McLeod of the North West Mounted Police named a new fort in Alberta after it.

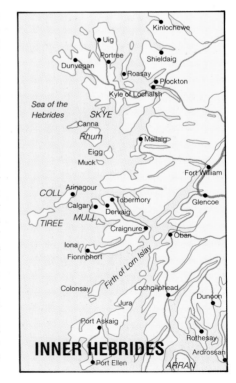

INNER HEBRIDES

Kinlochewe
Uig
Portree — Shieldaig
Dunvegan
Roasay
Plockton
Kyle of Lochalsh
Sea of the Hebrides
SKYE
Canna
Rhum — Mallaig
Eigg
Muck
Fort William
COLL — Arinagour
Calgary — Tobermory — Glencoe
Dervaig
TIREE — MULL
Craignure — Oban
Iona
Fionnphort
Firth of Lorn
Islay
Colonsay — Lochgilphead
Jura — Dunoon
Port Askaig
Rothesay
Ardrossan
Port Ellen
ARRAN

The Inner Hebrides 183

Preceding pages: the Isle of Mull; Tobermory, on Mull. Left, Iona Abbey.

Two castles are open to the public, both on the east, **Torosay**, with 19th-century Scottish baronial turrets and crenellations, is near Craignure and is still lived in by the Gutherie-James family. It's full of family memorabilia and is a friendly, non-imposing house. On wet days, of which there are many on Mull, you can leaf through old books in the drawing room. There's shapely Italian statuary in the grounds, fine clematis climbing on old brick walls, and a sweet-smelling rock garden.

The 13th-century **Duart Castle** on a dramatic headland overlooking the Sound of Mull is the MacLeans' stronghold. Mull belonged to the clan until it was forfeited when the MacLeans supported young Prince Charles Edward, who was beaten at Culloden in 1746. The castle was deserted for almost 200 years, then restored by Sir Fitzroy MacLean early this century. As a young Hussar, MacLean charged with the Light Brigade in the Crimea in 1854, and some of his mementoes are displayed in the Grand Banqueting Room.

Ferry tales: Mull is the jumping-off point for several other islands: Iona, Staffa, Coll and Tiree.

You feel a bit like a pilgrim as you board the serviceable little 10-minute shuttle to **Iona**. Cars and big coaches on day trips from the mainland line the ferry road at **Fionnphort** on Mull's southwest tip, for visitors must cross to the Holy Island on foot. Curiosity and a search for some intangible spiritual comfort draw well over half a million people from all over the world to this tiny three-mile island where Saint Columba and 12 companions landed from Ireland in the 6th century to set up the mission that turned Iona into the Christian centre of Europe.

In 1773 Dr. Samuel Johnson was impressed with the piety of Iona. The abbey, which had been suppressed at the Reformation, was still in ruins and there were not many visitors then. In the 1930s the low, sturdy building, about half a mile from the ferry, was restored by the Iona Community; visitors have increased ever since. Accept the

Two aspects of Mull: Tobermory Harbour (left) and Torosay Castle.

crowds and go round at your own pace. Some of the best restoration is the tiny cloister, especially the birds and plants on the slender replacement sandstone columns. They were meticulously copied from the one remaining medieval original. There's an unusual attention-grabbing modern bronze by Lipschitz in the green centre of the cloister.

The general store near the ferry has added bicycle hire to its varied services, so there's time in theory to see **Coracle Cove** where Columba landed in AD 563. Most visitors, with only a few hours to spend on the island, stay near the abbey where almost 50 European kings, chieftains and Lords of the Isles are said to be buried. Dr. Johnson, was sceptical, "the graves are very numerous and some of them undoubtedly contain the remains of men who did not expect to be soon forgotten".

There's a bird and seal sanctuary on the uninhabited **Treshnish Islands** off Mull's west coast. Privately-owned **Ulva**, nearby, is noted for its wildlife and walking.

Fingal's Cave on Staffa, accessible by ferry from Ulva, is a big attraction. The experience of going into the cave, if the weather is good enough for landing, is well worth the one-and-the-half-hour boat journey—tedious when the weather is bad. The primeval crashing of the sea, the towering height of the cave and the complete lack of colour in the sombre rocks makes a powerful impression. Even if the little 47-ft (14-metre) partially covered passenger launch can't land, it's worth making the journey just to see the curious hexagonal basalt rocks with the gaping black hole of the cave. Birdwatchers too have plenty to see.

The ferry from Oban for Coll and Tiree calls at Tobermory for additional passengers. There's the usual rivalry between these sister islands, most distant of the Inner Hebrides. People from Tiree can't understand why anyone wants to get off the ferry at Coll. The people of Coll maintain that the inhabitants of Tiree are permanently bent by the island's ceaseless wind.

Fascinating rock formations on Staffa.

Purists, or those against progress, feel **Coll** is too civilized. A young cyclist, camping near the glorious west coast beaches, complained that the island's only hotel had gone suburban when it installed a sauna; while a 75-year-old resident of **Arinagour**, the island's only village, where most of the population of 150 live, spoke with astonishment of the local café's advanced ideas—recently revitalised and repainted, it had emerged as a bistro.

Young families go to Coll for the simple holidays, pottering on uncrowded beaches. Much of the coast can be reached only on foot—although bicycles can be hired. This isn't an island for antiquities, and the restored medieval castle of **Breacachadh** is only sometimes open to the public.

The indefatigible Johnson commented on Coll's garden flowers, and in the mid-1800s the secretary of the Board of Fisheries arrived in great splendour—and at great public expense—in a large cutter with a crew of 23 to track the migratory habits of the unreliable herring. The silvery fish remain the darlings of many Hebridean songs and are the economic mainstay of many of the islands.

Tiree's Gaelic name, *Tir fo Thuinn*, means "land below the waves". It's a good description of this flat, sunny island whose two hills are only 400 ft high (120 metres). One of the islands' most eccentric visitors was Ada Goodrich Freer, who claimed telepathic gifts and an ability to receive messages through sea shells. She spent three weeks on Tiree in 1894 investigating Highland second sight. Although she spoke no Gaelic, she was finally defeated not by the language but by the monotonous diet of tea, eggs, bread and jam provided by the Temperance hotel.

Nowadays windsurfers, who call Tiree the Hawaii of the North, are attracted to the island by the great Atlantic rollers that break on the long, curving silver beaches.

Some people find **Colonsay** too bland. On the other hand, a woman

Tiree farming: the wind never seems to drop.

from Oban claims it to be her favourite island simply because it has no distinguishing features. She finds Mull too pretty and doesn't care for the lowering Cuillins of Skye. Colonsay, 40 miles (64 kms) southwest of Oban, is just right. It has its antiquities, seven standing stones and six forts, and excellent wildlife—birds, otters and seals. It has good white beaches and isn't over-mountainous. Visitors are few as there are no organised day-trips and, because the ferry calls only three times a week, accommodation has to be found either at the one hotel or with families providing bed and breakfast.

The island, eight miles (12 kms) long and three miles (four kms) at its widest, has a population of 120 and is one of the largest British islands still in private hands. It is warmed by the Gulf Stream, and the gardens of **Colonsay House**, open to the public, have a variety of exotic plants. According to legend, the island's wild goats are descended from survivors of the Spanish Armada ships wrecked in 1588.

At low tide it's possible to walk across muddy sands to tiny **Oronsay** off the southern tip of Colonsay; alternatively there are boat trips. Oronsay is about two miles (three kms) square and has a population of six. Its fine 14th-century priory is the biggest medieval monastic ruin in the islands, after Iona.

Skye lark: People disparage **Skye** for its commercialism. The island has the heavy burden of the over-romanticised legend of Bonnie Prince Charlie and is easy to reach. The crossing from the Kyle of Lochalsh on the mainland to **Kyleakin** takes only five minutes, so the rash of souvenir and gift shops, particularly at **Broadford**, a rather dull place not far from Kyleakin but centrally placed for touring, is not unexpected. Skye, whose coastline is so irregular that no place is more than five miles from the sea, is dominated by the savage **Cuillin Hills**, actually mountains and Britain's answer to the Alps. The island has its wilderness. **Loch Coruisk**, completely encircled by the Black Cuillins, painted by the Roman-

tics and written about by Sir Walter Scott, is a strange dead place; a two-mile (three-km) stretch of lunar-like, still, dark waters. See it either from one of the approach walks to the Cuillins or initially by car along one of the prettiest drives on Skye, from Broadford to **Elgol**, then by boat. The fugitive Bonnie Prince Charlie finally left the Hebrides on July 4, 1746, from Elgol beach.

Skye attracts wild weather. The Cuillins are rarely clear, and most visitors see them through a veil of Celtic mist. But the richly wooded and lush Sleat peninsula on the southwest of the island is often sunny and looks more like southern England, especially at the **Clan Donald Centre**. There are mature trees and rhododendrons in the well-tended grounds. The MacDonalds were once one of the Scotland's most powerful clans and the Clan Donald Trust, formed in the 1970s, has members throughout the world. The Lord of the Isles once ruled from **Armadale Castle**, whose ruins have been turned into a museum with audio-visual presentations. Money has been poured into converting the old stables into an excellent restaurant, a good bookshop, a giftshop and two luxury self-catering apartments. There's a ranger service and guided walks in the grounds. The Centre has a transatlantic feel.

Dunvegan Castle, seat of the MacLeods for 700 years and Skye's only stately home, is at the other end of the island and is unmistakeably Scottish. Nothing like as smart and polished as the Clan Donald Centre, it has the bizarre appearance of a fake, for, although the building is genuine enough, it was given a most suburban-looking coat of stucco in the 19th century. Bonnie Prince Charlie's waistcoat and various clan trophies are displayed inside. The gardens, with plenty of mature trees, have an attractive little waterfall and subtropical plants.

Modern tourism has eroded the strict Calvinistic views of Skye. Sunday drinking, at least for visitors, is accepted and the capital, **Portree**, a nice little place on a picturesque bay, is cheerfully touristy seven days a week. Even the two folk museums of 19th-century life are open on Sundays. The **Old Skye Crofter's House** is at **Luib** on the Broadford/Sligachan road and the **Colbost Folk Museum** is four miles (six kms) outside Dunvegan on the B884. The museum illustrates how hard Skye was hit by the Clearances: gunboats were sent in 1882 to put down riots caused by the evictions.

The Sabbath is strictly observed on the small lush island of **Raasay**, just east of Skye. The ferry doesn't run on Sundays, when most of the population of 150, almost half of whom are over 60, are in church. There are two churches, one for the "Wee Frees", the other for a group of even stricter dissenters. In the 18th century the English burned all Raasay's houses and boats because the laird had sheltered Bonnie Prince Charlie after Culloden. Visitors can see the ruined **Brochel Castle**, home of the MacLeods of Skye and the grounds of **Raasay House**. When the exuberant Boswell stayed with Dr. Johnson at Raasay House, now an out-

Left, the Isle of Skye: the romantic image lingers. Below, peat cutter at work on the Isle of Islay.

door pursuits centre, he danced a jig on top of the Dun Can ridge, 1,500 ft high (500 metres).

Island-hopping: The small islands of Eigg, Muck, Rhum and Canna can be reached from Mallaig on the Sleat peninsula, the end of the "Road to the Isles". There's not a great deal to do on the islands. Mostly people go for the wildlife, for a bit of esoteric island-hopping or to stay at Britain's most inaccessible luxury hotel on Rhum. The islands are all different and, if you just want to see them without landing, take the little boat that makes the seven-hour round-trip four times a week in the summer, less often in winter. It's a service for islanders rather than a pleasure boat for visitors, and carries provisions, mail, newspapers and other essentials. Only those planning to stay are allowed to disembark. Other boat services run day-trips to some of the islands.

Eigg is famous for its laird, Yorkshire businessman Keith Schellenberg and his Games. These last for three days and involve all 70 inhabitants and any visitors lucky (or rash) enough to visit the island in July. Schellenberg's friends and relatives fly in from all over the world for water sports and more Scottish pursuits. The grand finale is a reenactment of the struggle between the Jacobites and the Hanoverians. The silver trophies awarded at the end are of course Eigg Cups.

Muck gets its unfortunate name (Gaelic for pig) from the porpoises or sea-pigs that swim round its shores. It's the smallest of the four islands, only two miles (three kms) long, and has neither transport nor shops. Visitors must bring provisions and be landed by tender. Eighty breeds of birds nest on Muck.

There's an incongruous Greek temple on the rugged island of **Rhum**: the mausoleum of Sir George Bullough, the island's rich Edwardian proprietor. His castellated **Kinloch Castle**, used as a convalescent home during the Boer War just after it was built, is now an opulent hotel. Both the hotel and the island are owned by the Nature Conser-

Islay whisky is known for its peaty taste.

vancy Council. There is ex-cellent bird watching and hill walking.

Graffiti adorn the rocks near the landing stage at **Canna**; it's at least 100 years old and records the names of visiting boats. The harbour's safe haven is one of the few deepwater harbours in the Hebrides. This sheltered island, most westerly of the four, is owned by the National Trust for Scotland and is particularly interesting to botanists. No holiday accommodation exists.

Islay's the place if you like malt whisky. There are over half a dozen distilleries on this attractive little island, most with tours. Islay, where Clan Donald started, was once the home of the Lord of the Isles. It has some good beaches on the indented north coast. Also on this side of the island is one of the best Celtic crosses in Scotland: the 9th-century **Kildalton Cross** which stands in the churchyard of a ruined and very atmospheric little chapel. **Port Askaig**, where the ferry from the Kintyre peninsula docks, is a pretty little place with a hotel, once a 16th-century inn on the old drovers' road a few steps away from the ferry.

Jura, Islay's next-door neighbour, is so close you can nip over for a quick inspection after dinner. Three shapely mountains, the Paps of Jura, 2,500 ft (800 metres) high, provide a striking skyline. Although palms and rhododendrons grew on the sheltered east side, it's a wild island inhabited by sheep and red deer and is much favoured by sportsmen, birdwatchers and climbers.

Ghia has one of the nicest hotels in the islands, bright, Scandinavian and beautifully neat and simple. No need to take a car on the three-mile crossing from **Tayinloan** to this small green island popular with yachting people: no walk is more than three miles from the attractive ferry terminal at **Ardminish** with its sparkling white cottages. One of the formal attractions is **Achamore Gardens**. Seals, barking amiably, cruise in the waters off the little used north pier.

Does a scarecrow also scare seagulls?

THE OUTER HEBRIDES

The Outer Hebrides, 40 miles (64 kms) west of the mainland, are known locally as the Long Islands. They stretch in a narrow 130-mile (208-kms) arc from the Butt of Lewis in the north to Barra Head in the south. Their eroded and often dramatic west coasts are relentlessly pounded by the cold Atlantic. Some visitors are thrilled by their wild bleakness, others find it disconcerting. Each island regards itself as the fairest in the chain. The people live mainly by fishing and crofting, though commercial fish farming is growing—mussels as well as the usual salmon and trout.

There are enormous flat peat bogs on Lewis and North Uist and the islanders cut turf to burn rather than to export to the garden centres of England. The men cut it during the summer and stack it *in situ*; when it has dried the women and children cart it home and stack it against the outside of the house for winter fires. A traditional blessing on Lewis is: "Long may you live, with smoke from your house."

Some turf cutters carry insularity to extremes. An old man on North Uist, surprised to hear that visitors were crossing to Harris and Lewis, pronounced: "Nothing much to see there, You're better off here."

Fierce loyalty: These climatically hostile Western Isles of few trees and stark scenery are the Gaidhealechd, the land of the Gael. When their Gaelic-speaking inhabitants change to English, as they politely do when visitors are present, they have virtually no accent and are among the easiest Scots for visitors to understand. They were fiercely loyal to Bonnie Prince Charlie. When, after the Battle of Culloden in 1746, the young man, with a £30,000 price on his head, dodged round the Outer Hebrides pursued by "Butcher" Cumberland, no-one betrayed him.

Harris and the larger **Lewis** are really one island. Turn north from the ferry terminal at **Tarbert** for Lewis;

south for Harris. (Beware of Tarberts in the Highlands, though: there are many of them and it's all too easy on this tricky bit of coast to end up at the wrong one. The name means a narrow spit of land over which a boat can be pulled from one stretch of water to another.) The tiny Tarbert on the narrow isthmus joining Harris and Lewis is technically in Harris, a land of bare hills and fierce peaks. The ferries from Lochmaddy on North Uist and Uig on Skye dock in this sheltered port neatly tucked into the hillside. There are a few shops, the Harris Hotel, a tourist office and sheds selling Harris tweed.

One of the islands' most impressive medieval churches, **St. Clement's** at **Rodel** on the southern tip of Harris, was restored in 1873. It stands in fields, locked; but the Rodel Hotel, famous for its "Royal Household" 12-year-old whisky, has the key.

Lewis has well-behaved sheep, a great many lochs, an inordinate number of boulders strewn randomly over the landscape, the famous standing stones

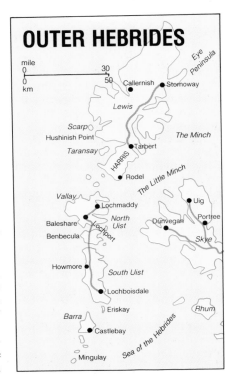

OUTER HEBRIDES

Farne, a remote corner of the Outer Hebrides.

of Callanish, very few trees, some dramatic cliffs, about 100 scattered villages, often with brightly coloured houses, and **Stornoway**, the only big town in the Outer Hebrides.

A woman in the hotel in Tarbert advised against Stornoway. "Nothing to see there," she said. "You're better off driving to Hushinish Point, especially in the evening when the salmon are rising." Visitors should try both. The ferry from Ullapool lands at Stornoway, a greyish, unremarkable market town. The liveliest part is the harbour where sometimes you can see thousands of silver fish, which will eventually be turned into fertiliser, being sucked by giant vacuum hoses straight from a boat's deck into waiting lorries.

The best view of the castellated mock-Tudor **Lews Castle** is from the harbour. It was built in the 19th century by Sir James Matheson, who made his money in Chinese opium. Like Lord Leverhulme after him, Sir James tried to change Lews. He imported soil to plant trees and shrubs, built roads and bridges and poured money into trying to reclaim the bogs that cover much of the island. But mostly the implacable country won. The grounds of Lews Castle, now owned by the Stornoway Trust, survived. There are chestnuts, laurel and silver birch and wild flowers in season. The house, a technical college, is not open to the public; there is a picnic area in the grounds.

The attempt by Lord Leverhulme (of Sunlight soap fame) to turn Stornoway into one of Europe's great fishing ports also failed. For, as the Highlands and Islands Developments Board, the government body that replaced these philanthropic individuals in the mid-1960s, found out, you can't impose an alien way of life on the islanders. Most are content to care for their sheep and cattle, do a certain amount of fishing and grow a few crops.

Lewis has its antiquities. The great circle of **Callanish** standing stones 16 miles (25 kms) from Stornoway on the west of the island, is reached by a dreary bog-pitted road. The 13 ritual stones, some 12 ft (three metres) high, are set in a circle like Stonehenge. Nobody is quite sure why they're there. Once, they were known as *Na Fir Breige*—the false men. They have been claimed as a Viking parliament, a landing base for UFOs and a site for predicting eclipses. The standing stones, duns, burial cairns on or just off the west coast road that bends round East Loch Roag and Little Loch Roag hint at how important the Western Isles were in prehistoric times.

The folk museum, in a former church at **Shawbost**, with an old red and blue farm cart and old furniture, fishing and crofting tools, was originally a project by local children. There are stupendous views from the massive ruins of **Dun Carloway** broch, built 2,000 years ago.

The drive from Tarbert to golden **Hushinish Point** is dramatic, particularly in the evening if you're lucky enough to see the setting sun silvering west Loch Tarbert and catching the peaks of Beinn Dhubh on Harris just across the water. The road goes straight through the well-maintained grounds of **Amhuinnsuidhe Castle** (pronounced *Avin-suey*), so close to the house you can almost see inside. This privately-owned pale turretted castle was built in 1868 and James Barrie began his novel *Mary Rose* here.

Language problem: The official tourist map of the Outer Hebrides (£2 from tourist offices) is essential for the Uists. Even though there is only one main road linking the three islands of North Uist, Benbecula and South Uist, most of the signposts are in Gaelic; the map gives them in English as well. The Lochmaddy tourist office has a free sheet of English/Gaelic names put out by the Western Isles Islands Council. As part of its policy of preserving one of Europe's oldest languages, the Council has put up Gaelic-only places names and signposts in the Outer Hebrides. In English-speaking Benbecula and in Stornoway on Lewis the signs are also in English.

Lochmaddy, where the ferry docks, is the only village on **North Uist**, and you're almost through it before you realise it's there. But to show its capital status it has a hotel and a bank. A small boy outside the "Wehaveit" general store told us quite seriously to expect the Uist roads to be different from the map, explaining that the constant movement of the bog made them change direction. Certainly at times the causeway road feels as springy as a dance floor.

The Uist archipelago of low bright islands dominated by the glittering sea is about 50 miles long and only eight miles at its widest (80 by 13 kms) and is so peppered with lochs that on the map the east coast round Benbecula looks rather like a sieve.

A circular road from Lochmaddy runs round the sparsely populated North Uist. At **Baleshare**, a strange beach on the west of the island, wild flowers grow in the cab of an abandoned dumper truck and cows wander close to a derelict van left where flower-spangled grass and stony beach merge. The paradox is that, although virtually no industry exists on the Uists, there's careless pollution. Empty whisky bottles sparkle among wild flowers; rust-

ing vehicles mar beauty spots.

A nature reserve lies beyond Baleshare at **Balranald** and, further on, standing stones lend interest to the wide sandy beach of **Vallay**. There are more standing stones at **Blashaval**. A sight-seeing drive of the 35-mile (56-km) circuit of North Uist from Lochmaddy takes just over an hour.

One of the easiest prehistoric sites to get to is the **Barpa Langass**, a 2,000-year-old chambered cairn near **Loch-port**, on the loch-covered east side of the island. This burial place of an island chieftain, not far from the Langass Lodge Hotel, is just a short walk from the A867. Nearby, the small loch **Obannam Fiadh** looks ordinary enough, but it has the pecularity that its waters are partly fresh and partly saline.

Although the Hebrides are renowned for their haunting Gaelic songs, it's not all that easy for visitors to get hold of them. Mostly they are handed down orally and it can be difficult to get the traditional Hebridean songs on paper. Older islanders feel the songs would be

debased if written down. But interest in the old music is growing locally.

The turf-cutter was right about **North Uist**, an island so full of lochs that they make up a third of its area. It's rich in prehistoric treasures. There's the remains of one of Europe's oldest potteries on the rocky islet of **Eilean-an-Tighe**—a "factory" that was virtually mass-producing high-quality pottery in Stone Age times. There are many standing stones on the island, while Scotland's last great battle with swords and bows and arrows took place on the **Carinish** promontory in 1601 near the ruined 12th-century Trinity Temple.

The east of tiny **Benbecula** is so pitted with lochs that most people live on the west coast. The antiquities are on this side too. There's the ruins of **Borve Castle** with three-metre-thick walls, one of the most important medieval ruins in the Outer Hebrides. Built in the 14th century by Lady Amie of the Isles, it was the home of the MacDonald of Clanranald, who once ruled Benbecula. Flora MacDonald, whose Hanoverian connections meant that she had to be persuaded to help Bonnie Prince Charlie escape, belonged to this family. A Royal Artillery base is sited on Benbecula and a small airport has flights to Stornoway and on to Inverness.

The most noticeable features of **South Uist** are the peat bogs, the abandoned roofless stone crofts and the meadows sprinkled with clover, buttercups and daisies. Small yellow irises shine everywhere. To see the best of the island, take the little feeder roads that run east west from the main single track road. Going south down the island's 22 miles (35 kms), you'll find, as with Benbecula, that the best is west. Look out on the loch-lined road to **Eochar** for the shell-covered old school bus in Flora Johnstone's garden. She so enjoyed sticking on the local shells in the 1960s that now she's starting on the walls of her cottage.

At **Howmore**, close to the low remains of ruined medieval chapels, some of the old white-washed thatched cottages still stand in flowery mead-

Sheep shearers at work on South Uist.

ows. They are now protected buildings and one is a youth hostel.

It is possible to see the cairn at **Airdh Mhuilinn** to the memory of Flora MacDonald from the main road. Islanders feel that the real hero of Charles Stuart's escape was Neil MacEachan, a local man from Howbeg; Flora was probably not the fervent Jacobite that legend portrays, as her stepfather was commanding the king's troops at the time of 1745 Rising.

Tiny **Lochboisdale**, South Uist's main village in the south of the island, is another ferry terminal. The Highlands and Islands Development Board which, along with the EEC, puts a great deal of money into the Western Isles, provided the tourist office in this pleasantly wandering little village, as it did in many other parts of the islands. The general store sells everything from carpets to clothes, from clocks to yesterday's papers.

Facing the main road near the artillery test-firing rocket range on the east coast is a modern, tall, narrow statue of the Virgin Mary put up on a slope of Rueval Hill in the 1950s by this predominantly Catholic community. South Uist and Barra are outposts of the "old faith".

The 3,000-year-old **Pollachar standing stone** at the southern tip of the island, where you can gaze across to Eriskay and Barra, is surrounded by wild orchids, clover and, in spite of two refuse bins, an accumulation of rubbish. There's a car ferry from **Ludag**, just along the coast from the Pollachar standing stone, across the one-and-three-quarters-mile stretch of water to **Eriskay**. The island, famous because of the hauntingly beautiful "Eriskay Love Lilt", is disappointing to see: just an unimpressive hump. For a fishing island only two miles by three with a population of around 200, it has had much fame. Bonnie Prince Charlie landed on the long silver beach on the west side on July 23, 1745. Two hundred years later the "Politician", a cargo ship carrying 24,000 cases of whisky, sank in the Eriskay Sound. Compton Mackenzie's *Whisky Galore* was a hilarious re-telling of the redistribution of the cargo.

The timetable for flights to **Barra**, the most southerly inhabited Hebridean island, must be the only one in the British Isles to state that arrivals are subject to tides. The small Logan Air-passenger planes servicing the island land on Cockle Strand, a runway that twice a day disappears under the incoming tide.

Fishing dominates Barra, as it always has. In the 1880s, choice Barra cockles were eaten in London. By the 1920s, Barra herring were so important that girls came from as far away as Yarmouth in England to work 17 hours a day in **Castlebay** gutting the silver darlings. In the past 20 years, lobster fishing has become important, with about 40 boats operating.

Although the islanders sometimes feel isolated, especially in winter when the boat from the mainland can't always get in, they are resourceful and self-reliant, even producing a weekly bilingual paper, the *Barra Bulletin*.

Coming out of her shell: Flora Johnstone of Eochar, South Uist.

CENTRAL SCOTLAND

Just who recorded that the Romans said "Behold the Tiber" at first sight of the Tay isn't clear, but certainly all roads lead to Perth, Scotland's one-time capital, and a superb centre for exploring Central Scotland.

Appropriately enough, the springs of tourist information are located in the city's old **waterworks**. The rotunda pump house and chimney topped with a fibreglass urn make a surrealist contribution to many paintings housed in another rotunda, the **Museum and Art Gallery**. Drama enough here in Sir David Young Cameron's landscape "*Shadows of Glencoe*", in the stuffed but still snarling wildcat, its bushy tail black-tipped, and in Perth's link with space, the Strathmore Meteorite of 1917. Take care from Pullar's, the original dry cleaners, who brought skilled workers here from Paris to teach employees how to do it, and take comfort from a Doulton stoneware whisky flask impressed "*The Fair Maid of Perth*". Sir Walter Scott's virginal heroine lived nearby in *Fair Maid's House*, the setting for his novel of the time of the battle of Clans on the meadow of the North Inch nearby.

Georgian terraces and imposing civic buildings line the riverside, but principal streets are uncompromisingly Victorian. No dullness, though. "All things bright and beautiful" on the bells of **St John's Kirk** heralds the hour strike in a belfry of 36 bells. One, the Ave Maria, was founded about the time of the Battle of Bannockburn in the early 14th century.

Away from the smart shops are surprises like the golden salmon that leaps over Mallock's fishing tackle shop. Next door David Campbell's grocer saucily offers "Robert Burns Shortbread Petticoat Tails", and the Auto Garden Chain Saw Centre promises peaceable massacre. Behind **High Street** the near-circular projections of house stairs play at castles, and rushing streams under stone bridges turn wheels for city mills to entertain customers of the Stakis City Mills Hotel.

Those with aesthetic tastes or presents to buy are catered for at **Caithness Glass**, where the mysteries of paperweight-making are revealed. Others can view blending, bottling and taste the product of **Dewar**'s, whose old premises do service for Perth's castle. Work off the effects at **Bell's Sports Centre**. History and tradition take the stage in the **Perth Theatre**, the longest established in Scotland.

Perth is ringed with castles, some still family homes, but many are romantic ruins like **Huntingtower**, three miles (four kms) west, where two linked towers are separated by the Maiden's Leap. Perhaps the resident colony of bats frightened her. An intriguing rooftop walk gives glimpses of hidden stairs and dark voids that must have struck terror into James I during his year's imprisonment. How often must he have lifted his eyes to these same painted ceilings?

Preceding pages, taking a dip in Loch Lomond. Left, Scone Palace. Below, a race on the River Tay

Scone Palace, two miles (three kms) north of Perth, was Scotland's Camelot and home to the much travelled **stone** on which 40 kings of Scotland were crowned. Brought here in the 9th century and taken to London in 1296 by Edward I, it was stolen in 1950 from beneath the Coronation Chair in Westminster Abbey and recovered from Arbroath. The Earl of Mansfield's home offers such diverse charms as six generations of family photographs, highland cattle, ornamental fowls and giant trees as well as a treasure house of period furniture, elegant porcelain and paintings.

Tickling and curling: A lake for all seasons, **Loch Leven** is heaven for trout anglers and the chosen wintering ground for wild geese and curling enthusiasts. On an island and reached by ferry from the lochside is ruined **Lochleven Castle**, which keeps open house in summer though it was once prison to the notorious Wolf of Badenoch and Mary Queen of Scots. After nearly a year, during which she suffered a mis-

carriage, Mary escaped by boat with the help of her jailer's son. The keys he threw in the lake were to be recovered 400 years later.

Falkland Palace, sitting cosily in the main street of its old Royal Burgh, was the favourite retreat of the Stuart kings. The streets themselves are full of love tokens. Stone lintels that top many doors carry the incised initials of those couples the houses were built for in the 1600s, the date and a heart. On one house front: "Contentment is great riches". Loving care everywhere here in the many laundered green spaces and carefully conserved weavers' houses.

Castle Campbell is rather impressively situated at the head of Dollar Glen, southwest of Perth. **Menstrie Castle,** near Stirling, links Scotland with Nova Scotia as the birthplace of Sir William Alexander, James VI's lieutenant. Near Crieff, **Drummond Castle** opens only its gardens and surprisingly they are Italian—statues, trees and shrubs dotting the parterre like pieces on a chessboard.

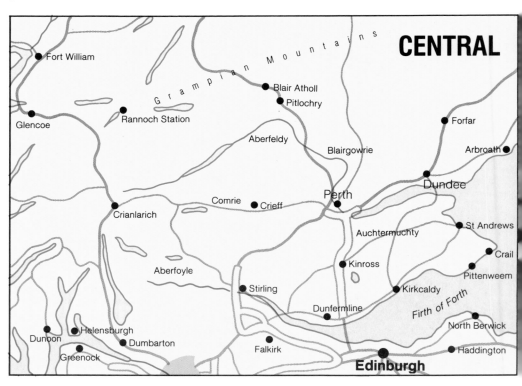

The King of Fife: The motorway that links Perth to Edinburgh does more than by-pass Fife, thrust out into the North Sea between the Firth of Forth and Tay. It by-passes an area rich in history, architecture and scenery. Its harbours nudge one another on a coast tilted towards Scandinavia, buildings and customs reflecting the thriving trade it enjoyed in the 17th century with the Baltic and the Low Countries.

Culross, where the Firth of Forth narrows, is a unique survival: a town of the 17th and 18th centuries that looks like a film set, and often is. Then it was a smokey, industrial town with coal mines and salt pans, manufacturing girdles and baking plates for oatcakes. Scottish parents often threatened their children with "I'll gar your lugs ring like a Culross girdle." A clip round the ear?

Sir George Bruce, who took over where the mining monks left off in 1575 went on to such success that James VI made Culross a Royal Burgh. Today, the town's wealth of old buildings with their crow-stepped gables and red pan-tiled roofs, many lovingly restored by the National Trust for Scotland, make it one of Scotland's finest showplaces. The **Town House**'s clock tower dominates the waterfront and the **Mercat Cross**, the tiny market place and oldest house, dated 1577. Wynds, or pathways, lead past the "**Palace**", the "**Study**", with its 17th-century Norwegian painted ceiling, and **Snuff Cottage** (1673) with the inscription "Wha wad ha thocht it". "Noses wad ha bought it" is the second line. Past the house with the Evil Eyes are the church, the ruined abbey and the magnificent Abbey House. One typical whitewashed cottage houses...an electricity substation!

Although **Dunfermline** was for 600 years capital of Scotland, burial place of kings, with a fine church and abbey, it owes its international importance to its humblest son, Andrew Carnegie. The great philanthropist opened the first of 3,000 free libraries here in 1881. The tiny cottage where he was born contrasts vividly with **Pittencrieff**, the

The gardens at Falkland Palace, a favourite retreat of the Stuarts.

mansion he left to the town on his death. Both are museums. In mock castellation the cut-out words "King Robert the Bruce" on the church tower advertise his burial here in 1329, "wrapped in a cloth of gold". The columns of the Norman nave, chevroned and diagonalled like Durham, preside over pewless space.

From the sublime to the grotto: at **Leven**, behind the esplanade and the parked oil rigs, are marvellous shell gardens. Begun in 1914, walls, walks, menagerie and aviary are patterned with shells, broken china and Staffordshire figures to make an antique dealer's fingers itch.

Kirkcaldy's all too evident association with coal and floor coverings may not appeal, but Lang Town, as it is often called, made important contributions to architecture, economics and literature. Robert Adam, Adam Smith and Thomas Carlyle were born here.

Lower Largo, its tiny harbour and inn stage-set beneath a viaduct, gave birth in 1676 to Alexander Selkirk,

Defoe's "Robinson Crusoe".

The original "Fifie" fishing boats were built at **St. Monans**, but the shipyard now builds only pleasure craft. A path leads away from the harbour to the 14th-century church with its feet on the rocky shore.

Pittenweem bustles with the business of fish. Above it, the old Royal Burgh snoozes with its memories of Augustinian monks and a tax collector whose robbery in 1736 led to riots in Edinburgh. Next door, almost, **Anstruther**, with a fisheries museum, and **Crail** end the run of picturesque harbours before Fife Ness is reached. The oldest Royal Burgh in East Neuk, Crail's crow-stepped gables and red-tiled roofs ensure that artists outnumber fishermen.

Sport of kings: There is a nice contrast in leaving the simplicities of Crail for the concentration of learning, religious importance and historical significance that is **St. Andrews**. Here, even golf qualifies as "Ancient" as well as "Royal", its Old Course laid out in the 15th century and the Royal and Ancient Golf Club formed in 1754. There are no fewer than four courses. It is not established whether John Knox played the game, but the damage to the cathedral following his impassioned sermons started neglect that reduced it to ruins. **St. Rule** nearby survives as a tower and St. Andrews Castle fared little better. Elsewhere, the **West Port** spans a main street and steeples abound, but not for climbing, as Dr. Johnson found. The **University**, whose buildings line North Street, is the oldest in Scotland. The most touching connection with the past is a flourishing thorn tree in the quadrangle of St. Mary's College. It was planted by Mary Queen of Scots.

Cryptic note for gourmets: Dr. Johnson and Boswell, Hebrides bound, had a good supper at Glass's Inn of "Rissered haddocks and mut chops". They had previously had tea at **Cupar**, which is on the road back to Perth. **Auchtermuchty** has surviving thatched cottages once used by weavers, with straw thatch as thin as a child's Christmas crib. Abernethy's tea shop

Dunfermline Abbey, burial place of kings.

keeps the key to the Pictish, chimney-like church tower, built when horns not bells summoned the faithful. At its base is an incised Pictish stone.

Lochs, rivers and mountains: Westward from Perth, roads follow rivers in the ascent to the lochs and watershed of the Grampians. At **Crieff** good taste demands visits to **Glenturret**, the oldest distillery in Scotland and the glass workshops. What romance attaches to the **Drummond Arms** as the scene of Prince Charles Edward's council of war in 1746 is a little dimmed by its having been rebuilt since. Five miles (eight kms) southeast of Crieff the oldest public library in Scotland, the **Innerpeffray Library**, has a Treacle Bible, so called because "Is there no balm in Gilead?" is translated into "Is there no treacle in Gilead?"

Comrie's situation on the River Earn where two glens meet makes it an attractive walking centre. Earthquakes too! The Highland Boundary Fault divides the Lowlands from Highlands here and earth tremors were bad enough

to damage houses in 1839. The road joins Loch Earn with magnificent mountain scenery till **Lochearnhead** is reached. Beyond here the high peaks have it—**Ben More**, **Ben Lui** and **Ben Bhuidhe**—until the lochs reach in like fingers from the coast of the Western Isles. Crianlarich is a popular centre with climbers and walkers. For those on wheels, **Ardlui** is a beautiful introduction to Loch Lomond. The largest lake in Britain, full of fish and islands, it is best known and loved through the song which one of Prince Charles Edward's followers wrote on the eve of his execution. There are fairies at the end of the Loch in Fairy Glen in the **Balloch Castle Country Park**.

The road back to **Aberfoyle** traverses the Queen Elizabeth forest park and leads to the splendid wooded scenery of the **Trossachs**, best viewed from the summer steamer on **Loch Katrine**. Scott's "Lady of the Lake" and "Rob Roy" brought Victorians flocking here. You expect to meet Dr. Finlay in the streets of **Callander**: the "Tanno-

Students at St. Andrews Castle.

chbrae" of the television series provides more potent images now than Scott and J. M. Barrie.

Doune's 15th-century castle is remarkably complete with two great towers and hall between. In Ruskin's judgement—and who would challenge that?—the west front of Dunblane's 13th-century cathedral is a perfect example of Scotland's church architecture. But how did the three Drummond sisters buried here come to meet their deaths, as the tombstone tells us, by poisoning in 1501?

The Scots are so obsessed with golf that Mary Queen of Scots could go off to play when her husband had just been assassinated. At Gleneagles the moorland courses have been described as a golfer's paradise and it's not hard to see why.

Follow the mill trail: Auchterarder's situation to the north of the Ochil Hills is a convenient point at which to hit the Mill Trail. Thanks to good grazing and soft water, Scotland's world-famous tweeds, tartans and knitwear have been produced here in the Hillfoot's villages since the 16th century. From the Heritage Centre in Auchterarder, with the only surviving steam textile engine and Tillicoultry's handsome Clock Mill powered by waterwheel, to the most modern mills in Alloa and Sauchie, producing designer knitwear with famous labels, the trail links modern technology with the cottage production of the past in a fascinating way. Amongst so much weaving there is much learning: Dollar is home to the Dollar Academy, founded in 1818.

From Perth, the motorway north bypasses Bankfoot's raspberry canes and motor museum. At Dunkeld, cross Telford's fine bridge over the Tay's rocky bed for the charm and character of this old ecclesiastical capital of Scotland. Cathedral and town were fought over and the Highlanders defeated in 1689. Dunkeld Little Houses replaced those ruined, but only the choir of the cathedral in its superb setting was restored. A delightful local museum in the Chapter House introduces Neil

Entertainment: below, 19th-century style at Pitlochry Theatre; and right, medieval style—a pageant at Arbroath.

Gow, the celebrated fiddler. For good measure there is an ell, the Scottish yard, fixed to a house in the square. Romantics will feel at home at **The Hermitage**, a mile west of the town. Built in 1758, this is the centrepiece of a woodland trail beside the River Braan on the Duke of Atholl's estate, a folly poised over a waterfall. Wordsworth wrote a verse about it and Mendelsohn sketched it. It was a favourite haunt of Beatrix Potter.

At the foot of the Highlands is **Blairgowrie**. Matter-of-fact, it reserves its charm for anglers and lovers of raspberries and strawberries. Buy your bagpipe, kilt, sporran or feather bonnet at Piob Mhor's. At **Meikleour** the road to Perth is bordered by a beech hedge, nearly 99 feet (30 metres) high and 1,980 feet (600 metres) long and planted in 1746.

Aberfeldy and **Loch Tay** are easily achieved from Dunkeld by the stone bridge General Wade built in 1733. Here the world-renowned Black Watch Regiment became part of the British Army in 1740. Picnic in view of the Moness Falls. Mecca of salmon and salmon fisheries, Loch Tay has impressive **Ben Lawers** above it and the beginnings of the River Tay at its foot.

Seek out **Pitlochry** for spectacle. The Festival Theatre, famous as the "Theatre in the Hills" and magnificently situated overlooking the River Tummel, is an attraction in itself. However, it is upstaged by the dam at the hydroelectric power station where in spring and summer thousands of migrating salmon can be seen through windows in a fish ladder.

Beyond the **Pass of Killiecrankie**, where Soldier's Leap recalls the battle of 1689, is **Blair Atholl**, key to the Central Highlands. Scottish at its most baronial, Blair Castle's white walls owe too much to Victorian restoration. This most visited historic house is home to the 10th Duke of Atholl and the Atholl Highlanders, Britain's only private army, so perhaps it is still unwise to cross swords with the Clan Murray!

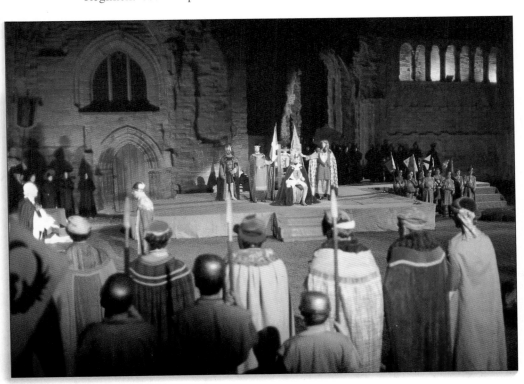

THE EAST COAST

If the silhouette of mainland Britain resembles "a witch riding on a pig"—with Scotland the witch and England and Wales the pig—then the crone's bony, jutting forehead is to be found in that lean coastline between the firths of Tay and Moray. Scotland's east coast and its hinterland are often neglected by indolent tourists, but reward industrious ones.

The east coast, after all, is probably the most industrious (but not industrial) region of the country. Its ports and coastal villages have given Scotland its fishing industry. Its agriculture, from the rich croplands of Angus to the famous beef farms of Aberdeenshire—the largest stretch of uninterrupted farmland in Britain—has been hard won and hard worked. "Our ancestors imposed their will on Buchan," says the writer John R. Allan of that particularly flinty outcrop buffeted by the North Sea, "…an idea imposed on nature at great expense of labour and endurance, of weariness and suffering."

It is, therefore, the east coast of Scotland which most physically and visibly exemplifies that which is most dogged and determined (and perhaps dour) in the Scottish character; and that which best knows how to exploit its assets. The northeast port of Peterhead, for example, is already the busiest fishing harbour in Europe but has also turned itself into a major berth for North Sea oil supply vessels; while the gentle, wooded valley of the River Spey is not only the centre of malt whisky production but with its "Whisky Trail" has made tourist capital out of its celebrated local industry.

For all its pragmatism, for all its gritty devotion to the work ethic, the coast and countryside between the neat and businesslike Firth of Tay and the sunny, sandy, open-mouthed Moray Firth is a land of rare and subtle loveliness. Here you can learn to live without the majestic wilderness and Gothic melodrama of the West Highlands and their archipelago (although you will find echoes of their atmosphere in the Grampian glens of Angus or the outriders of the Cairngorms which reach into Aberdeenshire) and explore the versatility of our dealings with the land and the sea. Here the scale is human and the history consequently dense.

Tale of two cities: The east coast cities are Dundee and Aberdeen. They are of comparable size (about 200,000), separated only by 70 miles (110 km), yet they couldn't be more different. Dundee has been the sad exception to the general rule of east coast energy and enterprise. Despite a vigorous industrial past rooted in textiles, shipbuilding and the jute industry (or perhaps because of it) Dundee, until recently, has long had the feel of a city down on its luck; whereas Aberdeen, the Granite City, is as solid and unyielding as its name suggests, a town of such accustomed prosperity and stout self-confidence that it assumed its new title of oil capital of Europe in the manner of one

Preceding pages, Dundee at night. Left, making Portsoy marble, obtained from a vein of serpentine.

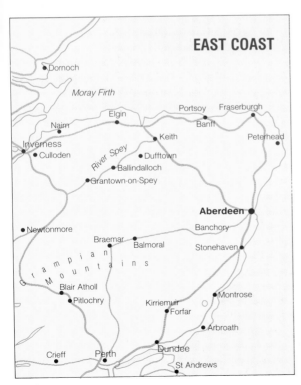

EAST COAST

doing the multinationals a favour.

Topographically, **Dundee** promises more than it fulfills. It has a magnificent position on the Tay estuary. It is dominated by an extinct volcano called the Law, and it has been fancifully called (sometimes in a spirit of satire) the Naples of the North. From the south side of the estuary, from the spectacular approaches of its road and rail bridges (look into the waves and see the forlorn piers of the original rail bridge which collapsed below a train, losing all passengers, at the height of a Wagnerian tempest in 1879) you can be persuaded that its setting merits the comparison.

There are other points of similarity. Like Naples, Dundee has had its share of slums and deprivation; like Naples, it is a port with a long maritime history (it was once the centre of the Scottish wine trade, and a leading importer of French claret). Unlike Naples, it has dealt its own history a mortal blow by destroying its past in a series of insensitive, speculative and sometimes shady developments. (In the 1970s the city's local authority was plagued by a succession of corruption scandals.)

"Perhaps no town in Scotland has been oftener sacked, pillaged and destroyed than Dundee," wrote an 18th-century historian, commenting on the fact that since the 11th century, Dundee had the habit of picking the losing side in the various internecine and international conflicts which afflicted Scotland. The city's own fathers—and the new **University of Dundee**—completed the process in the 20th century. A distinguished Scottish newspaper editor refused to set foot in Dundee after its graceful 17th-century town house was demolished to make way for the mediocre **Caird Hall** (concerts and civic events) in the 1930s.

Today, there is little left of antiquity to offer the history-conscious tourist: the 15th-century **Old Steeple**; the venerable **Howff graveyard**, which occupies land given to the city by Mary Queen of Scots; the **East Port**, remnant of Dundee's fortified wall. But, showing new initiative—and in the spirit of

Dundee: Shopping as it used to be.

212

enterprise which is revitalising its economy through sunrise industries like electronics and computer technology—Dundee is now capitalising on its maritime past.

The central Victoria Dock has long been the home of H.M.S. Unicorn, the oldest British warship still afloat and one of the only four frigates left in the world. To this attraction Dundee has recently added R.R.S. Discovery, the ship which carried Captain Scott's 1901-04 expedition to the Antarctic. It was, in fact, built in Dundee, which had a high reputation for the building of clippers and whalers around the turn of the century, and which annually sent its own fleet of whalers north to the Arctic. Both ships are now museums and there is a whaling exhibition at the **Broughty Ferry Museum** in the attractive seaside suburb of Broughty Ferry.

Dundee, therefore, is worth a visit—but not a long one. And it's worth the affectionate corner it occupies in the Scottish heart for the one great cultural gift it has bequeathed the nation: the *Sunday Post*. This folksy, idiosyncratic, highly successful newspaper (it goes all over the world) is produced by the long-established Dundee publishing house of D.C. Thomson, which has given Scotland its two most enduring comic-strip institutions, "Oor Wullie" and "The Broons", and given Britain the immortal children's comics *The Beano* and *The Dandy*.

And the city's hinterland is reason alone for visiting Dundee. The county of Angus is an eloquent fusion of hill, glen, farmland, beaches and cliffs and its towns and villages reach back into the dawn of Scottish history. The twin hills near **Brechin** (which has a 12th-century cathedral and one of the only two Celtic round towers remaining on the Scottish mainland) are ringed with concentric Iron-Age ramparts. There are Pictish sculptured stones in the churchyard of **Aberlemno**, while the former Royal Burgh of **Arbroath**, a fishing port and holiday resort moving into light industry, had its origins in a Pictish settlement.

The Disovery: Carried Captain Scott to the Antarctic.

Arbroath Abbey, now a handsome ruin, dates back to 1178 and was the scene, in 1320, of a key event in the troubled history of Scotland: the signing of the Declaration of Arbroath. There, the Scottish nobles reaffirmed their determination to resist the persistent invasions of the English and preserve the liberty and independence of their country. (The most noble and dignified sentiments of the Declaration are chiselled into the base of the enormous bronze statue of Sir William Wallace, the Scottish patriot, in Aberdeen's Union Terrace).

Arbroath's red cliffs and harbour at the Fit o' the Toon (*foot of the town*) remain atmospheric, and you will find there the local cottage industry of smoking haddock to produce the celebrated Smokies. The **Signal Tower** complex, built in 1813 to serve the families of the keepers of the lonely Bellrock Lighthouse, now houses a museum. In its heyday, the flagstaff sometimes signalled personal messages to the Bellrock. If a keeper's wife gave birth to a child, trousers or a petticoat would be hoisted to tell him whether the baby was a boy or girl.

Between Arbroath and Dundee is the resort of **Carnoustie**, which has a famous golf course and a lot of sand, while 13 miles (22 km) to the north is the elegant town of **Montrose**, built at the mouth of a vast tidal basin which is the winter home of pink-footed Arctic geese and pink-cheeked ornithologists. Inland, the county town of **Forfar** (where King Malcolm Canmore held his first parliament in 1057) is a striking point for the gloriously underused and somehow secretive glens of Angus, and lies close to what must be considered the county's star attraction: **Glamis Castle**, the exquisite fairy-tale home of the Earls of Strathmore and Kinghorne and a royal residence since 1372.

Glamis was the childhood home of Queen Elizabeth and the Queen Mother; Princess Margaret was born there; and it was claimed by Shakespeare for the legendary setting of "Macbeth". ("Hail Macbeth, Thane

Glamis Castle: interior grandeur and exterior splendour.

of Glamis!") It is now discreetly open to the public and four 17th-century cottages in the village of Glamis have been turned into the **Angus Folk Museum**, indicating the nature of domestic and agricultural life over the past 200 years.

A visit to Glamis can easily be combined with a visit to **Kirriemuir**, birthplace of the writer J.M.Barrie and the "Thrums" of his novels. The house in which the author of "Peter Pan" was born is now maintained as a museum by the National Trust for Scotland and you can see there Barrie's first theatre—the wash-house. Kirriemuir is also the gateway to **Glen Prossen** and **Glen Clova**, from where the committed walker can penetrate deep into the heart of the Grampians to **Glen Doll** and pick up the old drove roads over to Deeside. These ancient routes were used by armies and rebels as well as cattle drovers and look deceptively easy and appealing walks on the Ordnance Survey map. But the Grampians can be as treacherous as any Scottish hills; the drove roads have claimed the lives of seven walkers, caught in blizzards, over the past two decades.

To the southwest is **Glen Isla** and to the north **Glen Lethnot** (passage of a "whisky road" used by smugglers to outwit Revenue men in the old days) and graceful, meandering **Glen Esk**, which is reached through the pretty village of **Edzell** with its remnants, in the shape of a walled renaissance garden, of the ancestral home of the Lindsay family.

Edzell lies on the Angus boundary with the county of Kincardine, and here the countryside begins to alter subtly. It lies, too, on the western edge of the **Howe of the Mearns**, which means something special to lovers of Scots literature. This is the howe, or vale, which nurtured Lewis Grassic Gibbon, whose brilliant trilogy "A Scots Quair" gave the 20th-century Scottish novel— and the Scots language—its most distinctive voice. "Sunset Song", "Cloud Howe", "Grey Granite"—his lilting, limpid prose sings in your ears as you cross these rolling fields of rich red

earth and granite boulders to a coast that becomes ever more riven and rugged as you near **Stonehaven**—and the big skies, luminous light, spare landscape and chilly challenge of the northeast.

"The Highland Fault meets the sea at Stonehaven, and when you cross it you say goodbye to ease and amplitude," writes John R. Allan, the northeast's most eloquent advocate. "By the stony fields and diffident trees you may guess you have come to a soil very roughly ground through the mills of God." The A92 to Aberdeen now by-passes Stonehaven, but this solid, dignified if plain little fishing port-turned-seaside resort is worth a visit for the drama of its cliffs and **Dunottar Castle**, standing on its own giant rock above the town.

In the dungeons of these spectral ruins Covenanters were left to rot and the Scottish Regalia—the "Honours of Scotland"—were concealed in the 17th century from Cromwell's Roundheads. Popular history has it that, when Dunottar was besieged, the wife of the minister of nearby Kineff Church smuggled the Honours out of the besieged castle with the crown in her lap and the sceptre disguised as a distaff, and hid them in the church.

From Stonehaven to Aberdeen is a clear, high, exhilarating run of 15 miles (24 km) along the cliffs. But why not let the Granite City and the coast be the climax to your northeast tour and take, instead, the A987 to the lower Dee valley? Called the Slug Road for the steepness of its incline from Deeside, it deposits you near the little town of **Banchory**, where you can watch salmon leaping at the **Bridge of Feugh** and visit the late 16th-century tower house of **Crathes**, which is the complete castle, still furnished with period pieces and wall hangings as it was when it was the family seat of the Burnetts. (Aberdeenshire is said to have more castles, both standing and ruined, than any other county in Britain.)

The **Dee valley** is justly celebrated for its expansive beauty and the pellucid, peat-brown grace of its river, and at the handsome village of **Aboyne**, be-

Dunottar Castle: Covenanters were once left there to rot.

tween Banchory and Ballater (see page 237) you begin to tread on the rougher hem of the Eastern Highlands. Deeside's Royal associations make it the tourist honeypot of Aberdeenshire at the expense or perhaps the sparing of Donside. The valley of Aberdeen's second, lesser known river is equally rewarding, and felt by many to be the more subtle and characterful riverway of the two.

Ancient times: From Banchory you can strike over to Donside on the A980, passing through the village of **Lumphanan**, alleged to be the burial place of the doomed King Macbeth whose history has so often been confused with Shakespeare's fiction. **Macbeth's Cairn** does not, however, mark the grave of the king. Not only is it a prehistoric cairn, but it has now been established that Macbeth, like so many of the early Scottish kings, was buried on Iona. You can see at Lumphanan, however, one of Scotland's earliest medieval earthworks, the **Peel of Lumphanan**, and a few miles farther

on **Craigievar Castle**, the most sublime expression of the Aberdeenshire school of castle-building, now in the hands of the National Trust for Scotland but once the 16th-century family home of the Forbes.

Donside's metropolis is the little country town of **Alford**, now promoting itself as a tourist centre. It can offer the **Alford Valley Railway**, a narrow-gauge passenger railway which runs during the summer months; **Grampian Transport Museum** and nearby **Kildrummy Castle**, a romantic 13th-century ruin which featured prominently in the Jacobite Rebellion of 1715 and which now slumbers exotically in a Japanese water garden. Highlight of the Donside summer is the **Lonach Highland Gathering**, traditional games of a kind more authentic than the glitzy gathering at Braemar.

Both Dee and Don have their sources in the foothills of the **Cairngorms**, that lonely, savage massif which dominates the Eastern Highlands. There is no direct route through its lofty bulk, but from Deeside and Donside you can pick up the road which scuttles round it and give yourself one of the most thrilling journeys in Scotland.

At the hamlet of **Cockbridge**, beside the austere, curtain-walled castle of Corgarff, the A939 becomes the Lecht Road, which rises precipitously to some 2,000 ft (600 metres) before careering giddily down into the village of Tomintoul. In winter, the Lecht is almost always the first main road in Scotland to be blocked with snow, encouraging an optimistic ski development at its summit. A mile or so to the north of that summit, look out for the **Well of the Lecht**. Above a small natural spring, a white stone plaque, dated 1745, records that five companies of the 33rd Regiment built the road from here to the Spey. Its straightness testifies to their precision as Government troops extended control over the Highlands after the Jacobite Rebellion of 1745.

Tomintoul, at 1,600 ft (500 metres), is one of the highest villages in Scotland and a pickup point for the "Whisky Trail" which, if you have the energy and

Harvesting the barley: The area is rich in croplands.

the interest, can take you meandering (or perhaps reeling) through seven famous malt whisky distilleries in and around the Spey Valley. The trail (you can get maps in any of the local tour offices) is about 70 miles (110 km) long, and you can spend an hour in each distillery with guides who will admit you to some of the secrets of The Glenlivet, Tamdhu, Glen Grant or Glenfiddich, and offer samples.

Strathspey—*strath* means valley— is one of the loveliest valleys in Scotland, as much celebrated for the excellence of its angling as for its malt whisky industry. When you descend from the grim uplands of the Lecht passage through Tomintoul to the handsome granite town of **Grantown-on-Spey**, you see a land gradually tamed and gentled by natural woodland, open pastures and the clear, comely waters of the River Spey itself. The mountains are never very far away, but you can view them in comfort and style from the Strathspey Railway and the steam train which runs through the valley during the summer months.

Grantown, like so many of the small towns and large villages in this area, was an 18th century "new town", planned and built by its local laird. It makes a good centre for exploring Strathspey and it's also within easy striking distance of the Moray Firth, and the leading resort and former spa town of Nairn. The route from Grantown (the A939) takes you past the island castle of **Lochindorb**, once the lair of the Wolf of Badenoch—Alexander Stewart, the notorious outlawed son of Robert II, who sacked the town of Forres and destroyed Elgin Cathedral.

Nairn, when the sun shines—and the Moray Firth claims to have the biggest share of sunshine on the Scottish mainland—is a splendid place, even elegant, with fine hotels and golf courses, glorious beaches and big blue vistas to the distant hills on the north side of the firth. It is also at the heart of this amiable region's most picturesque and interesting attractions. On its doorstep is **Cawdor Castle**, 14th-century home of

Craigievar: a sublime example of local castle building.

the Thanes of Cawdor (more Macbeth associations); up the coast are the ghostly **Culbin Sands**, which in a great sandstorm of 1695 finally overwhelmed the village of Culbin, which lies buried beneath them; and on the Ardersier peninsula is awesome **Fort George**—one of the outstanding artillery fortifications of Europe—built to control and intimidate the Highlands after the 1745 Rebellion.

Blasted heath: The most poignant and atmospheric reminder of Charles Edward Stuart's costly adventure, however, is **Culloden Moor**, which lies between Nairn and Inverness. Culloden was the last battle to be fought on British soil and here the Jacobite cause was finally lost to internal conflicts and the superior forces of the Hanoverian Army. It is a melancholy, blasted place—in effect, a war graveyard where the Highlanders buried their dead in communal graves marked by rough stones bearing the names of each clan. It becomes even more melancholy when you learn that, although the battle

lasted only 40 minutes, the Prince's army lost 1,200 men to the King's 310, and that "Butcher" Cumberland's Redcoats performed with such enthusiasm that they slaughtered some of the bystanders who had come out from Inverness to watch.

The coast and countryside to the east of Nairn is worth attention—a combination of fishing villages like **Burghead** and **Findhorn** (now famous for the Findhorn Foundation, an international "alternative" community whose life and work, based on meditation and spiritual practice, have turned the sand dunes into flourishing vegetable gardens). And there are pleasing, dignified towns built of golden sandstone like **Forres**, **Fochabers** and **Elgin**, the ancient capital of Moray. Elgin's graceful cathedral dates back to 1224 (it was rebuilt after its destruction by the Wolf of Badenoch in 1390) and, although now partially ruined, is undergoing restoration. With its medieval street plan still well preserved, Elgin must be counted one of the loveliest

Blooms in the prosperous heartland of Aberdeenshire.

towns that can be found in Scotland.

The **River Spey**, which debouches at Spey Bay (site of the Tugnet Ice House, built in 1830 to store ice for packing salmon and now housing an exhibition dedicated to the salmon fishing industry and wildlife of the Spey estuary) marks something of a boundary between the fertile, wooded country and sandy coast of the Moray Firth and that plainer, harsher land which pushes out into the North Sea.

Decision time: Here the motoring tourist, with Aberdeen in his sights, is faced with a choice. You can either cut the coastal corner by driving straight through the prosperous heartland of Aberdeenshire by way of **Keith**, **Huntly**, **Inverurie** and yet more Aberdeenshire castles (Huntly, Fyvie and Castle Fraser, to name but three); or you can hug the forbidding littoral of Banffshire and Buchan and see for yourself John R. Allan's "stony fields and diffident trees", and the workmanlike ports of **Buckie**, **Fraserburgh** and **Peterhead**, and that whole chain of grey, grimly-forged fishing villages and harbours which has harnessed this truculent coast into something productive.

You will then discover that there are pockets of prettiness, hollows of warmth to be found among its cliffs and bays, as well as gusty, spectacular seascapes, rich bird life and the enduring fascination of working harbours, fish markets and museums dedicated to maritime history. Still the leading contributor to the British fishing industry, this was also the Herring Coast in the days of the great silver shoals which fed Scotland and beyond, and gave Banffshire and Buchan most of its income. There is even a "Fishing Heritage Trail" which you can follow.

Banff itself is a town of some elegant substance with a Georgian centre, while the 16th-century merchants' houses around **Portsoy** harbour have been agreeably restored. This village is also distinguished for the production and working of Portsoy marble, and a pottery and marble workshop are installed in one of the harbour buildings,

Looking for a bargain at Turriff Show.

while there is beauty and drama to be found in **Cullen** with its striking series of 19th-century railway viaducts and rare sweep of sand.

Between Macduff and Fraserburgh, where the coast begins to take a right-angle bend, tortuous minor roads link the precipitous villages of **Gardenstown**, **Crovie** and **Pennan**, stuck like limpets to the cliffs, and south of Peterhead the sea boils into the **Bullers O' Buchan**, a high circular basin of rock which Dr. Johnson described as a "monstrous cauldron" before insisting on sailing into it "through the high arch in the rock which the tempest has driven out".

Close by are the gaunt clifftop ruins of **Slains Castle**, said to have ignited the imagination of Bram Stoker and inspired his novel *Dracula*. It is certainly true that Stoker spent holidays at the golfing resort of **Cruden Bay**, where the craggy shore begins to yield to sand until, at the village of **Newhaven** and the mouth of the River Ythan, you find the dramatic dune system of the Sands of Forvie nature reserve. From there south, an uninterrupted stretch of dune and marram grass reaches all the way to Aberdeen.

Granite city: Aberdeen inspires strong emotions. You are either convinced that it is indeed "the silver city by the golden sands", and that its own conceit of itself is well deserved (the city's Book of Remembrance contains the sentiment, "Aberdeen to Heaven—nae a great step"); or you find its exposed interface with the North Sea and its granite austerity wintry of aspect and chilly of soul.

But if Aberdeen is either loved or loathed, even those who affect to dislike it do so with ambivalence. The northeast's most famous writer, Lewis Grassic Gibbon, had this to say about the city where he worked as a journalist, and about its stone: "It has a flinty shine when new—a grey glimmer like a morning North Sea, a cold steeliness that chills the heart…Even with weathering it acquires no gracious softness, it is merely starkly grim and uncom-

THE IMPACT
OF BIG OIL

The North Sea oil bubble may not have burst, but it has certainly been deflated; the days when it was assumed that the "black gold", under the North Sea would cure all Scotland's social and industrial ailments have long gone. The huge oil revenues (£7.5 billion a year at the last count) have disappeared into the maw of the British Treasury, and precious little has come back across the border. As one Scottish nationalist put it: "Scotland must be the only country on Earth to discover oil and become worse off."

Which is not quite true. Scotland may have no access to the revenues, but it has acquired a mature, technologically advanced industry which employs around 67,000 people and under-writes another 30,000 jobs all over the country. The offshore oil industry almost (but not quite) makes up for the thousands of jobs lost in traditional heavy industries like coal, shipbuilding, engineering and steel.

Crude oil is now flowing from 32 oilfields off the east coast of Scotland, and another 10 are waiting the thumbs up from the oil companies. The fields range in size from established giants like Forties, Brent and Ninian to barely economic mini-fields like Arbroath and Ivanhoe-Rob Roy. Many are in the deep, stormy waters of the East Shetland Basin, while others lie under the shallower seas east of Edinburgh. The North Sea has been producing just under 120 million tonnes of oil a year, but the gravy train is already slowing down only 12 years after it started to roll.

The early days between 1972 and 1979, however, were astonishing. Nothing like it had been seen in Scotland before. Hitherto unheard-of oil and engineering giants like Brown & Root and UIE fell over themselves to find sites in Scotland. Every week new schemes were announced for supply bases, refineries and petrochemical works. Scotland was galvanised. While local farmers made fortunes selling low-grade farmland to Edinburgh financiers, the Scottish National Party (SNP) startled Britain by getting 11 members elected to parliament in 1974 on the crude but effective slogan "It's Scotland's Oil."

Heady days, but they didn't last. By the late 1970s the industry had settled down and the SNP had run out of political steam. And, when the price of oil slumped in 1985-86 from $40 to less than $10 a barrel, recession struck the east coast. As company after company went out of business or drew in their horns, the number of jobs in the oil industry collapsed from a high of 90,300 in 1984 to around 67,600 in mid-1987.

But recent reports of the demise of Aberdeen have been greatly exaggerated. The old Granite City remains the oil capital of Europe, the town which services most of the 25,000 men working offshore and the place where every oil company, exploration firm, oil-tool manufacturer and diving company has a foothold. The American presence in Aberdeen is such that many of Aberdeen's "oilies" are more familiar with Houston and New Orleans than they are with the streets of London.

Aberdeen Harbour is still the biggest concentration of oilfield supply bases in Scotland, and Aberdeen Airport sees more helicopter flights than any airport in the world (although recent worries over the safety of long-range "Chinooks" have diverted some traffic back to Sumburgh Airport in Shetland). There are other supply and service bases at Lerwick, Wick, Peterhead, Montrose and Dundee and a fabrication yard at Arnish point near Stornoway on the Herbridean island of Lewis.

The yards where the giant production platforms were built have suffered badly from the boom-to-bust nature of the oil industry. The four west coast yards which were built at Hunterston, Ardyne Point, Portavadie and Loch Kishorn have all gone out of business. In fact the £15 million yard at Portavadie in Argyll never won an order, and has lain totally unused since it was built in 1975. On the east coast the yards at Nigg Point on the Cromarty Firth, Ardersier near Inverness and Methil on the Firth of Forth are now vying desperately with one another for orders.

The thousands of miles of pipeline along which Britain's oil flows comes ashore in Scotland at three points: on the island of Flotta in Orkney, at St. Fergus north of Aberdeen, and at Sullom Voe in Shetland. Sullom Voe is the biggest of the three terminals, with a "throughput" of 1.2 million barrels of oil a day from the oilfields of the East Shetland Basin. For 12 years the tiny Shetland Islands Council has been arguing with the oil giants over the rent for Sullom Voe. The council asked for £100 million a year; the companies offered £300,000.

Sign of the times: In the early days industrial Scotland had high hopes of "downstream" developments such as oil refineries and petrochemical plants. But very few came about, and those that did employed very few people. There are gas separation plants at Sullom Voe and St. Fergus and a huge new petrochemical works at Mossmorran in Fife, which converts natural gas liquids into "product" (butane, propane, ethane, etc), then ships it out via a tanker terminal at Braefoot Bay on the Firth of Forth.

But it's a sign of the times that both the Cromarty Firth and the Firth of Forth are now heavily used to "stack" redundant drilling rigs and pipe-laying barges. And industrialists have been scouting the east coast for a site to break up unwanted drilling rigs and platforms into scrap.

promising…One detests Aberdeen with the detestation of a thwarted lover. It is the one haunting and exasperatingly lovable city in Scotland."

Aberdeen itself is largely indifferent to the opinions of outsiders. Its infuriating complacency, however, has been its strength, and will almost certainly be its salvation when the North Sea oil wells run dry and the city re-focuses on its own considerable resources of sea, land and light industry. Its reverse side is self-reliance.

Of all Britain's cities Aberdeen is the most isolated. It comes as a shock to drive through miles of empty countryside from the south and, breasting a hill, find revealed below you the great grey settlement clasped between the arms of Dee and Don, as if it were the simple, organic extension of rock and heath and shore instead of a complex human artifice. On the sea's horizon you might see a semi-submersible oil rig on the move; in the harbour, trawlers jostle with supply vessels; and there are raw new ribbon developments of housing and warehousing to the north and south of the city. But otherwise Aberdeen, in its splendid self-sufficiency and glorious solitude, remains curiously untouched by the coming of the oil industry.

Granite endures. Much of historic Aberdeen remains, although most of its imposing city centre dates only from the 19th century with the building of **Union Street**, its main thoroughfare, in the early 1800s and the re-building of **Marischal College**, part of the ancient University of Aberdeen, in 1891. The façade of Marischal College, which stands just off Union Street in Broad Street, is an extraordinary fretwork of pinnacles and gilt flags in which the unyielding substance of white granite is made to seem delicate. The building itself is the second largest granite building in the world—the largest is the Escorial in Madrid.

Union Street's die-straight mile from Holborn Junction skirts the arboreal churchyard of St. Nicholas, Aberdeen's "mither kirk", and terminates in the **Castlegate**, which is virtually the same

A North Sea oil rig: no place for the faint-hearted.

square which has occupied that space since the 13th century. Its centrepiece is the 17th-century **Mercat Cross**, with its sculptured portrait gallery of the Stuart monarchs. The cross is the focus of Aberdeen's long history as major market town and import-export centre. For centuries fishwives from **Fittie**, the fishing village at the foot of the Dee, and farmers from the expansive hinterland brought their produce to sell round the cross, while more exotic products from Europe and the New World were hefted up the hill from the harbour by porters from the Shore Porters' Society, Britain's oldest company. (Founded in 1498, Shore Porters now concentrate on furniture removals.)

Aberdeen's oldest quarter and civic origins, however, lie to the north of the city centre on the banks of the River Don, whose narrow, sandy estuary was never developed as harbour and port in the manner of its larger twin, the Dee. Although Aberdeen was already a busy port when it was granted a royal charter in the 12th century by King William the Lion, its earliest settlement was to be found clustered around **St. Machar's Cathedral** in Old Aberdeen, once an independent burgh. The cathedral, founded in the 6th century, is one of the oldest granite buildings in the city (although it has a red sandstone arch which is a remnant of an earlier building) and the cobbled streets and lamplit academic houses surrounding it are atmospheric and peaceful. Here, too, is Aberdeen's first university, **King's College** (founded in 1495 by Bishop Elphinstone), with its graceful crown tower, and a nearby bridge, the **Brig O' Balgownie**, which Aberdeen owes to Robert the Bruce.

Aberdeen's history has often been self-protective; the city gave the Duke of Cumberland, later to become infamous as "Butcher" Cumberland, a civic reception as he led his Hanoverian army north to confront Prince Charles Edward Stuart's Jacobites at Culloden. But it is to its credit that it offered protection to Robert the Bruce during Scotland's Wars of Independence in the

Left, oil meets granite in Aberdeen. Right, Story Book Glen.

14th century. In return, Bruce gave the "Freedom Lands" to the city (which still bring it an income) and ordered the completion of the Brig O' Balgownie, whose building had been interrupted by the wars.

Today, besides all its other activities, Aberdeen confidently promotes itself as a holiday resort, and indeed it is one of the few cities to be recommended for a family holiday with young children. The sands are authentically golden, and there is a vast sweep of them between the mouths of the two rivers and many dunes beyond. But don't expect to sunbathe often or comfortably on them: the northeast gets a major share of Scotland's sunshine, but Aberdeen's beach is open-backed and exposed to every bitter breeze from the North Sea.

Its parks, however, are glorious, wonderfully well kept and celebrated, like many of the other open spaces, for their roses. (Aberdeen has won the "Britain in Bloom" competition so often that it gets regularly banned from entering.)

Hazelhead, on the city's western perimeter, **Duthie Park**, with its extensive winter gardens, and **Seaton Park** on the River Don are probably the most superior open spaces, but all have above-average play areas and special attractions for children during the summer. There is also a well-run permanent funfair at the beach, and a few miles inland in the Dee Valley one of the most attractive small "theme parks" in the country: **Anderson's Story Book Glen**, with its lifesize and giant tableaux of many favourite childhood characters.

A lively theatre, a vigorous art gallery, a well-stocked museum, a succession of festivals and games—you could go on listing the more obvious attractions of Aberdeen. But the real interest for the serious tourist lies in the character of Britain's most northern city, in the rich, robust dialect of its people and their cocky but cautious nature which has had long experience in handling rewards won by their own unremitting industry.

Mormond Hill in Aberdeenshire: part of Britain's early warning system.

THE NORTHERN HIGHLANDS

Nowhere in Britain is the bloodied hand of the past so heavily laid as it is in the Highlands. The pages of its history read like a film script—and have often served as one! There are starring roles for Bonnie Prince Charlie, Flora MacDonald, Mary Queen of Scots, the Wolf of Badenoch and Macbeth, with a supporting cast of clansmen and crofters, miners and fisher folk, businessmen and sportsmen. On the soundtrack, the skirl of the pipes is heard…

The cameras could find no point better at which to start turning than **Inverness**, the natural "capital" of the Highlands. It is assured of that title by its easily fortified situation on the River Ness where the roads through the glens converge. Shakespeare used it for location shots and sadly maligned the man who was its king for 17 years, Macbeth. His castle has disappeared, but from Castlehill a successor dominates the city: a pink cardboard cut-out like a Victorian doll's house that makes Flora MacDonald in bronze shield her eyes and her dog lift a paw. There are kind words, however, at the foot of the statue from Dr. Johnson.

In the nearby **Museum**, the death mask of Flora's Bonnie Prince shares cases with Mr. Punch in his "red Garibaldi coat", Duncan Morrison's puppet figure that once delighted local children. Traditions are strongly represented here in silversmithing, taxidermy and the making of bagpipes and fiddles, but reserve your enthusiasm for a 7th-century Pictish stone depicting a wolf—magic! Inverness is sentimental at heart. Preserved in front of the **Town House**, on a busy street uphill from the river, is the **Clach-na-Cuddain**, a stone on which women rested their tubs of washing. **Abertarff House**, rescued from years of neglect by the National Trust for Scotland, is now its Highland Office, with a chimneypiece marriage lintel of 1691 in the gift shop.

Here be monsters: From an area of

Inverness rich in industrial archaeology the **Caledonian Canal** climbs through six locks like a flight of stairs to the "Hill of Yew Trees", **Tomnahurich**. This Highland waterway, which joins the North Sea and the Atlantic Ocean through the Great Glen, was dreamt of by a local seer a century before it was built; he predicted: "Full-rigged ships will be seen sailing at the back of Tomnahurich." Now you can set sail here in summer on the "Scot II" for a trip on **Loch Ness** and enjoy "a wee dram in the lingering twilight". No doubt the dram will help you when you come to "watch out for the Monster". Occasional expeditions to find Nessie aid the local economy.

Castle Urquhart is more tangible, a picturesque ruin on the loch's edge bearing the scars of having been fought over for two centuries. Further, at **Foyers**, Britain's first hydro-electric scheme, built to provide power for a now defunct aluminium factory, feeds power into the National Grid.

Dr. Johnson, on horseback, praised

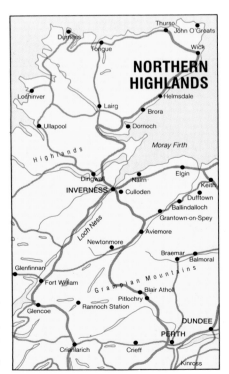

Preceding pages, Suilven, Scotland's Matterhorn. Left, Inverness.

the lochside road, which "between birch trees, with the hills above, pleased us much", and took a dram with an old woman who shared her earth hut with her goats. Later, at a public house called the General's Hut, he dined with Boswell off "mutton-chops, a broiled chicken, bacon and eggs and a bottle of Malaga".

At **Fort Augustus** the canal descends in another flight of locks to the Great Glen Exhibition, which is all about Nessie. The garrison was established after the Jacobite Rising of 1715, but, swords to ploughshares, became a monastery and school. What have a hansom cab and the clock tower in common? Both were designed by Joseph Hansom.

Turn right at **Invergarry** for the beauty of glen and mountain on the road to the Kyle of Lochalsh and Skye. Seven heads for seven brothers on the "Well of the Heads" monument record the murder of two sons of a 17th-century chieftain and a reprisal in the deaths of seven brothers, whose heads were washed in the well before being presented to the chief.

After **Loch Lochy**, the Caledonian Canal reaches the sea in the eight locks of "Neptune's Staircase". Energetic people leave Achintee Farm, just outside **Fort William** for the climb up **Ben Nevis**, Britain's highest mountain. The Fort itself was demolished, not by the Jacobites but by the railway. The secret portrait of Bonnie Prince Charlie, and his bed, are among the Jacobite relics in the West Highland Museum. Telford's road by **Loch Eil** is the romantic "Road to the Isles" of the song, and at **Glenfinnan** was begun "that arduous and unfortunate enterprise" recorded on the monument surmounted by a kilted Highlander at the place where Prince Charlie raised his standard in 1745.

Seaports and spas: At the northern end of the Great Glen the road crosses the neck of the **Black Isle**, which is neither island nor black but forest and fertile farmland, and is bisected by new roads built to serve the oil centres on the

Loch Ness: inspiration for monster fantasies.

north shore of the Cromarty Firth. **Cromarty**, at the extreme tip of the Isle, lost face as a Royal Burgh through declining fortunes as a sea port and trading community, but has recently earned rightful popularity as a place where visitors can literally step back into history in the unspoilt old town. Early geologist Hugh Miller is its scholarly most famous son. His thatched fisherman's cottage, now a museum, is in marked contrast to the houses of rich 18th-century merchants. Privilege reigns in the East Kirk, where there are two wooden "lofts" or galleries of 1700, both beautiful but one ornate for the laird and the other simple for ordinary folk. **Muir of Ord** takes us back to the Great North Road and **Dingwall**, one-time centre of government. Was Macbeth really born here?

Though Scotsmen had long known the local sulphur and chalybeate springs at **Strathpeffer**, it took a doctor who had himself benefited to give substance to "miracle" recoveries and incidentally recognize their profitable po-

A ploughing contest near Inverness.

tential. Dr. Morrison opened his pump room around 1820 and the new railway brought thousands to fill the hotels, attend concerts in the spa pavilion and, if they felt inclined, enjoy "low-pressure subthermal reclining manipulation douche". Strathpeffer had arrived. Given the right weather, it might have become another Salzburg. A couple of wars intervened and the spa declined; but, like all things Victorian, it is enjoying something of a revival as a resort of character that has been likened to an Indian hill station.

Beyond the town the roads diverge, the more southerly winding through Strath Bran and **Achnasheen**. The scenery here is the stuff of photomurals, with **Kyle of Lochalsh** at this end of the rainbow that leads across the sea to Skye. Achnasheen's other leg points to **Kinlochewe** at the head of Loch Maree and close to the National Nature Reserve of Ben Eighe. The mountain itself is a fascinating pudding of old red sandstone topped with white quartzite. In the pine forests there is a good chance of

THREAT TO THE ENVIRONMENT

One man's wilderness is another's development potential. This age-old conflict of interests has suddenly turned into a bitter dispute between conservationists and business interests in the Highlands as commercial foresters talk about expanding the 13 percent of Scotland that is tree-covered to 30 percent by the end of the century.

At the centre of the controversy is the Flow Country of Caithness and Sutherland in the far north, so called because the peat bogs which cover it appear to be moving like a slowly advancing glacier. This extraordinary landscape, one of Europe's last remaining wildernesses, is a breeding ground for many of Britain's most important wading-birds such as the rare greenshank, the merlin and the black-throated diver. Yet vast new forests of lodgepole pine and sitka spruce are marching across the peatland, destroying the birds' habitats. It is, say environmentalists, like another of the invading armies that have punctuated Scotland's turbulent history.

The forestry industry argues that the new plantations help cut Britain's import bill for timber, but the true propulsion for the accelerating afforestation is that it provides generous tax concessions for wealthy investors. Sportsmen, pop stars and television personalities have been identified as being

among the backers behind the latest tree-planting schemes, and the fact that most of them live in London serves to deepen the locals' resentment.

One TV personality, Magnus Magnusson, who is of Icelandic descent, finds himself on the other side of the argument as president of the Royal Society for the Protection of Birds. "This is wanton vandalism of one of our greatest national assets," he says. "My ancestors were accused of rape and pillage, but I think even they would be ashamed of what is going on." The RSPB points out that Britain contains a seventh of the world's undisturbed peatland and that most of that acreage is to be found in Scotland. "The mosaic of lochs, rivers, pools, peat mosses and heather moorland is ideal for species which live in open spaces," the society says.

So remote is this vast area of soggy open moorland and low, featureless hills that until recently only a handful of bird-watchers and fishermen realised the extent to which "tax-avoidance forestry" was advancing. Planting in Scotland requires no planning permission and the investment companies behind the schemes kept an understandably low profile. The other major planter, the Forestry Commission, has traditionally possessed such wide powers that it is known in the Highlands as "a state within a state".

The Flow Country, thanks to its magical landscape, provided a potent focus for pressure groups wishing to draw the media's attention to the problem. But elsewhere in Scotland huge numbers of conifers have been planted by other forestry companies. Around a fifth of the south-west region of Dumfries and Galloway is now forested, and hill farms in the Borders area have also had to make way for trees. Islanders on Arran, in the Clyde estuary, began calling their island "Little Finland" as more of it disappeared under the encroaching conifers.

The debate is far from one-sided, however. Many Scots, bemused to find that familiar areas have become "eco-systems", are impatient with the conservationists. The Highlands and Islands Development Board argued that a ban on forestry and other land uses would kill prospects for as many as 2,000 local jobs and would jeopardise the economic future of whole communities. The Highland Regional Council agreed: what was the point of having no trees, it asked, if there were no jobs and no people? That outcome, after all, would simply continue the melancholy history of the Highlands, whose inhabitants left because the land could not sustain them, or because they were forcibly cleared out by the landowners to make way for sheep or grouse, or because an English king was trying to destroy the clan system. In less than 200 years the proportion of Scotland's population that lives in the Highlands has plummeted from 20 to 5 percent.

The conservationists had an answer. Forestry employs relatively few people, they said, whereas tourism provides 100,000 jobs in Scotland. And tourists are not going to come to gaze at a landscape of lodgepole pine.

seeing rare and protected wildlife: deer, wildcat, pine marten and golden eagle. Nature trails begin in the car park.

Eastern promise: From **Dingwall**, where gilded mortar-and-pestle signs still signal a chemist's shop, road and rail cling to the east coast. Near **Alness**, on a hill, is a replica of the Gate of Negapatam in India, which General Sir Hector Munro, hero of its capture, had built by local men, thus simultaneously alleviating poverty and satisfying pride. Had he lived today instead of in the 18th century, North Sea oil would have solved his unemployment problem. The place is dormitory to **Invergordon** on Cromarty Firth, which offered shelter to Britain's navy through two world wars and finally suffered the closure of its naval base in 1956. For better or worse, certainly for richer or until the oil lake dries up, the choice of Nigg Bay for the construction of oil rig platforms brought dramatic changes to the area.

Tain's memories are older, going back to 1066, when it became a Royal Burgh. Though St. Duthac was born and buried here, it didn't save the two chapels dedicated to him from disastrous fires—or guarantee sanctuary. The Stuarts made up for it all: James IV came often, and James V with bare feet.

Wonderland of Sutherland: Cross **Bonar Bridge** and nothing, as Lewis Carroll's Alice would have said, is the same. Motorists adjust to the pace set by single-track roads and the sheep that share them. Railway buffs settle back in their seats to enjoy spectacular views of heather-covered moor and loch. This is Viking country, closer in character to Scandinavia than to England.

At **Invershin** is a superbly situated castle without a burden of history. Retainers, some heavy-laden, come and go beneath the towers and battlements with which it is over endowed. It was built as late as 1914 for the Duchess of Sutherland and is now a youth hostel. The **Falls of Shin** nearby provide a heart-rending spectacle. From a platform built over the cascading river salmon can be seen attempting their

Left, unspoilt Lochalsh. Below, off to a lamb sale at Lairg.

summer passage upstream to their spawning grounds. Many fail their great leap, slithering backwards. Others, by tremendous exertion of body, fins and tail, drive up the rocks to the pools above—an affecting sight that rouses human onlookers to cheers.

"All roads meet at Lairg," it's said. Sometimes in August it seems all the sheep in Scotland do as well. **Lairg** is in the heart of the Sutherland crofting country and the lamb sales identify it as a major market-place. Mirrored in the quiet waters of Loch Shin, an Iron Age hut circle on the hill above the village keeps company with the council houses below and, at **Kinvonvie**, a crofter's experiment in restoring grass to the uplands.

The eastern spoke from Lairg's hub reaches the coast at Loch Fleet and **Dornoch**, where some regard Royal Dornoch, opened in 1616, as offering better golf than the Old Course at St. Andrews. Not a sporting chance, though, for Janet Horn: 100 years later she was burnt as a witch (the last to be sentenced in Scotland) for having the Devil shoe her daughter after she had turned her into a pony. Dornoch Castle's surviving tower suffered the indignities of use as a garrison, courthouse, jail, school and private residence. Now it's a hotel.

Golspie lives in the shadow of the Sutherlands. An oversize statue of the First Duke looks down from the mountain; a stone in the old bridge is the rallying point of the clan; and nearby is the Duchess's **Dunrobin Castle**, an improbable confection of pinnacles and turrets that doesn't know whether it is a schloss or a château. The prehistoric fort at Carn Liath a little further along the coast is a nice antidote. **Brora** passes as a resort. It boasts a bijou coal-mine nearly 400 years old that gets called up for national service; the fuel crisis of 1974 was the last time it came out of retirement.

Havens, harbours, herring: The goldrush that brought prospectors to the burns of **Helmsdale** in the 1860s proved a flash in the pan. More reward-

A crofter's life, near Applecross.

ing is the country that lies ahead, **Caithness**, for centuries so remote from the centres of Scottish power that it was ruled by the Vikings. Trade links were entirely by sea and in the boom years of the fishing industry scores of harbors were built. The fishing fleets have gone; the harbours remain.

The road to **Berriedale** twists spectacularly past the ravines of the Ord of Caithness and on to **Dunbeath**, where a few lobster boats are a reminder of past glories. **Lybster** offers more bustle, but at **Mid Clyth** leave the road at a sign, "Hill o' Many Stanes", for a mystery tour. On a south-facing hillside are 22 rows of small stones, thought to be Bronze Age. For star sightings, perhaps? There are more stones in the Whaligoe Steps at **Thrumster**; the fishwives used to carry laden creels up the 365 steps of the cliff face and walk the six miles (10 kms) to Wick market.

Herring were the backbone of **Wick**'s prosperity. More than 1,000 boats once set sail to catch the "silver darlings". Now the near-deserted quays give the harbour a wistful charm. Maybe the disappearance of the herring explains why the fishermen were so superstitious: aboard ship, no-one mentioned salmon by name—they were "red fish". The evasions went further: rabbits were "four footers", pigs were "sandy Campbells" and the minister was "the man in the black coat". Where we "touch wood", they touched iron, saying "caul iron". What is clearly the most celebrated product of Wick? Caithness glass.

For cross-country record breakers, **John O' Groats** has a natural attraction. It also has incomparable cliff scenery in the towering "stacks" of **Duncansby Head**. Across the Pentland Firth the Orkney Islands lie "like stranded whales". A Dutchman, Jan de Groot, came here in 1500 under orders from James IV to set up a ferry service to Orkney to consolidate his dominion over this former Scandinavian territory. Jan's response to requests from his eight sons as to who should succeed him was to build an octagonal house

Sutherland's hiking country, looking towards Suilven.

with eight doors and with an octagonal table in the middle so that each sat at the "head". A mound and a flagstaff commemorate the site.

The approaches to **Thurso** are heralded by the Caithness "hedges" that line the fields, the flagstones that were once shipped from local quarries to every corner of the old Empire. The streets of Calcutta were paved by Caithness. It is hard to find Thurso harbour attractive. **Fisherbiggins**, the old fishermen's quarter, is a facsimile reproduction from 1940, but elsewhere there is pleasant Victorian town planning. **Scrabster** is Thurso's outport, with a ferry to Orkney. The site of Scotland's first nuclear power station at **Dounreay** was chosen for its remoteness. Besides electricity it generates traffic, spawns housing development and boosts the local economy. Roll up, roll up for "Caithness's high-technology tourist attraction", as a brochure puts it.

The furthest point: It's an odd feeling: nothing between you and the North Pole except magnificent cliff scenery. At **Tongue** the sea loch pokes deep into the bleak moorland, and near **Durness** the Alt Smoo river drops from the cliff into the Caves of Smoo. Look out for cooties, sea cockies, tammies and tommienoories (puffins by another name).

The return to Lairg can be made south from Tongue on the lovely road through **Altnaharra**, where crosses, hut circles and Pictish brochs abound. From Durness the road joins the western coast at **Scourie**, where mermaids are mistaken for seals and palm trees grow. **Ullapool** is a resort for all seasons, beautifully situated on Loch Broom facing the sunset, an idyll that has to be shared with too many others in July and August.

Herring inspired the British Fisheries Society in 1788 to build fisher cottages and improve the harbour. Today, harbour facilities are still being improved, a car ferry serves Stornaway in Lewis and trips leave the pier for the deserted but delightfully named **Summer Isles**.

Balmoral Castle, the Queen's holiday home in Aberdeenshire.

Smoking is good for the health at **Achiltibuie**. Fish and game to be cured are "steeped in spicy aromatic brines which gently permeate and cure the raw materials. Treacle, juniper berries, bay leaves and rum add subtlety and character as the flavours develop". What palate could resist such a description?

Downhill racing: It's doubtful if the Clan Grant, whose war cry was" Stand Fast Craigellachie", could have resisted the forces at work in **Aviemore**, below their rallying place. It has become a holiday complex, a quiet Speyside halt transformed in 20 years into a year-round resort by the opening of roads into the Cairngorms and chairlifts for the skiers. Brewers built the centre; hotels, restaurants, a theatre, ice rinks and go-cart tracks followed. In summer you could be "magicked" abroad when Aviemore goes German for the Beer Fest with oompah music, sauerkraut, bratwurst, fräuleins and foaming tankards. The Highlands fight back with nail hammering, haggis throwing, barrel hurling and, of course, the Games.

More sober delights can be had in wining and dining on a steam train of the Highland Railway en route from the town to Boat of Garten.

Appropriately enough, **Glenlivet** is at hand. Visiting Speyside in 1822, George IV was told his favourite malt whisky was unobtainable. The honour of Rothiemurchus was saved by Elizabeth Grant, who produced bottles from her own bin "long in wood, mild as milk, and the true contraband gout in it". Grant's father was made a judge.

Duck your head to enter the Blackhouse in the Highland Folk Museum at **Kingussie** and another world. A peat fire fills this replica of an Isle of Lewis stone house with pungent smoke. You know how the salmon must have felt in the Victorian corrugated-iron smokehouse nearby. In the museum is ideal equipment for a strolling player: a chanter walking-stick and bagpipes from Waterloo.

Royal haunts: Blame **Braemar** on Queen Victoria. She loved it. The village is best enjoyed in September when the Highland Gathering brings people from all over the world to watch cabers tossed, stones put and hammers thrown, as well as the daring intricacies of sword dancing and the Highland fling. Fairy-tale Braemar Castle's surprising charm and intimacy stem from being lived in.

And then there's **Balmoral**. If the Gaels called it Bouchmorale ("majestic dwelling") before Prince Albert's rebuilding, what superlatives would they have found for the new Scottish baronial palace? Since 1855 it has been a royal residence, though in midsummer the Queen shares her gardens with the public and her prayers with her subjects at nearby **Craithie** church. **Ballater** continues the royal progress down the Dee, and this is where the family pops down to the shops. London's Bond Street can produce no more "By Appointment" signs than here. Against the backdrop of forest, mountains and castles, what more fitting place to bring down the curtain on an extravaganza which began as a melodrama and ends as a musical comedy?

Tartanry again, this time at Aviemore's leisure complex.

ORKNEY

Six miles (12 kms) of sea separate the northeast corner of Scotland from an archipelago of 70 islands, about one-third of which are inhabited. This is Orkney (the word means "seal islands" in old Icelandic) which extends over 1,200 square miles (3,100 sq. kms). If you believe there are more islands it may be because you have drunk too well of the products of Orkney's two distilleries or are counting seals—both common and grey—which abound in these waters.

In few places in the world is the marriage of landscape and seascape so harmonious. On halcyon summer days, the blues of the sky and of the sea complement the greens of rolling pastures and the gold of fields of grain. Later, when zephyrs blow, scudding cumulus clouds are matched by the white horses of waves.

The "ey" is Old Norse for islands and one should refer to Orkney and not "the Orkneys" or "the Orkney islands". It also announces an ancient affiliation with Norway, an affiliation historical rather than geographical, for Norway lies 300 miles (480 kms) to the east. Orkney was a Norwegian appendage until the end of the 15th century and the true Orcadian is still more a Norse than a Scot.

To Orcadians, Scotland is the *sooth"* (south) and never the "mainland" for that is the name of the group's principal island: when inhabitants of the smaller islands visit the largest, therefore, they journey to **Mainland**, and when they travel to the United Kingdom they are off *"sooth"* to Scotland. Not that there are many of them to travel: the population is about 19,000, of whom one-quarter live in the capital, Kirkwall.

Shortest flight: Travel within the archipelago is by ferries and more often by planes. The Loganair flight between Westray and Papa Westray is the shortest commercial flight in the world. In perfect weather conditions, it takes only one minute.

To wander these islands is, for the dedicated lover of archaeology, a taste of paradise: for the uninitiated it is the threshold of a world of wonder. Orkney offers an uninterrupted continuum of mute stones from Neolithic times (about 4500 BC) through the Bronze and Iron ages to about AD 700, followed by remains from the days when the islands were occupied successively by Celts and Vikings.

On average, every square mile (2.6 sq. kms) has three recorded items of antiquarian interest. The key to these is often kept at the nearest farmhouse and payment is made by placing money in an honour-box. Anyone interested to scrape away with a toothbrush—after first contacting the appropriate authorities—is almost assured of unearthing artefacts.

One in six of all seabirds that breed in Britain nests in Orkney, which boasts about 30 major seabird cliffs. Every nook, every cranny, every ledge of

Papa Westray
North Ronaldsay
Westray
Sanday
Rousay
Eday
Stronsay
Birsay
MAINLAND
Shapinsay
Stromness
Maeshowe
Kirkwall
Scapa Flow
Flotta
Burray
HOY
South Ronaldsay
Pentland Firth
ORKNEY

weathered sandstone is jammed with nesting birds: guillemots and razorbills, shags and storm petrels, gannets and gulls. Puffins pop in and out of their earth burrows while cormorants flap above the water or, after diving, perch on an exposed rock and hoist their wings to dry.

Fishing is excellent and varied. Wild brown trout abound in myriad lochs where, thanks to an ancient Norse law, you don't need a permit to fish. As a bonus, in spring, late summer and autumn, sea-trout (similar to salmon) leave the sea to spawn in burns and lochs. In recent years the potential for sea angling has been realised and lucky anglers catch 200-lb (90-kg) skate and halibut and a variety of other species.

City sights: **Kirkwall** is dominated by the 12th-century **St. Magnus Cathedral**. Construction began in the Norman style but a healthy leavening of Gothic features attests to more than 300 years of building. Facing the cathedral is the ruined **Bishop's Palace**, a massive structure with a round tower reminiscent of a castle. Here, in the 13th century, the great Norwegian king, Haakon Haakonson, lay dying while Norse sagas were read aloud to him. Nearby is a third ancient building, the **Earl's Palace**, a romantic gem of renaissance architecture. It is roofless: in the 17th century its slates were removed to build the town hall.

Other Kirkwall attractions are the **Tankerness House Museum** which presents the complete story of Orkney from prehistory to the present; the **Orkney Library**, the oldest public library in Scotland, and a golf course.

War and peace: South of Kirkwall is the great natural harbour of **Scapa Flow**. Here, the captured German fleet was anchored after World War I and here the fleet was scuttled. Only six of the 74 ships remain on the bed of this deep, spacious bay which is bliss for the scuba-diver, a peaceful cornucopia for the deep sea angler.

The island of **Flotta**, at the south of Scapa Flow, is a North Sea oil terminal. This is the Orcadians' only concession

Kirkwall Harbour: familiar to sailors in both world wars.

to black gold and it is enough. Mining for uranium near Kirkwall has been firmly rejected.

Fifteen miles (24 kms) west of Kirkwall is picturesque **Stromness**, Orkney's second town. A well on the main street testifies that, in the 17th century, Stromness was developed by the Hudson Bay Company whose ships made this their last port of call before crossing the Atlantic. Stromness has a good Art Centre, a museum, an indoor swimming pool and a golf course.

Most of Mainland's major archaeological sites are to the north of Stromness. Crawl into awesome **Maeshowe,** the most magnificent chambered tomb in Britain, which dates from 3500 BC. Within is a spacious burial chamber built with enormous megaliths on some of which are incised the world's largest collection of runic hieroglyphics. These are the grafitti of Vikings who entered the tomb in the 12th century.

Near Maeshowe are the **Ring of Brodgar** and the **Standing Stones of Stenness**, the remains of two of Britain's most spectacular stone circles. When the former was completed, about 1200 BC, it consisted of 60 standing stones set along the circumference of a circle about 340 ft (103 metres) in diameter. Today, 27 stones, the tallest of which is 14 ft (four metres) still stand. The four giant monoliths of Stenness are all that remain of that particular circle of 12 stones erected about 2300 BC.

Skara Brae, Britain's Pompeii, sits on the Atlantic coast alongside a superb sandy beach. The settlement, remarkably well preserved, consists of several dwelling houses and connecting passages and was engulfed by sand 4,500 years ago after having been occupied for 500 years. Skara Brae is a quintessential Stone Age site; no metal of any kind was found: all furniture—beds, chairs—are made of stone.

Five miles (eight kms) north is **Birsay** with the 16th-century **Earl's Palace**. Opposite is the **Brough of Birsay**, a tiny tidal island (avoid being stranded) which has rich remains of

Chapel built in Orkney by Italian prisoners during World War II.

Norse and Christian settlements.

A further eight miles (13 kms) east, and guarding Eynhallow Sound, is the **Broch of Gurness**. Brochs are Iron Age (100 BC to AD 300) strongholds built by the Picts. These structures, unique to Scotland and ubiquitous in Orkney, were circular at their base and their massive walls tapered gently inwards to a height of about 60 ft (18 metres).

Echoes of war: The principal southern islands are South Ronaldsay, Burray, Lamb Holm, Hoy and Flotta. Technically, the first three are no longer islands, being joined to Mainland by the **Churchill Barriers**. These were built by Italian prisoners during World War II after a German submarine penetrated Scapa Flow and sank the battleship Ark Royal.

On **Lamb Holm** enter some Nissen huts and be astonished at the beautiful chapel built with scrap metal by these prisoners. An unusual Wireless Museum at St. Margaret's Hope on **South Ronaldsay** has its devotees.

Hoy, the second largest island of the archipelago, is spectacularly different. The southern part is low-lying but at the north stand the heather-covered Cuilags (1,420 ft/426 metres), from where all Orkney, except Little Rysa, can be viewed. A stroll along the 1,140-ft-high (367-metre) **St. John's Head**, which teems with seabirds (beware the swooping great skuas) and boasts some rare plants, is sheer delight for the geologist, ornithologist and botanist or for those simple creatures who just like to ramble. Immediately south of St. John's Head is the **Old Man of Hoy**, a 450-ft (135-metre) perpendicular sandstone column which constantly challenges the world's rock-climbers.

Northward-bound: And so to the northern islands. Fertile **Shapinsay** is so near Mainland that it is called suburbia. Also near Mainland, but further west and readily reached by local ferry are **Rousay** and **Egilsay**. Rich archaeological finds have earned the former the sobriquet "Egypt of the North".

Visit the remarkable 76-ft-long (23-

Ring of Brodgar: 3,000 years ago there were 60 stones.

metre) Neolithic **Midhowe** chambered tomb, aptly named the "Great Ship of Death", which has 12 burial compartments on either side of a central passage. Nearby is the magnificent **Midhowe Broch**. Ascend the summit of Mansemass Hill and stroll to Ward Hill for superb views of **Eynhallow**, medieval Orkney's Holy Island, between Rousay and Mainland.

On Egilsay an unusual round church, which has affinities with similar buildings in Ireland, marks the 12th-century site of the martyrdom of St. Magnus.

Low-lying **Sanday**, with its white beaches, has room for a golf course but not to the exclusion of archaeological remains. Most important is the Quoyness chambered cairn, standing 13 ft high (three metres) and dating from about 2900 BC. It is similar to, but even larger than, Maeshowe. **Stronsay**, another low-lying island with sandy beaches, was formerly the hub of the prosperous Orkney herring industry. **Eday** may be bleak and barren yet is paradise for bird watchers and has the customary complement of archaeological edifices.

Westray, the largest northern island, is unique in that its population is increasing. This is largely because of a successful fishing fleet which contradicts the allegation that the Orcadian is "a farmer with a boat". **Noup Head** is Westray's bird reserve and splendid view point. The island also has a golf course and the ruined renaissance **Notland Castle**. Papa Westray's **North Hill Nature Reserve** is home to arctic terns and skuas. At **Knap of Howar** are considerable remains of the earliest standing dwelling houses in northwest Europe (approximately 3000 BC.) Their occupants, archaeologists have found, had "a strong preference for oysters".

On the most northerly island, **North Ronaldsay**, a dyke around the island confines sheep to the shore, leaving better inland pastures for cattle. Seaweed, the sole diet of these sheep, results in dark meat with an unusually rich flavour: an acquired taste.

Orkney boasts the world's shortest commercial flight: it lasts one minute.

SHETLAND

The writer Jan Morris called them "inset islands". In those two words she defined the mystery of the **Shetland Islands**, whose remoteness (200 miles to the north of Aberdeen) means that maps of Britain usually relegate them to a box in the corner of a page. "This has subtly affected our concept of them," wrote Morris. "They are much, much further away than most people suppose. They are much more foreign places, much harder, older and more distinct."

In many ways the 20 or so inhabited islands scarcely seem part of Britain at all. It comes as a surprise to see the extension of U.K. road numbering: what on earth is a small island doing with an A970? The declining population of 23,000 people doesn't regard itself as British, or even as Scottish, but as Norse. The nearest mainland town is Bergen in Norway. Norwegian is

taught in the schools. The heroes of myths have names like Harald Hardrada and King Hakon Hakonsson.

Wildlife wonders: The islands, dotted over 70 miles (112 km) of swelling seas, are a geologist's and bird-watcher's paradise, and appeal to hardy walkers. Spring comes late, with plant growth speeding up only in June. Rainfall is heavy, mists are frequent and gales (record gust: 177 miles/285 km an hour) keep the islands virtually treeless. But conditions change rapidly, hence the islanders' advice: "If you don't like the weather, wait a minute." It's never very cold, even in mid-winter, thanks to the caresses of the North Atlantic Drift; and in mid-summer (the "Simmer Dim") it never quite gets dark. (A game of golf gets under way at midnight on midsummer's eve.)

The late-January festival of Up-Helly-Aa is loosely based on a pagan fire festival intended to herald the impending return of the sun. A procession of *guizers* (men dressed in winged helmets and shining armour) parades through the streets carrying burning torches with which they set fire to a replica of a Viking longship. It is an authentic fiesta and visitors aren't encouraged; for one thing, there would be no-one to look after guests since everybody is too busy celebrating.

At other times, the Shetlander is exceptionally hospitable and talkative. When he says, "You'll have a dram", it's an instruction rather than an enquiry and you're unlikely ever to be offered a larger glass of whisky. It's worth attending a folk concert, not just for the drink but because the islands are full of astonishingly accomplished fiddlers.

Oil boom: Two check-in counters confront passengers at **Sumburgh Airport** on the main island, **Mainland**: one is for fixed-wing aircraft, the other for helicopters. North Sea oil generates the traffic and at one time threatened to overwhelm the islands. But the oil companies, pushed by a determined local council, made conspicuous efforts to lessen the impact on the environment and, although half of Britain's oil flows through the 1,000-acre (400-

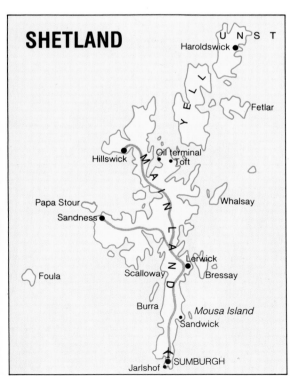

hectare) **Sullom Voe** terminal at the southern tip of Mainland, they seem to have succeeded beyond most islanders' expectations. The 16 crude oil tanks, each holding 21 million gallons (95 million litres) were painted mistletoe-green, 124 species of birds have been logged within the terminal boundary, and outside the main gates a traffic-sign gives priority to otters.

Sheep outnumber people by eight to one. "They eat everything," says one islander. "The place would be covered in wildflowers if it weren't for the wretched sheep." Shetland ponies are more loved. They were carefully bred to keep their legs short so that they could pull carts through Britain's coal mines, but these days they graze freely, their manes tangled by the wind, or are sold as children's pets. But it's birds that dominate Shetland. Because of the lack of woodlands there are fewer than 50 breeding species, but no lack of numbers. Filling the sky and the cliff ledges are 30,000 gannets, 140,000 guillemots and 300,000 fulmars. There are over 3,000 pairs of great skua (known locally as bonxies), piratical birds who will dive-bomb intruders during the breeding season. It's the puffins everyone wants to see, however; they begin to arrive in May and before long there are 250,000 of them. Take a small boat round the islands and, as well as the birds, you can find seal colonies, porpoises and dolphins.

Ancient mound: A concentrated anthropological history of the islands is located at **Jarlshof**, a jumble of buildings close to the airport. Waves of settlers from the Stone, Bronze and Iron Ages built dwellings here, each one on the ruins of its predecessor. The Vikings built on top of that and medieval farmsteads later buried the Viking traces. At the end of the 19th century the site was just a grassy mound, topped with a medieval ruin. Then a wild storm laid bare massive stones in a bank above the beach and the archaeologists moved in. Hearths were found where peat fires burned 3,000 years ago. Today old wheelhouses (named be-

A Viking festival sets Lerwick alight every January.

cause of their radial walls) have been revealed and an exhibition area fleshes out Jarlshof's history.

En route to the capital, Lerwick, 27 miles (43 km) to the north, the offshore island of **Mousa** is home to sheep and ponies, and also to a spectacularly well-preserved *broch*, a round dry-stone tower more than 40 ft (13 metres) high.

Lerwick looks no more planned than Jarlshof was. The old town has charm, with intimate stone-paved alleys leading off the main street of granite houses and dignified shops (no chain stores here). But little attempt has been made to blend in newer commercial premises and housing estates; ugly jerry-building predominates. The windows of the baronial-looking **town hall**, presented to the town by Norway, Holland and Germany as thanks for Shetland's kindness to seamen, are a reminder of Lerwick's relationship with the elements. It huddles round the harbour, as if preparing itself for the next gale, and gulls screech as if in warning.

For centuries the miniature metropolis has been a crossroads of the North Atlantic for fishing fleets from Spain, Holland, Norway, Germany and Russia, and a babel of accents can still be heard. One of the town's most famous sons, Arthur Anderson, went on to co-found the P&O shipping line in the 19th century; the **Anderson Educational Institute**, the island's only senior secondary school, was endowed by him.

The sea dominates the **museum**, sited above the library in Hillhead. It has a good collection of harpoons, decorative 19th-century sea chests, and coins found in shipwrecks dating back 400 years. More information would be useful about the purpose of certain implements on display, such as trussing drivers, flensing knives, shivs, pluckers and flinchers. The museum also houses various Victorian trinkets and lace shawls, and a collection of 5,000-year-old beads, pots and pumice stones found when excavating Sumburgh airport.

Six miles (10 km) from Lerwick, in a sheltered bay, is the old fishing port of **Scalloway**, once Shetland's capital. Its main feature is the gaunt ruins of an early 17th-century castle built for Earl Patrick Stewart, a nephew of Mary Queen of Scots. So tyrannical was the earl that he is reputed to have used a mixture of eggs, blood and human hair as building plaster.

Deep voes (*inlets*) poke into the Shetland Islands like long fingers so that no part of the watery landscape is more than three miles from the sea. As you drive across Mainland's moors, meadows and hills, dramatic sea views abruptly materialise. Shetlanders were always more sailors than farmers; but at **Tingwall**, north of Lerwick, an **Agricultural Museum** lays out in an old farmyard a rare collection of old peat-cutting tools and cooking pots.

Island-hopping: Small ferries connect a handful of smaller islands to Mainland. **Yell**, a peaty place, has a local museum and craft centre and a knitwear centre selling genuine rather than generic Shetland garments. **Unst**, the U.K.'s most northerly island, has an important nature reserve at Hermanness and a Royal Air Force base. **Fetlar's** name means "fat island", a reference to its fertile soil. **Whalsay** is prosperous, thanks to its notably energetic fishermen. The **Out Skerries,** a scattered archipelago, have a thriving fishing fleet. The peacefulness and abundant wild flowers of **Papa Stour**, a mile of turbulent sea west of Mainland, once attracted a transient hippy colony.

Foula, 14 miles (23 km) to the west of Scalloway, must be Britain's remotest inhabited island and most winters are cut off for several weeks by awesome seas. The spectacular 1,200-ft (370-metre) cliffs are home to storm petrels, great skuas and a host of other seabirds.

Another staging-post for the birds is provided by **Fair Isle**, 20 miles (32 km) to the south-west, halfway to Orkney. This self-reliant island, now owned by the National Trust for Scotland, has an observatory to monitor the birds' movements and is home of Fair Isle sweaters, whose distinctive geometric patterns can be dated back 2,000 years to Balkan nomads.

A WEE DRAM

At the end of the most sophisticated dinner parties in London, guests are invariably offered a choice of brandy or port but seldom a glass of Scotch. Familiarity, perhaps, has produced contempt for the native product—or, the Scots would argue, the English are showing their customary ignorance of all things Scottish. The prejudice is an ill-founded one because good malt whiskies have a wider range of flavour and aroma than brandy and—an extra bonus—are less likely to make the over-indulger's head throb the morning after. Snobbery probably accounts for the attitude, too, for Scotland's unique drink has never quite managed to cultivate the exclusive image of Cognac.

For one thing, there's a lot more of it on the market. Scotch is one of Britain's top five export items: even the Vatican, on the most recent annual reckoning, bought 18,000 bottles. Because of overproduction in the late 1970s, manufacturers have been less keen on nourishing an upmarket image than on shifting stocks, and have created for the export market a variety of cheap brands with bogus-sounding names. A few more expensive brands then need to be heavily promoted as offering "something special".

Toddler's tipple: The lowly origins of Scotch may also be partly to blame for its fluctuating fortunes. In the 18th century, it was drunk as freely as the water from which it was made, by peasants and aristocrats alike. A spoonful was given to new-born babies in the Highlands and even respectable gentlewomen might start the day with "a wee dram". The poorest crofter could offer the visitor a drink, thanks to the ubiquity of home-made stills which made millions of gallons of "mountain dew" in the remote glens of the Highlands. Even in Edinburgh, no-one needed to go thirsty: excise officers estimated in 1777 that the city had eight licensed stills and 400 illegal ones.

Preceding pages: Hercules Irvine, crofter; whisky maturing under the eye of the Customs officer. Left, Scotland's magnificent obsession. Right, tools of the whisky distiller's trade.

Yet something as easy to make cannot be made authentically outside Scotland. Many have tried, and the Japanese in particular have thrown the most modern technology at the problem; but the combination of damp climate and soft water flowing through the peat cannot be replicated elsewhere. Indeed no-one—not even the most experienced professional taster —can agree on what elements create the best whiskies. Is the water better if it runs off granite through

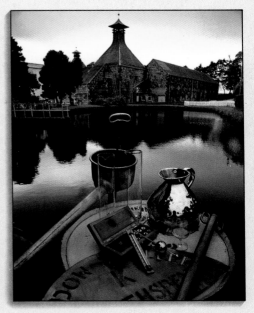

peat, or if it runs through peat onto granite? Does the secret lie in the peat used to dry the malt in a distillery's kiln? Or does it lie in the soft air that permeates the wooden casks of whisky as the liquid matures for anything from three to 18 years? The arguments continue—over a glass or two of the debated liquid, of course.

Some historians believe that the art of distilling was brought to Scotland by Christian missionary monks. But it is just as likely that Highland farmers discovered for themselves how to distil spirits from their surplus barley. The earliest known reference to whisky occurs in 1494, when Scottish Exchequer Rolls record that Friar John Cor purchased a quantity of malt "to make aquavitae".

These days there are two kinds of Scotch whisky: *malt*, made from malted barley only; and *grain*, made from malted barley together with unmalted barley and maize. Most popular brands are blends of both types of whisky—typically 60 percent grain to 40 percent malt.

A single malt, the product of one distillery, has become an increasingly popular drink, thanks largely to the aggressive marketing by William Grant & Sons of their Glenfiddich brand. But sales of single malts still account for only one bottle in 20 sold

the water, doesn't have to be local) is soaked in tanks of water for two or three days. It is then spread out on a concrete floor or placed in large cylindrical drums and allowed to germinate for between eight and 12 days. Next it is dried in a kiln, ideally heated by a peat fire. The dried malt is ground and mixed with hot water in a huge circular vat called a mash tun. A sugary liquid, "wort", is drawn off from the porridge-like result, leaving the remaining solids to be sold as cattle food. The wort is fed into massive vessels containing up to 45,000 litres of liquid, where living yeast is stirred into the mix in order to convert the sugar in the wort into crude alcohol.

around the world, and most of the production of single malt distilleries is used to add flavour to a blended whisky.

So automated are Scotland's 100-plus distilleries that the visitor, sipping an end-of-tour glass of the product he has watched being manufactured, is left with an image of the beautifully proportioned onion-shaped copper stills and a lingering aroma of malted barley—but not with any clear idea of the process by which water from a Highland stream is transformed into *usquebaugh*, the water of life.

What happens is this. To make malt whisky, plump and dry barley (which, unlike

After about 48 hours, the "wash" (a clear liquid containing weak alcohol) is transferred to the copper pot stills and heated to the point at which alcohol turns to vapour. This vapour rises up the still to be condensed by a cooling plant into distilled alcohol which is then passed through a second still. (One thing that distinguishes Scotch whisky from Irish whiskey, apart from the spelling, is that Scotch is distilled twice and Irish three times.)

The trick is to know exactly when the

The mashing process in which malt is mixed with hot water, with yeast then added.

whisky has distilled sufficiently. Modern measuring devices offer scientific precision, but the individual judgement of an experienced distiller is hard to beat. Some smaller distilleries, it was once said, were so afraid of disturbing any element in the delicate environment that they wouldn't allow cobwebs to be swept off the vat-room rafters.

Once distilled, the liquid is poured into oak casks which, being porous, allow air to enter. Evaporation takes place, removing the harsher constituents of the new spirit and enabling it to mellow. Legally it can't be sold as whisky until it has spent three years in the cask and a good malt will stay casked for at least eight years.

It wasn't until the 1820s that distilling began to develop from small family-run concerns into large manufacturing businesses. What accelerated the change was the invention in 1830 by Aeneas Coffey of a patent still. This was faster and cheaper than traditional methods. More importantly, it did not need the perfect mix of peat and water, but could produce whisky from a mixture of malted and unmalted barley mashed with other cereals.

The real thing: But was the resulting grain whisky real Scotch? Some dismissed it as flavourless surgical spirits; others approved of it as "lighter-bodied". The argument rumbled on until 1905, when one of London's local authorities decided to test in the courts whether pubs could legally sell the patent-still (as opposed to the pot-still) product as "whisky". Even the courts couldn't agree. It was left to a Royal Commission to deliver the verdict that both drinks were equally wholesome and could call themselves whisky.

The Distillers Company, which was to swallow up more than 40 distillers until it too was taken over in 1986 by Guinness, lost no time in capitalising on the Royal Commission's decision. It advertised its patent-still grain whisky as "light, delicate, exquisite — not a headache in a gallon" and pitched its appeal particularly at city dwellers, claiming somewhat dubiously that pot-still whisky was "too strongly flavoured for most people in sedentary occupations".

The industry's future, however, lay in a marriage between malt and grain whiskies. Blending tiny amounts of 30 or 40 malt whiskies with grain whisky, distillers found,

could produce a palatable compromise between taste and strength. What's more, an almost infinite variety of combinations was possible, enabling each brand to claim its own unique taste.

The truth is that most people, in a blind tasting of blends, would be hard-pressed to say whether they were drinking Bell's, Teacher's, Dewar's, Johnnie Walker or J&B. Pure malt whiskies, on the other hand, are more readily identifiable. The experienced Scotch drinker can differentiate between Highland malts, Lowland malts, Campeltown malts and Islay malts, and there is certainly no mistaking the bouquet of a malt such as Laphroaig, which is usually described as tasting of iodine or seaweed.

So which is best? Whole evenings can be whiled away in Scotland debating and researching the question, with no firm conclusions being reached. It all comes down to individual taste. The one point of agreement is that a good malt whisky should not be drunk with a mixer such as soda or lemonade which would destroy the subtle flavour— though ice and water can be added. After dinner, malts are best drunk neat, as a liqueur. Blended whisky, on the other hand, is refreshing in hot weather when mixed with soda.

In sales terms, Glenfiddich leads the market in single malts, exporting 6 million bottles a year to 185 countries. The Scots themselves tend to favour Glenmorangie, which is matured in old Bourbon casks, charred on the inside, for at least 10 years to produce a smooth spirit with hints of peat smoke and vanilla. The most popular malt in the United States is The Macallan, produced on Speyside and matured in 100 percent sherry casks seasoned for two years in Spain with dry oloroso sherry; connoisseurs argue that the 10-year-old is a better drink than the more impressive-sounding 18-year-old.

The brave should sample Glenfarclas, whose legendary 105 proof spirit made the *Guinness Book of Records* for its strength (over 60 percent alcohol). Those desiring a more diluted sample need only take one of the many distillery tours on the Scotch Whisky Trail. Because whisky "breathes" while maturing in its casks, as much as 4 million gallons (20 million litres) evaporate into the air each year. All you have to do is inhale.

PORRIDGE, HAGGIS AND COCK-A-LEEKIE

Scotland, as the writer H.V. Morton once remarked, is the best place in the world to take an appetite; and although, on a permanent basis, the local diet has its hazards—many believe it to be the main cause of the country's internationally appalling level of heart attacks and strokes—the seafood at least can hardly fail to be good for the health. Certainly, lobster, large langoustines and giant Orkney scallops do wonders for the most jaded of appetites.

No doubt Mr. Morton's was coaxed also by the Scottish air, which in the Highlands (and even the Lowlands) remains remarkably pure. Indeed, it has traditionally helped determine the nature of the Scottish kitchen. It is vigorous and sometimes blustery air, calling for the inner warmth and energy produced by porridge (the Scottish equivalent of Italian *polenta*, though grey rather than yellow), by broth and haggis, by baps, butteries, barley bannocks, girdle scones, oatcakes and other examples of local baking; plus whisky and pot after pot of tea.

So at least the story goes—although the rise of Chinese and Indian restaurants and an increasingly international outlook on food have influenced Scottish taste in recent years almost as much as English. Scottish cookery still has its roots in the soil, however, especially in some of those isolated hotels and restaurants far from the main cities. There, real Scottish cuisine is something the proprietors are genuinely proud of serving. Elsewhere, Scotland has its own unedifying brand of fast food. "Scotch eggs", for example, are hard-boiled eggs wrapped in sausage meat and then fried; the result is as appetising as a greasy cannonball.

The fashionable restaurants may differ little from their English counterparts—though steak and game, if not vegetables, do tend to be better north of the River Tweed—but historically the real Scots kitchen is no more like the English than the Portuguese is like the Spanish. That expert in the art of

Scots gastronomy, F. Marian McNeill, has rightly scolded that expert in the art of French gastronomy, André Simon, for referring to Scottish dishes under the heading of "English fare". Many good things come out of England, she admitted, but porridge isn't one of them.

If flour, even in these days of *nouvelle cuisine* and meat still form the basis of English cookery, meal and fish from the basis of Scottish, along with bakery, which

can sometimes be stodgy, heavy and mass-produced but is often really delectable. Until recently in Scotland there were fewer restaurants than tea rooms, where people ate not only lunch and afternoon tea but also "high tea". The latter consisted perhaps of fish and chips and an array of scones and cakes.

Such establishments, sometimes with a piano trio providing gentle music, flourished in Edinburgh and Glasgow until after World War II, and their atmosphere can still be sampled in the elegantly renovated Willow Tea Room in Glasgow's Sauchiehall Street, originally designed by the great Charles Rennie Mackintosh. The tables and

Left, fishermongers in Rothesay, on the Isle of Bute. Right, Scotland's most maligned native dish.

chairs may no longer be the real thing, but they look good and the place still reeks of *art nouveau*, as also do a few Glasgow pubs (such as the Griffin opposite the King's Theatre, in spite of modern attempts to interfere with its *Jugendstil* beauty).

It is also significant that biscuit-making remains an extensive and popular industry in both Edinburgh and Glasgow and as far north as Kirkwall in Orkney (where the oatcakes are arguably the best in the land). Good orange marmalade is another of Scotland's gifts to the world's breakfast and tea tables—though the theory that the name "marmalade" derives from the words *Marie est malade* (referring to the food given to Mary Queen of Scots when she was ill) must be considered far-fetched.

Flavourful fish: Kippers, too, are a treat. The best of them are from Loch Fyne or the Achiltibuie smokery in Ross and Cromarty, where their colour emerges properly golden, not dyed repellent red as they are in so many places. Finnan-haddies (*alias* haddock) are a tasty alternative, boiled in milk and butter. Salmon and trout, sadly, are just as likely to come from some west-coast or northern fish farm as fresh from the river, but the standard remains high. If you're buying from a fishmonger, ask for "wild" salmon, more flavourful than the farmed variety.

The beef of the Aberdeen Angus remains the most famous in the world, though Clive Davidson of the Champany Inn near Linlithgow—which serves, according to the *Good Food Guide*, the best steak in Britain—would challenge its supremacy, naming Scots Blue-Grey ("the ugliest beast you ever saw") as a more than worthy rival, and pope's eye as a better cut than the more fashionable but flabby fillet. Good Scottish meat, he claims, should be hung for at least four weeks or even for eight—unlike supermarket steak, which is not aged at all—and should never be sliced less than one-and-a quarter inch thick.

Venison, pheasant, hare and grouse are also established features of the Scottish kitchen. Admittedly, the romance of eating grouse after it has been ritually shot on or around August 12 should be tempered (if you are honest with yourself) by this bird's quite depressing fibrous toughness, which makes grouse shooting seem, at least to a gourmet, an unutterable waste of time.

As for haggis—though it, too, is hardly a gourmet delight—it does offer a fascinating experience for brave visitors. Scotland's great mystery dish is really only a sheep's stomach stuffed with its minced heart, liver and lights, along with suet, onions and oatmeal. After being boiled, the stomach is sliced open, as spectacularly as possible, and the contents served piping hot. Butchers today often use a plastic bag instead of a stomach; this has the advantage that it is less likely to burst during the boiling process, resulting in the meat being ruined. But no haggis devotee would contemplate such a substitute.

The tastiest haggis, by popular acclaim, comes from Macsween's of Edinburgh, who also make a vegetarian haggis. (That's progress, as the Orkney poet George Mackay Brown would cynically say.) Small portions of haggis are sometimes served as starter courses in fashionable Scottish restaurants, though the authentic way to eat it is as a main course with chappit tatties (potatoes), bashed neeps (mashed turnips) and a number of nips (Scotch whisky, preferably malt). This is especially so on Burns Night (January 25), when supper is ceremonially accompanied by poetry reading, music and Burns's own "Address to the Haggis"; or else on St. Andrew's Night (November 30), when haggis is again attacked with gusto by loyal Scots the world over.

Many of Scotland's national dishes have names as rugged as Scottish speech. No adventurous eater should pass up the chance to sample fare with such names as feather fowlie (a chicken soup), cock-a-leekie (a soup made from chicken and leeks, but authentic only if it also contains prunes), hugga-muggie (Shetland fish haggis, using the fish's stomach), Arbroath smokies (smoked haddock stuffed with butter), crappit heids (haddock heads stuffed with lobster), partan claws (giant crab claws, preferably not torn by fishermen from the living crustacean), stovies (potatoes cooked with onion), carageen mould (a Hebridean dessert), cream crowdie (a mixture of cream, oatmeal, sugar and rum), or hattit kit (an ancient Highland sweet made from buttermilk, milk, cream, sugar and nutmeg).

Though the Scots are said to like far more salt in their soup—and with their fish and vegetables—than the English, they also possess an exceptionally sweet tooth, as some of the above dishes confirm. This is also seen in their penchant for fizzy lemonade and the Glaswegian's favourite thirst-quencher, Irn-Bru, a sparkling concoction said to be "made from girders".

Real cheese, at last fighting back against the marketing boards' anonymous mass production, has been making progress in Scotland. Lanark Blue, hand-made from unpasteurised ewe's milk, has been one recent success, worth looking out for in go-ahead restaurants. Unpasteurised (hard) Teviotdale or (soft) Bonchester from the Border country make a welcome change from tinted Scottish Cheddar; and if you

least on the rail link between London and Edinburgh. Hot savouries have always tended to have mysterious, sometimes misleading, names. Scotch woodcock, for instance, is no more a bird than Welsh rarebit is a rabbit; a woodcock, in this context, is a portion of anchovies coated with scrambled eggs and served (like most savouries) on small fresh slices of toast. At best it rounds off a meal most piquantly, as also do Loch Fyne toasts, where kipper fillets replace the anchovies.

Many hotels and restaurants, encouraged by a "Taste of Scotland" scheme devised by the Scottish Tourist Board, offer their customers supposedly authentic menus, often

fancy something almost as creamy as France's *crème fraîche* there's always Caboc from the Highlands, with its oatmeal coating.

Cheese before pudding, as a running-order reflects Scotland's Auld Alliance with France, as does the amount of fine claret to be found on the wine-lists of good restaurants and hotels and in many homes. But pudding before savoury is also an admirable tradition, for a long time almost defunct but now showing happy signs of revival, not

Bread is increasingly mass-produced but can be delectable.

with flowery descriptions of dishes in self-consciously broad Scots. However good the intentions, these may be no more reliable than some of their English counterparts. Scottish cuisine at its best tends to have a French accent; it is a marriage between fine local ingredients and French flair. This is the hallmark of David Wilson's cooking at the Peat Inn, in Fife—widely hailed as Scotland's best restaurant. The Auld Alliance is something which he and others like him believe in. Not only has it helped to give Scotland a culinary vocabulary—the Scottish "ashet" derives from the French *assiette*—but it still inspires chefs.

263

In spite of its puritanism and thunderings from the kirk against "vain outer show", Scotland is unique among the British provinces in having a distinctive painterly tradition. The art of Protestant northern Europe tends to be tormented and morbid and, given a Calvinist shadow of guilt and sin, one would expect Scottish painting to be gloomily angst-ridden. Instead, as if in defiance of all the kirk represents, it is extroverted, joyful, flamboyant, robust—much more sensuous (if less complex) than English art with its inhibiting deference to the rules of good taste.

It's significant that young Scottish artists have mostly by-passed the Sassenach (English) capital to study abroad, those from Edinburgh in Rome, the Glaswegians a century later in pleasure-loving Paris. Growth of the arts in Scotland is linked to the relative importance of its two major cities, and the rivalry between them (culture versus commerce) has resulted in aesthetic dualism: where Edinburgh's painters are rational and decorous, raw but dynamic Glasgow has produced exuberant rebels.

The Enlightenment: Before the 18th century, Scottish art scarcely existed. There was no patronage from the kirk, which forbade idolatrous images, or from the embattled aristocracy. In a country physically laid waste by the Covenanter wars and mentally stifled by religious fanaticism, painters were despised as menial craftsmen.

The return of peace and prosperity, however, gave rise to a remarkable intellectual flowering, the Edinburgh Enlightenment, which lasted, roughly, from 1720 until 1830 and caused the city to be dubbed the "Athens of the North". The rejection of theology for secular thought was accompanied by a new enthusiasm for the world and its appearance, the brothers Adam evolving a style in architecture and design which was adopted all over Europe and has remained to this day the

Preceding pages, Wilkie's Pitlessie Fair. Left, Raeburn's popular Rev. Robert Walker skating on Duddingston Loch. Right, Ramsay's portrait of David Hume.

classic model of elegance and grace.

A need arose, meanwhile, for portraits to commemorate the city's celebrated sons. Though the earliest portrait painters, Smibert and Aikman, achieved modest recognition as artists not craftsmen, Allan Ramsay, son of a poet and friend of the philosopher, David Hume, expected to be treated as an equal by the intellectual establishment, many of whose members he immortalised with his brush.

Considering the visual austerity of his background—Edinburgh had no galleries, no art school and only a few enlightened collectors—Ramsay's rise to fame is astonishing. Leaving home to study in Italy, he returned to London in 1739 and was an instant success, finally ending up as court painter (in preference to Reynolds) to George III. Despite his classical training, Ramsay cast aside impersonal idealism for "natural portraiture", concentrating on light, space and atmosphere and the meticulous rendering of tactile detail: ribbons, cuffs, the curl of a wig, the bloom on a young girl's cheek. Above all, he was interested in the character of this sitters, combining formal dignity with intimacy and charm. The refined distinction of his best work, such as the portraits of his two wives, has earned him an honourable position in the history not just of Scottish but of British art.

His achievement was rivalled in the next generation by Sir Henry Raeburn, knighted in 1822 by George IV and made King's Limner (*painter*) for Scotland. Raeburn also studied in Italy and his *oeuvre*, like Ramsay's, is confined to portraiture with an emphasis on individual character, the fiddler Neil Gow or a homely matron receiving the same attention as a scholar or fashionable beauty. But his style is broader and more

Equally novel was David Allan's transfer of the pastoral tradition of nymphs and shepherds into scenes from Scottish rural life. He was followed by David Wilkie whose "Pitlessie Fair" (painted at 19) was the start of a career which earned him a knighthood and outstanding popularity, his "low-life" comedies, like "The Penny Wedding", creating a taste for such subjects that persisted throughout the Victorian era.

Though no one equalled Raeburn and Wilkie, there was a new public interest in the arts, which continued to flourish in Edinburgh during the 19th century. Notable in landscape are David Roberts with his views of the Holy Land and, later, William McTag-

painterly, the poses more dramatic: Judge Eldin looking fierce in his study, the Clerks of Penicuik romantically strolling, the Rev. Robert Walker taking a turn on the ice.

Raeburn is the first Scottish painter of national renown to have remained in his native Edinburgh and, in doing so, he established the arts in Scotland and their acceptance by the public. Increased prestige led to ventures in other *genres*, especially landscape. Though Alexander Nasmyth painted an italianate Scotland, gilded and serene, the choice of local vistas rather than a classical idyll in the manner of Claude was startling in its novelty.

gart, "the Scottish Impressionist". The academic mainstream, however, was confined to historical melodrama, sentimental cottagers and grandiose visions of the Highlands as inspired by Walter Scott.

The Glasgow Boys: The 1880s saw a new departure when a group of students, nicknamed the Glasgow Boys, united in protest against Edinburgh's stranglehold on the arts. Due to rapid industrial expansion, Glasgow had grown from a provincial town into "the second city of the empire" and, in contrast to 18th-century Edinburgh, there were galleries, an art school and lavish collectors among the new rich (like William

Burrell) who were anxious to buy status through cultural patronage.

Initially, though, the Glasgow Boys scandalised their fellow citizens. Rejecting the turgid subjects and treacly varnish of the academic "glue-pots", they abandoned their studios to paint in the open air, choosing earthy, peasant themes that lacked "message" or moral and gave offence to the genteel. The public, devoted to gain, godliness and grand pianos (whose legs were prudishly veiled) was both affronted and bemused by Crawhall's lyrical cows, the voluptuous cabbages tended by Guthrie's farm hands, the indecent brilliance of the rhubarb on Macgregor's "Vegetable Stall".

Royal Scottish Academy, while Hornel retreated into orientalism. Today, there is a revival of interest (and investment).

New experiments: Although they became, latterly, as doctrinaire as the hated "glue-pots", the Glasgow Boys had an important influence on younger artists, giving them the courage to experiment through their flamboyant handling of paint and colour. Oppressed by the Calvinism, philistinism and drabness of Scottish life, rebels of the next generation, led by Peploe, Cadell, Hunter and Fergusson, again fled to Paris where they became intoxicated by the decorative art of Matisse and the Fauves (wild beasts). Discarding conventional realism,

Influenced by Whistler and the European Realists, most of the Glasgow Boys left Scotland in disgust to study in Paris—where they were subsequently acclaimed. This success abroad tickled civic pride (what Edinburgh artist could compete?) and the canny burghers, who had once been so hostile, began to pay high prices for their pictures. Sadly, the Glasgow Boys now lost their freshness and became respectable: Lavery a fashionable portrait painter, Guthrie a conservative president of the

**Left, Lorimer's Ordination of the Elders.
Above, MacGregor's Vegetable Stall.**

they flattened form and perspective into a dancing, linear rhythm, with colour an expression of a pagan *joie de vivre*. The Fauves' English imitators were never as uninhibited as the Scots, who sold well both in Paris and London.

As with the Glasgow Boys, fame abroad brought the Scottish Colourists belated success at home. Peploe and Hunter returned to paint a Scotland brightened by gallic sunshine and the witty Cadell to transform Glasgow housewives into flappers of the Jazz Age.

A gloomier fate, though, awaited the architect and designer, Charles Rennie

Mackintosh, who is by far the most important figure of this period and, as an originator of *art nouveau*, has an international standing. Glasgow School of Art, his architectural masterpiece, is one of the city's most remarkable buildings and the Glasgow Style he initiated in furniture and the decorative arts is now admired the world over. Yet in his day "Toshie" was dismissed as a drunken eccentric and was such a failure professionally that he abandoned architecture and a public which had mocked him to paint watercolours in France. These watercolours, nonetheless, have a refinement of sensibility that is rare in Scottish art: hauntingly poetic, mysterious and exquisite.

Modern times: From the 1930s onwards, Scottish painters have performed creditably though landscape (the Scots have an unbounded pride in their lochs and glens) has tended to predominate. In a country where intellectual achievement allied to public service is so highly esteemed, it's curious that the arts in Scotland have mostly been devoted to the expression of simple emotion and visual pleasure, avoiding politics, social comment or even a cerebral interest in stylistic experiment. In the 1950s, Colquhoun and MacBryde adopted Cubism not for formal reasons but as a means of conveying romantic melancholia.

Since World War II, while modern trends have been pursued with characteristic vigour, there's been a loss of optimism and sparkle. More poignant than the Modernists is Joan Eardley, who turned her back on artistic fashion to paint urchins in the Glasgow back streets, then, after settling in a remote fishing village, sombrely elemental landscapes.

John Bellany, the son of a fisherman, is unusual in that he has the tormented vision one might expect, but rarely finds, among artists brought up under Calvinism. Overwhelmed, after a visit to Buchenwald, by human wickedness, he gave up modish abstracts to return to figurative art of a tragic, often nightmarish monumentality. Bellany's work has made a profound impact in Germany and northern (Protestant) Europe.

Another post-war change is that German Expressionism, with its energy and gloom, has replaced the hedonistic influence of the French, especially in recent times when Glasgow School of Art has produced a new group of rebels. Known (unofficially) as the Glasgow Wild Boys, they have also rejected Modernism for gigantic narrative pictures with literary, political or symbolist undertones. The most successful, Adrian Wiszniewski and Stephen Campbell, have been rapturously received in New York. Wiszniewski, a Pole born in Scotland, has adapted Slavic folk art to express nostalgia for the past, disenchantment with the present. Campbell, combining macho brutalism with whimsy, draws his inspiration from P.G. Wodehouse and Bram Stoker. Their great *tableaux*, however, lack Bellany's morbid passion; although affecting social "concern" and apparently doom-laden, the most striking quality of these young painters is their anarchic ebullience.

Campbell's move to New York is symptomatic of an inevitable drift from the provinces to the cosmopolitan centres of the art world. In spite of this, painting in Scotland retains an almost aggressive vitality. Self-confidence is also boosted by superb municipal collections, notably the Burrell, which has replaced Edinburgh Castle (scoring for Glasgow) as Scotland's principal tourist attraction.

Left, Guthrie's "A Hind's Daughter". Right, "Eardley's Street Kids".

The days when Billy Connolly, the Glasgow comedian, could dismiss Scottish folk music as four Aran sweaters singing "the Wild Rover" are, thankfully, over. It's not just that the performers have ditched their woolly jerseys in favour of tee-shirts and jeans; the sound of Scottish music has changed dramatically in the past 20 years.

Nothing has been more dramatic than the forging of an alliance between two previously alien schools. On the one hand: the inheritors of the bagpipe tradition, regarded until then as a musical law unto themselves, reared on raw, warrior iron, nurtured on centuries of exclusivity. On the other: the freebooting young adventurers of the folk-music revival, ready to play and sing anything that had its roots embedded somewhere in Celtic culture.

The pipers who joined the folk groups were regarded as renegades by the piping fraternity—all those years of training in the supreme art going to waste! But for the folk musicians, the bagpipe provided much-needed instrumental beef in an increasingly noisy market-place.

Whether the piping Establishment have benefitted is debatable. They are a gritty, stubborn lot, much given to internecine warfare over the etiquette and mystique of piping disciplines which have been handed down lovingly, like family heirlooms, through the generations. Discipline still rules OK at the big sponsored competitions, where pipers from all over the world challenge each other at what in the Gaelic is called *piobaireachd* (pibroch).

Just to confuse the uninitiated, *piobaireachd* has another title, *ceol mor* (Great Music). This is a truly classical music, built to complex, grandiloquent proportions and actually playable only after years of study and practice. Those who *can* play it do so by memory, in the manner of the great Indian raga players. The pipe music that most of us are familiar with—stretching from "Mull of Kintyre" to reels, marches,

jigs and strathspeys—is referred to by the classicists as *ceol beag* (Small Music).

Great or Small, much of it has survived thanks to patronage rather than household popularity. The earliest royal families in Scotland are credited with having a piper, or several, on their books, and no upwardly mobile landlord of ancient times could afford to be without his piper. But it was in the warring Highland clan system that the pipes flourished, both on the domestic scene and

the battle ground. The blood-tingling quality of the Great Highland Bagpipe, with its three resonant drones, was quickly recognised by the early Scottish regiments, and the military connection remains to this day. Even now, the Scots still use the pipes to soften up the English at soccer and rugby internationals. Sometimes it seems to work.

With the pipes pouring forth on every big public occasion, there's no serious dispute about their role as bearers of the country's national music. But piping can offer nothing to compare with the phenomenal resurgence of Scots fiddle music, which had thrived only in geographical pockets until the folk-

Left, international pipers at a Highland Games. Right, a ceilidh in full swing.

music revival got its full head of steam in the 1960s. Today, it's reckoned that there are more fiddlers in Scotland than ever before.

The fiddle has been part of Scottish music for more than 500 years—King James IV had "fithelaris" on his payroll in the 15th century. As a vehicle for dance music it left the pipes standing. The fiddle reached its Golden Age in the 18th century, when Scots musicians sailed to Italy to study and brought back not only the tricks of the classical trade but, perhaps more significantly, a steady supply of exquisite violins, which were soon copied by enterprising local craftsmen.

At the same time, the dancing craze had

Scott Skinner, born in 1843. Classically trained, and technically virtuosic, the "King of the Strathspey" won international acclaim, and the arrival of recording in the later part of his career helped to spread the message—even as far as fiddle-packed Shetland, which had until then resolutely stuck to its own Norse-tinged style. (From Shetland comes the fiddling giant of the present day, Aly Bain—a sort of contemporary Niel Gow and Scott Skinner rolled into one.)

Another traditional instrument that has become increasingly popular is the *clarsach*, or Scots harp, which had fallen into virtual extinction until it was revived in the early 1970s by Alison Kinnaird and other

begun. Country fiddlers found their robust jigs and reels much in demand at posh balls and parties, and the first major collections of Scots fiddle tunes were published, making the music widely accessible. The Golden Age produced its golden boy—Niel Gow, a prolific composer and, by every account, an extraordinarily gifted player.

By the early 19th century, though, high society, as fickle as ever, had turned its fancy to the new polkas and waltzes that were flooding in from Europe. The rural fiddlers played on regardless, and it was the Aberdeenshire village of Banchory that produced the most famous Scots fiddler of all—James

young enthusiasts. Now, the *clarsach*, too, finds a place in the folk bands and there is a thriving Clarsach Society.

If the fiddle and the *clarsach* have fought their way back into the mainstream of Scottish culture, they were both a long way behind folksong in doing so. The classic narrative ballads and pawky bothy ballads had survived largely in the hands of farmworkers and the travelling folk (the tinkers) of Perthshire and the northeast. The advent

Sword dance performed at the Royal Scottish Country Dance Society's Edinburgh headquarters.

of the tape recorder enabled collectors like Hamish Henderson to bring their songs to the ears of the young urban folk revivalists. It was Henderson who discovered Jeannie Robertson, a magnificent traditional singer, living in obscurity in Aberdeen. She was the Bessie Smith of Scottish folksong, and her influence soon showed itself in the folk clubs that sprang up all over Scotland.

The folk clubs served, too, as spawning grounds for new songwriting, especially of the polemical brand, producing some of the best songs since Robert Burns. Burns is credited with more than 300 songs, many of them set to traditional fiddle tunes, and you can still hear them in all sorts of venues.

Many of the early folk clubs are still in existence—notably those in Edinburgh, Aberdeen, Kirkcaldy, Stirling and St. Andrews. The visitor should inquire about folk clubs in the vicinity. Sadly, the type of *ceilidh* that is laid on for tourists tends to be neither traditional nor contemporary but caught in a time-warp of kilt, haggis and musical mediocrity. In the Gaelic, *ceilidh* means a gathering. The Gaelic-speaking community, now mostly confined to the west Highlands and islands, holds its great annual gathering, the National Mod, in different parts of Scotland every year. There, you can sample some of the most beautiful singing you could hope to hear as young and old compete for much-coveted prizes.

Even the folk scene finds competitions stimulating. Since the 1960s there has been a steady growth in the number of folk festivals. From Easter until autumn, there's hardly a weekend when there isn't a folk festival somewhere in Scotland. In cities like Edinburgh and Glasgow, the festivals are among the biggest of their kind in the world; Edinburgh's lasts for 10 days. But there's nothing to beat the smaller traditional folk festivals in rural areas, where the atmosphere is friendlier and the talent tends to be local rather than imported. Among the best events are those at Keith (June), Auchtermuchty (August) and Kirriemuir (September). Shetland (April) and Orkney (May) are also famous for their annual celebrations of traditional music.

Every folk festival has its unofficial "fringe": invariably located in the bars serving the best whisky in town. Many a pub session can excel the finest organised *ceilidh*

or competition. Away from the festivals, Scottish pub sessions can be disappointing affairs. It's perhaps a hangover from the days when music was banned in licensed premises.

As for dancing, well, you are unlikely to find it in the pub for reasons of space, if nothing else. The cunning Irish centuries ago devised a way of dancing in tight cottage corners: they keep their arms rigid at the sides of the body. For the Scots, dancing is reserved for the village hall or the ballroom. Many of the traditional dances, including the famous Highland Fling, call for the raising of the arms to depict the antlers of the red deer—splendidly symbolic but treacherous at close quarters. Popular formations like the Eightsome Reel and the Dashing White Sergeant also involve much hectic birling among large groups.

Like the accordion-pumped music which fires these breath-sucking scenes, Scottish dancing has its more rarified moments. There are country dance societies in various districts, and when the members get together they dance with the kind of practised precision that must have been essential at the earliest Caledonian Balls.

It's good fun to go along to a village hop—usually advertised as a *ceilidh* or ceilidh-dance—and trip the heavy fantastic. You don't have to know the steps: the locals will hurl you in the right directions and there will be time for a soothing beer as the band move from "The Mason's Apron" to their idiosyncratic version of the latest Madonna record.

As it happens, Scottish rock has begun to sit up and notice its Celtic heritage. The pre-eminent folk-rock band are Run Rig, all-electronic but hitched musically to ancient Gaelic themes. In songwriting, too, folk music has made its mark in the rock venues. The leading singing songwriters—men like Eric Bogle, Rab Noakes and the brilliant Dick Gaughan—have found eager new audiences there, and their influence can be heard in the punkish protest music of groups like the Proclaimers.

Folk music in Scotland has its own poppy hybrids. Beware of the Fiddle Rally—up to 100 deeply unhappy fiddlers, aged from 14 to 94, sawing away at "Largo's Fairy Dance" in wooden unison. And watch out for Billy Connolly's four Aran sweaters: they're not *entirely* extinct.

GAMES HIGHLANDERS PLAY

Highland Gatherings, sometimes described as "Oatmeal Olympics", are much more than three-ring circuses. As the Gathering gets going a trio of dancers are on one raised platform; a solitary piper is on another; a 40-man pipe band has the attention, if not of all eyes, at least of all ears; the "heavies" are tossing some unlikely object about; two men are engaged in some strange form of wrestling; a tug-o'-war is being audibly contested and an 880-yard (800-metres) race is in progress.

Track events are the least important part of these summer games. The venue has been chosen for its scenic beauty rather than a "Tartan" track. At the Skye Games, milers literally become dizzy as they run round and round the track's meagre 130 yards (117 metres).

Everywhere the sound of pipes can be heard. It is not only the piper playing for the dancers; another solitary piper playing a mournful dirge in the individual piper's competition; or the 40-strong pipe band being judged in the arena. Around the arena, behind marquees, under trees, in any place which offers some slight protection to muffle the sound, those still to compete are busy rehearsing under the sharp ear of their leaders and coaches. It is amazing how the coach can stand in the centre of a circle of wailing pipes and immediately walk over to one set, incline his head towards them and tell their owner he is half-a-tone flat.

The solo pipers are undoubtedly the aristocrats of the Games and the highest honour—and the biggest prize—is awarded the pibroch winner. There are three competitions for solo pipers: pibrochs (classical melodies composed in honour of birthdays, weddings and the like); marches (military music); and strathspeys and reels (dance music). While playing a pibroch the piper marches slowly to and fro, not so much in time to the music, but in sympathy with the melody. On the other hand, when playing

Preceding pages, making music, Shetland style. Left, hammer throwing at a Highland meeting. Right, tossing the caber.

dance music, he remains in one position tapping his foot; and, understandably, when playing a march—for who can resist the skirl of the pipes?—he strides up and down the platform.

Most dancers at Games are female, although, occasionally, a thorn appears among the roses. Seldom are any girls older than 18 and competitions are even held for three- and four-year-olds.

King Malcolm Canmore is credited with

being responsible for one of the more famous dances seen at the Games. In 1054 he slew one of King Macbeth's chieftains and, crossing his own sword and that of the vanquished chieftain, performed a *Gille Calum* (sword dance) before going into battle. The touching of either sword with the feet was considered an unfavourable omen.

The origin of the Highland fling is also curious. A grandfather was playing the pipes on the moors and having his young grandson dance to them. Two courting stags were clearly silhouetted against the horizon. The grandfather said to the lad: "Can ye nae raise yer hands like the horns of yon stags?" And so originated the Highland Fling. The dance is performed without travelling (that is to say, on one spot) and the reason is that the Scot, like the stag, does not run after his women: he expects them to come to him. A more mundane explanation for the dance being performed on one spot is that it was originally danced on a shield.

In the dance called *Sean Truibhas*—the Gaelic for old trews (*trousers*)—the performer's distaste for his garb is expressed. This dance originated after Culloden when the wearing of the kilt was proscribed.

One of the original aims of the Games was to select the ablest bodyguards for the king

cms). Then there is the tossing of the 56-lb (25-kg) weight. In this event it is not distance but height that counts. The competitor stands below and immediately in front of a bar and with his back to it. Then, holding the weight in one hand he swings it between his legs and throws it up and, hopefully, over the bar. Tosses of more than 15 ft (4.5 meters) are not uncommon.

Caber tossing: The most unusual and spectacular event is tossing the caber, a straight, tapered pine-tree trunk shorn of its branches. It weighs about 125 lbs (57 kg) and is about 19 ft (six metres) long. The diameter at one end is about nine inches (23 cms) and at the other about five inches (13

or chieftain, and this is perpetuated in today's heavy events. The objects used in these have evolved from what would be found in any rural community such as a blacksmith's hammer or even a stone in the riverbed.

Hurling the hammer and putting the shot are similar, yet different, to these events as practised at the Olympics. At the "Oatmeal Olympics" the hammer has a wooden shaft rather than a chain and the weight of the shot varies. The 56-lb (25-kg) weight is thrown by holding, with one hand, a short chain attached to the weight; the length of weight and chain must not exceed 18 inches (45

cms). Two men struggle to carry the caber to a squatting competitor. They place it vertically with the narrower end in his cupped hands. The competitor gingerly rises and, with the foot of the caber resting against, and eight-ninths towering above, his shoulder, starts to run. This resembles the performance of an inebriate rather than an athlete. Finally, at an auspicious moment, the competitor stops dead, lets out an almighty roar, and thrusts his hands upwards. The wide end of the caber hits the ground; now is the moment of truth: will the quivering pole fall backwards towards the competitor or will it attain the perpendicular and then turn over completely and fall away from him?

But why does an empty-handed, puffing judge trot alongside the competitor? Tossing the caber is judged not on distance but on style. An imaginary clockface is involved, and the athlete is presumed to be standing at the figure 6 when he makes his throw. A perfect throw lands at 12; a somewhat less perfect one at 11 or at 1 and so on. Naturally, the athlete will attempt, after throwing, to swivel his feet so that his throw appears perfect. Thus the puffing judge.

Caber tossing is believed to have evolved from throwing tree trunks into the river after they have been felled. They would then float to the sawmill. It was important to throw the

How did the Games evolve? Some claim that they were first held in 1314 at Ceres in Fife when the Scottish bowmen returned victorious from Bannockburn. Others believe that it all began even earlier when King Malcolm organised a race up a mountain called Craig Choinich. The winner would receive a *baldric* (warrior's belt) and become Malcolm's foot-messenger.

A race up and down Craig Choinich is still a feature of the Braemar Games which is the highlight of the circuit. However, this isn't so much because of the calibre of the competition but because, since the time of Queen Victoria who revived the Games, they are invariably attended by the Royal Family.

trunks into the middle of the river or they would snag on the banks.

Colour codes: Colour is the keynote of the Games. All dancers and musicians are dressed in full Highland regalia, as are many of the judges and some spectators. Competitors in the heavy events all wear the kilt. The reds of the Stuarts, the greens of the Gordons and the blues of the Andersons all mingle with the green of the grass and the purple of the heather to produce a muted palette.

Two views of the Braemar Games: the judges deliberate; and the Royal Family, led by the Queen, inspect their subjects.

Highland Games are very much in vogue and new venues are constantly announced. Currently, more than 100 Gatherings are held during the season which extends from May until mid-September. In spite of the spectacular appeal of the great Gatherings (Braemar, Cowal, Oban), the visitor might find that the smaller meetings (Ceres, Uist in the Hebrides) are more enjoyable. These have an authentic ambience and competitors in the heavy events are certain to be good and true Scots and not professional intruders from foreign parts.

What's more, you may not even have to pay admission!

A FONDNESS FOR FESTIVALS

Those who imagine the Scots to be Calvinistic churls may be surprised to learn that the Scottish calendar is chock-a-block with local festivals. These are basically for the natives and are not mounted in order to attract the tourist. Indeed, at some, the tourist is scarcely welcome because his presence means that the service industries have to attend to his needs which doesn't leave them time to enjoy *their* festival.

Until the middle of this century Puritanical Scotland ignored Papish Christmas: offices, shops and factories all functioned as usual on December 25. *The* great event on the Scottish calendar was the night of December 31 (Hogmanay) and New Year's Day. Traditionally, as the bells struck midnight, the crowds gathered around the focal points of towns would join hands and sing "Auld Lang Syne" and then whisky bottles would be passed around before all dispersed to go first-footing.

It is important that the first-foot (that is, the first person to cross a threshold in the new year) should be a dark-haired person who brings gifts of coal and salt which ensure that the house won't want for fire or food in the coming year. Also, the first-foot will normally carry a bottle of whisky.

Hot stuff: Fiery New Year processions which will drive out and ward off evil spirits have been held for centuries at Comrie, Burghead and Stonehaven. At the Comrie Flambeaux procession, locals walk through the town carrying burning torches; at Stonehaven, participants swing fireballs attached to a long wire and handle. Some suggest that the swinging of fireballs is a mimetic attempt to lure back the sun from the heavens during the dark winter months.

The Burning of the Clavie at Burghead is held on the evening of January 11. (This is when Hogmanay falls according to the old-style calendar which was abandoned in 1752 but which still holds sway when deciding the date of many celebrations.) The ceremony

begins with the Clavie King lighting a tar-filled barrel which is then carried in procession through the town and from which firebrands are distributed. Finally, the Clavie is placed on the summit of Doorie Hill and allowed to burn for a time before being rolled down the hill. Fragments of the Clavie are treasured because they offer protection from the evil eye.

By far the greatest and most spectacular fire ceremony is held at Lerwick in Shetland

on the last Tuesday in January. Casual visitors are not welcome at Up-Helly-Aa, at which the Shetlanders remember their Norse heritage: invitations are required. Up-Helly-Aa begins with the posting of "The Bill", a 10 ft (three-metre) high Proclamation at the Market Cross and the displaying of a 30-ft (nine-metre) long model longship at the seafront.

Come evening, and with the Guizer Jarl magnificently dressed in Viking costume at the steering oar, the longship is dragged to the burning site. Team after team of guizers, each clad in glorious or grotesque garb and all carrying blazing torches, follow the ship.

Left, dressed up for the Galashiels Common Riding. Right, the climax of Lerwick's Up-Helly-Aa Viking festival.

When the burning site is reached the "Galley Song" is sung; the Guizer Jarl leaves the longship; a bugle sounds; and hundreds of blazing torchs are hurled upon and consume the hull while the song changes to "The Norseman's Home". Celebrations continue all through the night.

At nearby Kirkwall, capital of Orkney, those who survived the Hogmanay celebrations gather on New Year's Day at the Mercat Cross for the "Ba' Game". Sides are taken: the Uppies who were born south of the Cathedral and the Doonies, born north of the Cathedral. The two teams attempt to carry a leather ball, about the size of a tennis ball, against all opposition, to their own end of the

scale, on Christmas day. A similar "Ba' Game" is held at Jedburgh in the Borders early in February.

Evil spirits: A different kind of game can be seen at Lanark on March 1. Then, the church bells peal out and the children of Lanark, armed with home-made weapons of paper balls on strings, race three times around the church, beating each other over the head as they go. After the race, town officials throw handfuls of copper coins for which the children scramble. Whuppity Scoorie is claimed by some to be a ridding of the town of evil spirits by scourging the precincts of the church. A somewhat more mundane explanation is that the festival represents the chas-

town. The waters of the harbour constitute the Doonies' goal and the crossroads at the opposite end is the Uppies' goal.

A giant scrum forms and the teams shove and shove, with the scrum becoming so torrid that steam rises from its centre. Infringements? What are *they*? Mayhem reigns and the "Ba' Game" leaves Australian Rules looking like a Sunday afternoon picnic. A good game lasts for several hours. If the harbour goal is reached it is obligatory to throw the ball into the water and several players—irrespective of their allegiance—dive in after it and finally sober up. The game is also held, although on a more modest

ing away of winter and the welcoming of spring.

About six weeks later, older children—students at St. Andrews University—take part in the traditional Kate Kennedy pageant in which they play the parts of distinguished figures associated with the university or the town. Lady Kate, a niece of the founder of the university, was a great beauty to whom the students are said to have sworn everlasting allegiance. Women are banned from the procession and the part of Kate is always played by a first-year male student.

The Galashiels Braw Lads gallop out.

During the summer months, traditional fairs are held throughout the country. Until quite recently, farm employees who wished to change their jobs would seek out new employers at the Feeing Markets which were held at the end of each term. (The farming year was divided into three contractual terms.) These markets would also attract small stall-holders eager to part the labourer from his term's wages. Each June, such a market, enlivened with Highland dancing, country music and other entertainments is still held at Stonehaven.

Later in the month, a similar fair is held at nearby Garmouth. However, the excuse for the Maggie Fair is that it commemorates the landing of the "merry monarch", Charles II, at nearby Kingston, after he had been proclaimed King of Scotland following the execution of his father King Charles I.

August 1 is Lammas Day, or Lunasdal—the feast of the Sun God, Lugh—and was formerly an extremely popular day for local fairs. Such fairs are still held in August, although not on the first, at St. Andrews and at neighbouring Inverkeithing.

Also at this time a bizarre ritual occurs on the day before the South Queensferry Ferry Fair. A man, clad head to toe in white flannel, is covered with an infinite number of burrs until he becomes a moving bush. Bedecked with flowers and carrying two staves, this strange creature makes his way from house to house receiving gifts. One theory for this strange practice equates the Burryman with the scapegoat of antiquity.

Fleet of foot: In late August attention switches to the west coast where the ancient burgh of Irvine holds its Marymass Fair which dates from the 12th century. Horse races, which are very much a part of this fair, are said to be even older. These races are not only for ponies but also for Clydesdale carthorses which, in spite of their enormous size (they weigh about one tonne) are remarkably fleet of foot. The fair's fame is derived from the eponymous parish church yet an association with Mary Queen of Scots has arisen and the principal in the pageant is invariably dressed as Mary Stuart. The celebrations continue for a week.

Throughout the summer months the clippity clop of horses' hoofs is heard on the cobblestones of Border towns. The Riding of the Marches, first introduced in the Middle Ages, is the custom of checking the boundaries of common lands owned by the town. In some cases, the Riding also commemorates important local historical events which invariably involved warfare between the English and the Scots in the Middle Ages. The festivities often last for several days and are always stiff with protocol.

The highlight at all these festivals is the main Ride-Out—there may also be several minor Ride-Outs—which begins with a grand parade with brass and pipe bands and which usually ends with a similar parade. The Ride-Out is always led by a cornet bearing a banner and one of the great events is the Bussing of the Colours which is held, amidst much revelry, on the "Nicht Afore the Morn". This ceremony is seen at its best at Hawick, where the Cornet's Lass and her maids of honour, all clad in long gowns and picture hats, tie ribbons to the flag and exhort the cornet to carry it worthily.

The Selkirk Gathering, held in June, is the oldest, the largest and the most emotional of the Ridings. It concludes with the Casting of the Colours which commemorates Scotland's humiliating defeat at the Battle of Flodden from which only one Selkirk warrior returned. At the "casting", flags are waved in proscribed patterns while the band plays a soulful melody.

Each town—including Annan, Dumfries, Duns, Galashiels, Jedburgh, Lanark (scarcely a Border town), Langholm and Lauder—has its own variations of the ceremonies; and all have other activities which include balls, concerts, pageants and sporting events. At Peebles the Riding incorporates the Beltane Fair which is the great Celtic festival of the sun and which marks the beginning of summer.

Aberdeen also has its Riding of the Marches but "horses" of a different kind are involved in a mid-August festival on the island of South Ronaldsay in Orkney. The "horses" are young boys or girls dressed in spectacular costumes. Pulling beautifully wrought miniature ploughs, often family heirlooms, and guided by boy ploughmen, these "horses" turn furrows on a sandy beach. Prizes are awarded for the best turned-out "horses" and for the straightest and most even furrows.

And so, inexorably, the festive year rushes headlong towards another Hogmanay.

THE LURE OF THE GREEN TURF

Visit the 19th hole at any of Scotland's 400 golf courses and you're almost certain to hear a heated argument, over a dram or two of whisky, as to where the game of golf originated. The discussion doesn't involve geography but rather topography: the "where" refers to *which* part of Scotland. All know that, in spite of the Dutch boasting of a few old paintings which depict the game, it all began in Scotland hundreds of years ago when a shepherd swinging with his stick at round stones hit one into a rabbit hole. Little did that rustic know the madness he was about to unleash when he murmured to his flock: "I wonder if I can do that again?"

Few courses in the world have the characteristics of the quintessential Scottish course. Such a course, which borders the seashore, is called a links. It is on the links of Muirfield, St. Andrews, Carnoustie, Troon and Turnberry that the British Open—or "the Open"—is usually played.

The word links refers to that stretch of land which connects the beach with more stable inshore land, and a links course is a sandy, undulating terrain which borders the shore. One feature of such a course is its ridges and furrows which result in the ball nestling in an infinite variety of lies. Another feature is the wind which blows off the sea and which can suddenly whip up with enormous ferocity. A hole which, in the morning, was played with a driver and a 9-iron can, after lunch, demand a driver, a long 3-wood and a 6-iron.

Giant greens: Most golfers will immediately head for St. Andrews. Here, they will be surprised to find that the Old Course has two, rather than the customary four, short holes and that it has only 11 greens. Yet it is categorically an 18-hole course: seven greens are shared. This explains the enormous size of the greens, on which you can find yourself facing a putt of almost 100 yards (90 metres). Remember it is the homeward-bound player who has the right of way on these giant double greens.

At St. Andrews the Old Course is flanked

St. Andrews: a magnet for golfers from all over the world.

by the New on the seaward and by the Eden on the inland side. Tucked between the New and the white-caps of the North Sea is the shorter Jubilee course. Don't be too distressed if you fail to obtain a starting time on the Old: the New is even more difficult.

Ancient as is the Royal and Ancient Golf Club of St. Andrews it must bow the knee to the Honorable Company of Edinburgh Golfers which was formed in 1774 and which is generally accepted as the oldest golf club in the world. Their present Muirfield course which is at Gullane (pronounced *Gillun*), 13 miles (21 kms) east of Edinburgh, is considered by most of the world's top players to be the ultimate test of golf.

The rough here is ferocious and if, on looking around, you fail to see your partner, don't panic and think he has been abducted by the "wee folk". He will merely be out of sight in one of the nearly 200 pot-bunkers which litter the course.

Don't be too concerned if you can't obtain a starting time at Muirfield— indeed, possibly you should be thankful—for the tiny village of Gullane is also the home of the three challenging Gullane courses (simply called 1, 2 and 3) and to Luffness New. The latter is "New" because, for Scotland, it is just *that*, having been founded only in 1894.

Capital course: Back in the city of Edinburgh are more than a score of courses, two of which are home to very ancient clubs. The Royal Burgess Golfing Society claims to be even older than the Hon. Coy., while the neighbouring Bruntsfield Links Golfing Society is only a few years younger.

On the road from Gullane to Edinburgh you pass through Musselburgh where golf is known to have been played in 1672 and, most probably, even before that. Was this where Mary Queen of Scots was seen playing a few days after the murder of Lord Darnley, her second husband? Was Mary the world's first golf widow?

Glasgow, never outdone by Edinburgh, has nearly 30 courses. Outstanding among these are Killermont and Haggs Castle. The latter is less than three miles (five kms) from the city centre. While golfers thrill over birdies and eagles at Haggs their non-playing partners can enthuse over the renowned Burrell Collection which is less than half-a-mile (one km) away. Even closer to the Burrell is the excellent Pollok course.

Troon, 30 miles (48 kms) south of Glasgow and frequently the scene of the Open, is the kingpin in a series of nearly 30 courses bordering the Atlantic rollers. Here, without hardly ever stooping to pick up your ball, you can play for almost 30 miles. Troon itself has three courses. Then, to the north is Barassie with one and then Gailes with two courses. South of Troon are three courses at Prestwick—scene of the first Open in 1860—and Ayr, also with three courses. Fifteen minutes further down the "course" are the Arran and Ailsa links of Turnberry.

Golf widows will be delighted that Turnberry is a splendid spot from which to visit the Burns Country and Culzean Castle (pronounced *Cullane*), a gift from the people of Scotland to General Dwight D. Eisenhower, a former frequenter of the Turnberry links.

Over on the east coast is another remarkable conglomerate of courses with St. Andrews as its kingpin. About 30 miles to the north, across the Tay Bridge, are the three Carnoustie courses. The Medal course here, formerly scene of many Opens, has been called brutal, evil and monstrous. Then, 20 miles (32 kms) south of St. Andrews and strung, like a priceless necklace, along the north shore of the Firth of Forth, are the Elie, Leven, Lundin Links and Crail courses, of which the last named is claimed by golfstorians to be the seventh oldest in the world.

Other glittering gems are found in the northeast. Here are Balgownie and Murcar, two of Aberdeen's half-a-dozen courses, nearby Cruden Bay, Nairn which is close to Inverness, and Dornoch which stands in splendid isolation in the extreme northeast. The Balgownie and Cruden Bay clubs are both 200 years old and founders of the latter are probably turning in their graves at the new name of their club—the Cruden Bay Golf and Country Club.

Dornoch is, even for a Scottish course, under-played and is probably the most under-rated course in all Britain. Authorities believe that this course, all of whose holes have a view of the sea, would be on the Open rota if it was closer to the main centres of population. Incidentally, the last witch to be hanged in Britain suffered at Dornoch. Before the final deed was enacted she was ducked in a pond on the Dornoch short course at a hole which, not unexpectedly, bears the name "The Witch".

Down at the extreme southwest of the country is Machrianish, another underrated, under-played links which is far from the madding crowd. Here the turf is so naturally perfect that "every ball is teed, wherever it is". And, if the views from here, which include Ireland and the Inner Hebrides, seduce you then you might wish to make your way over the seas to Islay, which is renowned for both its whisky and its Machrie course.

Scotland, home of golf, also boasts some superb inland courses. Many *aficionados* consider the King's at Gleneagles to be the best inland course in all Britain. Certainly, nowhere in the world can there be a champi-

onship course set in such dramatically beautiful scenery. And the King's is but one of four courses which make up the Gleneagles complex. If these four aren't enough, a mere 30 miles to the north is Blairgowrie with its fabled Rosemount course. Here, among parasol pines, larches, silver birch and evergreens, you will come upon lost golf balls, partridges, pheasant and otter. The lake by the 16th tee is called the Black Loch and the pike in it are so large that they are reputed to kill the swans.

Golf can sometimes be a surprisingly dangerous game.

Soothing rain: Summer days in Scotland are long, and the eager beaver can tee off at 7 a.m. and play until 10 p.m.—easily enough time for 54 holes unless you're prone to slice, hook or pull. The rough of gorse, broom, heather and whin is insatiable, and a great deal of time can be lost searching for balls. If you attempt 54 holes in a day, have no fear of tiring, for the turf on Scottish courses is very springy and a joy to walk upon and seldom, even on a summer's day, does the temperature reach the seventies. However, be prepared for light rain, even in summer. The locals call it *brash* (a dialect word for light, soothing, pleasant rain) and you will soon find that you simply ignore it.

At many courses caddy cars are available. Caddies, on the other hand, are about as difficult to find as a haggis on the moors. If you can lay your hands on one of them (caddies, not haggis—you buy the latter in tins), you are in for a treat. The word, incidentally, comes from the French *cadet*, meaning a "young boy," and was used, especially in Edinburgh, to describe anyone who ran errands.

Club formalities: At the majority of courses no formal introduction is necessary: as a visitor, you just stroll up, pay your money, and play. Indeed, at some of the more remote country courses you merely deposit your money in the honour-box. Some clubs do ask that you be a member of another club. Others (certainly less than one in three) require an introduction by a member, although if you are an overseas visitor this formality is usually waived.

Note, however, that restrictions tighten up at weekends. And, joy of joys, at those courses to whose names you have thrilled—Turn-berry, Carnoustie, St. Andrews—no introduction is needed. This doesn't mean you will gain entry to the clubhouse—for it, rather than the fairways and greens, is the holy of holies at a Scottish course. The reason: the clubhouse is the private domain of a particular club whose members happen to make use of the adjacent course.

A round of golf can be enjoyed for under £2, although green fees on most courses are about £6. At the big-name courses, allow £15—or even more. Day tickets, permitting unlimited play, usually cost only about 50 percent more and, in some instances, are the same price as tickets for a single round.

HUNTING, SHOOTING AND FISHING

It seems to be one of nature's iron laws that valuable assets fall into the hands of the already rich. Valuable *natural* assets are no exception. While Scotland, therefore, may have been blessed with more natural assets—red deer, salmon, grouse and sea trout—than most small European countries, they are owned by a handful of ultra-rich estate owners, many of whom live a long way from Scotland. This means that "field sports" such as deer stalking, salmon fishing and grouse shooting are touchy political issues, bound up with memories of the Highland Clearances and the ownership and use of the land.

While many (probably most) Scots accept that sporting estates are now essential to the economies of remote Highland areas, they are inclined to resent the fact that they are owned and exploited by local aristocrats, southern financiers or oil-rich Arabs. And there's growing unease about the hard-nosed line being taken by the newer proprietors, some of whom are trying to recoup their investment as fast as they can, often at the expense of local interests.

For example, when the North of Scotland Hydroelectricity Board (always known as "The Hydro") sold its fishing rights on the River Conon north of Inverness to City of London financier Peter Whitfield for a reputed £1.5 million, the deal had the effect of clearing the locals off the river: Whitfield immediately divided his fishing into beats which he sold on a weekly timeshare basis at prices up to £15,000 a person per week. He found a ready market among rich southerners and Europeans, but none of the locals could afford that kind of money. "That river used to be part of the local community," says one irate local angler. "Our people have fished it for generations. Now we've been elbowed off to make way for strangers."

The bitterness voiced over the salmon fishing on the River Conon is echoed all over the Highlands. At the same time the Scottish

Preceding pages, fishing holiday. Left, trophies from hunts in Brodick Castle, Arran. Right, a Highlands gamekeeper.

Tourist Board and the Scottish Office relish the idea of wealthy sportsmen from England, Europe and the USA spreading their cash in the hard-pressed economies of the uplands. But more and more sporting landlords (especially the newer ones) are alienating the Scottish public by trying to keep walkers, mountaineers and ramblers off their vast estates by littering the countryside with "Keep Out" signs (which are legally meaningless in Scotland).

"I suppose the trouble is that most sporting estates were started up for the private pleasure of the owner and a few of his guests," says David Hughes-Hallett of the Scottish Landowners Federation (SLF). "That makes them hard to defend politically. But these days are long gone. Nowadays most sporting estates are commercial ventures which have got to make money to cover their costs."

Of course, the health of Scotland's field sports depends heavily on the state of the ecology. This often leads to an uneasy alliance between left-wing environmentalists and Highland estate owners. Both groups fret constantly about the effects of acid rain, the damage caused by tributyle tin to salmon and sea trout and whether the rapid growth of tax-break forestry is polluting the water courses with pesticides and herbicides. The industry took a nasty knock in 1986 when radiation from the Chernobyl accident descended on the Scottish uplands, and found its way into the fat and muscle of the red deer.

Stalking these red deer is one of Scotland's prime attractions to wealthy foreigners. At the last count there were more than 290,000 red deer in Scotland, most of them wandering north of the "Highland line" (between Dumbarton and Aberdeen), with a few small herds in the higher hills of North America descend on the Highlands to spend their days crawling on their bellies through heather and mud, often in sleet or snow, hoping to get near enough to jumpy stag to get off a clean shot. And it has to be a clean shot; if the beast is just wounded, the shooter will be dragged endlessly across the hills until the beast is properly killed.

It is a bruising and usually expensive business. A week's stalking (six days) costs around £1,500 and only the trophy (the head) belongs to the hunter; the venison belongs to the estate. Accommodation is extra and can cost anything from £100 a week for a self-catering chalet, to more than £100 a night at upmarket establishments like Mar Lodge in

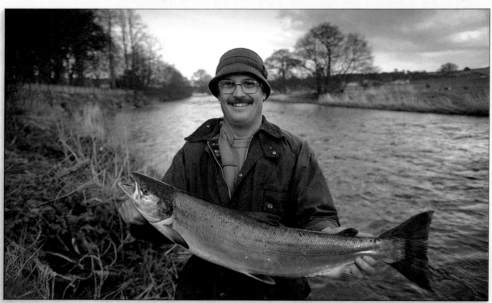

Dumfries and Galloway. With numbers now at an all-time high (there were only 150,000 in the 1950s), there are fears that there are just too many of the beasts. Sportsmen often claim they are doing the species a favour by "shooting out" the older stags and the weaklings. Around 40,000 red deer are shot in Scotland every year, 50 percent of which are hinds (females) culled by professional stalkers and foresters every winter to keep down the numbers.

Although the stalking season runs from July 1 to October 20, very little shooting is done before the end of August. Thereafter shooters from all over Britain, Europe and Deeside or Tulchan Lodge in Strathspey (both of which are owned by a Swiss businessman). Rifles can be hired, but most sportsmen bring their own. And a decent 0.270 or 7mm stalking rifle with telescopic sight can cost anything from £300 to £3,000.

John Ormiston of "Sport In Scotland", the biggest of the sporting-holiday agencies, reckons that the most enthusiastic deer hunters are the British and the Germans, followed by the Americans. "It's all a matter of tradition," he says. "The French and Italians

Above, a catch from the River Don. Following pages: Scottish thistle; a red deer.

prefer using shotguns." A more recent development is the shooting of roe deer bucks (males), usually in woodland, and often from "high seats" fixed in trees. "That's a bit less expensive," Ormiston says. "A red deer stag costs £250 to shoot. A roe deer buck costs around £180."

The "Glorious Twelfth" is the name given to August 12, the day the season opens on red grouse, and the moors of Scotland and northern England fill up with gents in expensive tweeds carrying even more expensive shotguns. Although there have been alarums sounded in recent years over the dwindling stocks of red grouse, things seem to be picking up again. At the end of 1987 estates in the Eastern Highlands were reporting the best season for almost 20 years, with some eight-gun parties bagging up to 200 "brace" (i.e. pairs) or birds in a single day.

Stalking the salmon: But, like deer stalking, grouse shooting doesn't come cheap. Driven grouse (grouse shot with the aid of beaters) can cost around £60 a brace. And even estate-reared pheasants can cost the shooter about £30 a brace. The cheapest shotgun will cost in the region of £250, while an over-and-under Purdy can cost the enthusiast more than £18,000.

But the upmarket sport *par excellence* has to be salmon fishing in one of Scotland's great east-coast salmon rivers such as the Spey, the Dee, the Tay, the Tweed or the Conon. One recent survey estimated that it costs the affluent angler around £3,500 to land an Atlantic salmon from a Scottish river. Certainly, a week's fishing on a good "beat" at the height of the season (July to September) on one of the classier rivers is likely to set the fisherman back between £1,500 and £2,000. If, that is, he is lucky enough to find someone willing to take his money; the supply is strictly limited and the demand is always high.

So high, in fact, that a number of London-based firms have taken to operating salmon beats on a timeshare basis. It works like this: a company such as Salar Properties (owned by financier Jim Slater) buys a large stretch of a good salmon river such as the Tay in Perthshire or the Forss in Caithness, divides it into beats, and then sells a week's fishing on the beats "in perpetuity" for up to £25,000 a week, (depending when the slot occurs in the season and on the quality of the fishing).

Despite the formidable sums involved, Slater has had no trouble peddling the weeks to wealthy *aficionados*.

With that kind of money at stake, the river proprietors are growing ever more anxious about the salmon stocks. They are right to be worried. In 1967 around 605,000 salmon were hauled out of Scottish rivers. By 1985 that figure had slumped to just over 270,000 and of those only 76,000 were caught by anglers. The rest were scooped up by netsmen using the traditional "net and coble" method of fishing, or stake nets which run out from the east coast beaches.

In an effort to make sure the dwindling numbers of salmon aren't intercepted before they can make their run up the rivers, some river proprietors have set up the Atlantic Salmon Conservation Trust. The idea is to raise several million pounds to buy out the coastal netting companies and increase the numbers of fish available to the anglers. The trust, founded in late 1986, quickly acquired 53 netting stations near the approaches to the River Spey and the River Nairn; most have been closed and the remainder will be shut down by 1990.

"Not that that would get rid of all the problems," says the trust. "An awful lot of salmon bound for Scottish rivers are being taken in drift nets off the coast of Greenland, Iceland and Faroes. And there's a lot of poaching going on and off the coast of Scotland with illegal fine-meshed nets."

Trout fishing: While salmon fishing may be the glamour end of the sport, many anglers feel that too much is made of it. They argue that the tourist authorities would do better to bang the drum about the brown trout fishing which is available on countless Scottish lochs, particularly on the west coast and the far north where the salmon are not so abundant.

"Our trout lochs are the most neglected resource we have," says Inverness fisherman, Allan Scott. "Brown trout weighing three or four lbs. (1.4 to 1.8 kgs) aren't uncommon. And in the deep lochs around Fort William you get the occasional ferox trout. They're giant brown trout, some of them weighing up to 20 lbs. (9 kgs). They're cannibals. Big-shouldered brutes that eat their own kind and prey on other fish. But a hell of an exciting fish to get on the end of your line."

TRAVEL TIPS

DESTINATION SCOTLAND

GETTING THERE

Air: Prestwick handles transatlantic flights to Boston, Halifax Nova Scotia, Minneapolis/St. Paul, New York (via Shannon) and Toronto. There are flights to Edinburgh and Glasgow from many European destinations including Amsterdam, Copenhagen, Dublin, Dusseldorf, Frankfurt, Gothenburg, Milan and Paris. In addition there are some direct flights to Aberdeen.

There are excellent air services from Glasgow and Edinburgh to London Heathrow (including no-booking-needed Shuttle flights) and to London Gatwick. British Airways has tended to dominate these routes and added insult to injury when it gobbled up British Caledonian, tartan-clad hostesses and all, in 1987.

Road: There are good motorway connections from England and Wales. The M1/M6 is the quickest route, though heavily congested at the southern end. The A1, a more easterly approach, is longer but may be a better bet if you plan to make one or two stopovers on the way. Edinburgh and Glasgow are about 400 miles (650 km) from London.

Rail: Inter-City trains provide a fast service from England and Wales. Up to 20 trains a day, including overnight sleepers, run from London to Edinburgh and another 10 from London to Glasgow.

Journey times from London to Edinburgh on the 125 mph (200 kph) trains are about five hours. Telephone numbers: London Euston 01-387 7070; London Kings Cross 01-278 2477.

Bus: There are daytime and overnight coach services from England to Scotland. The journey time is about eight hours from London to Edinburgh and Glasgow. Coach travel may not be so comfortable or fast as the trains but it is a good deal cheaper.

INSIDE SCOTLAND

GETTING ACQUAINTED

Climate: No matter what you say about Scottish weather you are bound to be wrong. There are those who rave about the cloudless fortnight they spent on Skye and those who have spent more than one holiday there and have yet to see the Cuillins.

With this word of warning, it can be said that the west is generally wetter and warmer than the east. Nowhere can the weather be depended upon. Summer is in Scotland a somewhat misleading expression.

Nevertheless, there have been occasions when people have been admitted to Aberdeen hospitals suffering from heatstroke and the best place for sunshine in Britain is the Hebridean island of Tiree. Equally, the coldest temperature ever recorded in Britain was at Braemar in the Highlands.

For what it's worth, Edinburgh's highest/lowest daily average temperatures in Celcius (Fahrenheit in brackets) are: Jan 6/1 (42/34), Feb 6/1 (43/34), Mar 8/2 (46/36), Apr 11/4 (51/39), May 14/6 (56/43), Jun 17/9 (62/49), Jul 17/9 (65/52), Aug 18/11 (64/52), Sept 16/9 (60/49), Oct 12/7 (54/44), Nov 9/4 (48/39), Dec 7/2 (44/36). April, May and June are usually drier months than July, August and September—but take a good umbrella whenever you go.

Clothing: Given the climate, it follows that one should never be without a raincoat or a warm sweater. Neither, in summer, should you be without light clothes. For those attracted to the excellent opportunities for hill-walking and rock-climbing it is essential to come properly prepared. In the mountains the weather can change very quickly. Each year people suffer serious and needless injury through setting out without adequate equipment. The Highlands are no place to go on a serious hill walk in a T-shirt and tennis shoes.

Time: Scotland, like the rest of the U.K., follows Greenwich Mean Time. In spring the clock is moved forward one hour for British Summer Time and in autumn moved back again to GMT. Especially in the north of Scotland this means that it is light until 10 p.m. and after in June and early July.

When it is noon GMT, it is 2 a.m. in Honolulu; 4 a.m. in Los Angeles and Vancouver; 5 a.m. in Calgary; 6 a.m. in Chicago, Houston and Winnipeg; 7 a.m. in New York, Toronto, Montreal and Lima; 8 a.m. in Caracas, Santiago and Halifax; 9 a.m. in Buenos Aires, Montevideo and Rio de Janeiro; noon in London, Dublin and Accra; 1 p.m. in Amsterdam, Belgrade, Copenhagen, Gibraltar, Lagos, Madrid, Malta, Oslo, Rome and Stockholm; 2 p.m. in Alexandria, Athens, Cairo, Cape Town, Helsinki, Istanbul, and Leningrad; 3 p.m. in Baghdad, Moscow, and Nairobi; 3:30 p.m. in Tehran; 4 p.m. in Mauritius; 5 p.m. in Karachi; 5:30 p.m. in Bombay, Calcutta, Colombo and New Delhi; 6 p.m. in Dacca; 6:30 p.m. in Rangoon; 7 p.m. in Bangkok and Jakarta; 8 p.m. in Hong Hong, Manila,

Peking, Perth and Singapore; 9 p.m. in Tokyo; 9:30 p.m. in Adelaide; 10 p.m. in Melbourne and Sydney; midnight in Christchurch and Wellington.

Shopping: Most shops are open 9 a.m. to 5:30 p.m. with some shops in the larger cities opening late on Thursday evenings. In the smaller towns there is often an early closing day, though few towns are without a "wee shoppie" which stays open all hours and can provide food and drink and assorted necessities.

Money: The British pound sterling is divided into 100 pennies. The coins used are 1p, 2p, 5p, 10p, 20p, 50p, and £1. One of the minor pleasures of living in Scotland is that the £1 coin is not nearly so common as in England and the £1 note still circulates along with notes of £5, £10, £20, £50 and £100.

Scotland has its own banks, The Royal Bank of Scotland, the Bank of Scotland and the Clydesdale and they still issue their own notes which circulate alongside Bank of England notes. If you are travelling to England, you should find that Scottish banknotes are accepted there, though occasionally a shop will refuse to take them. English banks will readily change Scottish notes for you.

Don't expect consistent opening hours. The Royal Bank and the TSB Bank are open 9:30 a.m. to 3:30 p.m. Monday to Friday in the cities with most of these banks

also opening from 4:30 p.m. to 5:30 p.m. on Thursday. The Bank of Scotland opens from 9:30 a.m. to 4:45 p.m. except on Thursday when it closes at 3:30 p.m. but re-opens from 4:30 p.m. to 5:30 p.m. The Clydesdale is slightly different again, opening from 9:30 a.m. to 4 p.m. each day except Thursday when it shuts at 3:30 p.m. but re-opens from 4:30 p.m. to 5:30 p.m. In rural areas banks may close from 12:30 p.m. to 1:30 p.m. and may not be open later on Thursdays.

Eurocheques and Eurocard can be used at banks and travellers cheques can be cashed at banks, bureaux de change and many hotels, though the best rates are normally available at banks.

Access (alias Mastercard) and Visa are the most commonly acceptable credit cards, followed by American Express and Diners Club. Small guest houses and bed and breakfast places will want payment in cash.

Telephones: There are many public telephone boxes but up to one in four are out of order at any one time. Those in pubs, hotels and public buildings are most likely to work.

The minimum charge is 10p. A recent useful innovation is the Cardphone which is a special type of public phone which does not take cash but instead is operated by a card rather like a credit card in size. Phonecards for £1, £2, £4 and £10 can be bought at post offices and shops displaying the phonecard sign.

Direct dialling is possible to most parts of the world.

The following telephone services are free:
Directory inquiries 192
Operator services 100
Emergency i.e. Police, fire and ambulance, 999

Postal Services: Main post offices are open from 9 a.m. to 5:30 p.m. Monday - Friday and from 9 a.m. to 1 p.m. on Saturdays. Sub-post offices (which often form part of another shop) keep similar hours, though they usually close for a half-day during the week.

At the time of writing letters for delivery within the United Kingdom require either an 18p stamp (first class) or a 13p stamp (second class). Airmail letters to the U.S.A. cost 31p, to Europe 22p, to Asia, India, Australia, New and Zealand 34p.

Newspapers: *The Scotsman* is the national newspaper and, indeed, the only Scottish quality newspaper. It has good coverage of both Scottish and other U.K. news and foreign news as well as material on the arts and business. The *Glasgow Herald* has some pretensions to being a quality newspaper but it is somewhat too parochial to be accorded this status.

Dundee boasts the *Dundee Courier*, one of the few newspapers in the U.K. which do not carry news on the front page. Aberdeen's *Press and Journal* has a reputation for excessive parochialism epitomised by the apocryphal headline on what proved to be a story

about the sinking of the Titanic: "Aberdeen man lost at sea".

Top mass-market seller is the *Daily Record*. English daily papers circulate widely in Scotland.

The four main cities have evening papers which concentrate on sport and entertainment listings. Scotland's most popular Sunday newspaper is the *Sunday Post*, from the same stable as the *Dundee Courier*. It defies classification: perhaps the most useful comment on it would be that it tries to be useful and inoffensive.

Throughout Scotland there are many local weekly papers, which may be entertaining and informative if you are interested in a particular region, or interested in newspapers.

Magazines: Scotland is poorly served by magazines. *Radical Scotland* is the only current affairs magazine and is monthly. The *Edinburgh Review* is a literary review of consistent quality. The English weeklies are widely available — which may account for the paucity of indigenous material.

Radio and Television: Radio and TV are excellent, for the most part. Radio Scotland is the main BBC radio service and national BBC radio stations also operate in Scotland; so it is possible to hear the excellent Radio 4 UK (a mixture of news, current affairs and light entertainment) as well as the classical music channel on Radio 3. BBC Radio 2 concentrates on light enter-

tainment and sport.

BBC Radio 1 and the local radio stations run by both the BBC and commercial companies offer wall-to-wall pop and light music, interspersed with breathless news summaries. Local stations tend to provide a tedious diet of pop music but can be useful sources of local traffic news and other important information.

Television services are provided by the BBC and commercial companies. BBC1 is a general TV service, mirrored (though with a more down-market emphasis) by the commercial ITV network. BBC2 and its commercial stablemate, Channel 4, recognise the existence of more specialist audiences.

Holidays: Strictly speaking, there is only one Public Holiday which applies throughout Scotland— Ne'er Day (or New Year's Day to Sassenachs). Lest it be thought that this is evidence of the Protestant ethic in Calvinist Scotland it should be added that Christmas Day, December 26 and January 2 are taken as holidays. Most towns and cities in Scotland have official local holidays, which varies from place to place.

The Bank Holidays, so beloved of the English and which are actually public holidays for them, do not apply in Scotland. Scottish Bank holidays are only holidays for banks, although they may coincide with particular local holidays.

Language: English in one form or another is spoken in

Scotland. There are various regional dialects and local expressions used. Glaswegians appear to assume that anyone whose name they do not know is called "Jimmy". In most parts of Scotland the uninitiated could be forgiven for thinking that the name "Ken" was unusually popular; in fact, the Scots use "ken" at the end of sentences as the English are wont to use "do you know". The Scots have a tendency towards understatement which is well illustrated by the phrase "it's no bad"—than which there is no greater compliment.

In the Highlands and the islands Gaelic is still spoken and is the first language to some of the older people. Nowhere is it anyone's only language.

Health: It is advisable to have medical insurance. Citizens of EEC countries are entitled to medical treatment under reciprocal arrangements and similar arrangements exist with some other countries. No matter which country you come from, you will receive immediate emergency treatment free at a hospital casualty department.

Emergency services such as police, ambulances, the fire service or lifeboats can be reached by dialing 999.

Although Scotland isn't normally associated with mosquitoes, an aggressive breed of midge exists in parts of the west coast and calls for a tough repellent.

Current Information: 220 volts is standard. Hotels usually have dual 220/110 volt sockets for razors.

Tourism Information: General postal enquiries: Scottish Tourist Board, PO Box 15, Edinburgh EH1 1YU.

The Scottish Tourist Board has its Scottish Travel Centre in South St Andrew Street in the centre of Edinburgh. Other tourist information is provided by local tourist boards throughout Scotland. The main offices are set out below.

Edinburgh and the Lothians
Town House
Dunbar
Tel: (0368) 63353

The Borders
Scottish Borders Tourist Board
Municipal Buildings
High Street
Selkirk, TD7 4JX
Tel: (0750) 20550

The South-west
Dumfries and Galloway Tourist Board,
Douglas House,
Newton Stewart, DG8 6DQ
Tel: (0671) 2549
Ayrshire and Burns Country Tourist Board
39 Sandgate, Ayr
Tel: (0292) 284196

Glasgow
Greater Glasgow Tourist Board
35-39 St Vincent Street
Glasgow G1
Tel: (041) 227 4880.

Firth of Clyde Islands
Isle of Arran Tourist Board, Tourist Information Centre,

Brodick Pier,
Brodick, Isle of Arran Tourist Board
Tel: (0770) 2140
Rothesay and Bute Tourist Board,
The Pier, Rothesay
Isle of Bute PA20 9AQ
Tel: (0700) 2151

West of the Clyde
Fort William and Lochaber Tourist Board
Cameron Centre
Cameron Square
Fort William, PH33 6AJ
Tel: (0397) 3781

Inner Hebrides
Oban Mull and District Tourist Board,
Boswell House,
Argyll Square,
Oban, Argyll
Tel: (0631) 63122
Isle of Skye and South West Ross Tourist Board,
Portree,
Isle of Skye IV51 9BZ
Tel: (0478) 2137.

Outer Hebrides
4 South Beach Street
Stornoway,
Isle of Lewis PA87 2XY

Central Scotland
Aviemore and Spey Valley Tourist Board,
Main Road
Aviemore PH22 1PP
Tel: (0479) 810363
Inverness, Loch Ness and Nairn Tourist Board,
23 Church Street,
Inverness IV1 1EZ
Tel: (0463) 234353
Loch Lomond and the Trossachs Tourist Board,
PO Box 30,
Stirling
Tel: (0786) 75019
St Andrews and Fife

Tourist Board,
South Street
St Andrews
Fife KY16 9JX
Tel: (0334) 72021
Perthshire Tourist Board,
PO Box 33,
George Inn Lane,
Perth PH1 5LH
Tel: (0738) 27958

The East Coast
City of Aberdeen
Tourist Board,
St Nicholas House,
Broad Street,
Aberdeen AB9 1DE
Tel: (0224) 632727
City of Dundee
Tourist Board,
Nethergate Centre,
Dundee DD1 4ER
Tel: (0382) 27723.
Kincardine and Deeside
Tourist Board,
45 Station Road,
Banchory AB3 3XX
Tel: (033 02) 2066

Northern Highlands
Caithness Tourist Board,
Whitechapel Road, Wick,
Caithness
Tel: (0955) 2596
Ross and Cromarty
Tourist Board,
Gairloch,
Ross-shire IV21 2DN

Tel: (00445) 2130
Sutherland Tourist Board,
The Square,
Dornoch IV25 3DS
Tel: (0862) 810400

Orkney
Information Centre,
Broad Street, Kirkwall,
Orkney KW15 1DH
Tel: (0856) 2856

Shetland
Market Cross,
Lerwick, Shetland
Tel: (0595) 3434

London
The Scottish Tourist Board
runs a Scottish Information
Centre at 19 Cockspur
Street, London on the south-
west side of Trafalgar
Square.
Information about Scotland
is available through the British Tourist Authority as
listed below:

Europe
52 Rue de la Montagne
Bergstraat, 1000 Brussels.
Tel: (2) 511 43 90; Moner-
gade 3, 1116 Copenhagen
K6. Tel: (1) 12 34 41/12 07
93. 6 Place Vendome, 75001
Paris. Tel: (1) 296 3552/
4760; Neue Mainzer Str. 22,

6000 Frankfurt am Main.
Tel: (69) 2380711/12/13; c/
o British Airways, 112
Grafton Street, Dublin 2.
Tel: 778 176; Via S Erfemia
5, 00187 Rome. Tel: (6) 678
4998; Leidesplein 5, 1017
PS Amsterdam. Tel: (20)
254771; Mariboesgt 11,
Oslo 1. Tel: (2) 41 23 90;
Torre de Madrid 6/4, Plaza
de Espana, 28008 Madrid.
Tel:(1) 248 65 91; For visitors: Malmshillnadsgatan 42
(1st floor), For mail: Box
7293, S-103 90 Stockholm
40. Tel: (8) 42 52/21 24 44;
Limmatquai 78, 8001, Zu-
rich. Tel: (1) 47 42 77/97.

North America
94 Cumberland Street, Suite
600, Toronto, Ontario M5R
3N3. Tel: (416) 961 8124;
John Hancock Centre (Suite
3320), 875 N. Michigan
Avenue, Chicago, Illinois,
60611. Tel: (312) 7870490;
Plaza of the Americas, North
Tower, Suite 750, Lock Box
346, Dallas, Texas 75201.
Tel: (214) 720 4040; 612
South Flower Street, Los
Angeles, California 90017.
Tel: (213) 623 8196; 3rd
Floor, 40 West 57th Street,
New York, NY 10019. Tel:
(212) 581 4708.

ON THE MOVE

TRANSPORT

Air: There is a network of
air services within Scotland
which is especially valuable
if going to the islands. Flying
saves a lot of time to these
destinations and also can
give a different perspective
on the countryside.

For internal Scottish serv-
ices, these are the relevant
airport telephone numbers:
Loganair services:
Aberdeen: 0224-723306
Glasgow: 041-889 3181
Inverness: 0667-62332
Orkney: 0856-3457
Shetland: 059-584 246
British Airways services:
Aberdeen: 0224-722331

Edinburgh: 031-333 1000
Glasgow: 041-887 1111
Inverness: 0463-232471
Wick: 0955-2215

Ferries: The wise visitor
books boat before bed in the
Scottish islands, writes
Dymphna Byrne. For the island-studded west coast—
the Hebrides and the islands

of the Clyde—get the Caledonian MacBrayne summer timetable. This, running from May to October, is as long and narrow and as incomprehensible to the first-time visitor as a Chinese scroll.

Locals whip through it with ease. The rest of us, not knowing Kilchoan from Kyleakin, take a day to plot a route. Summer booking is vital to avoid the nerve-wracking, time-consuming "standby" queue.

Caledonian MacBrayne, a fusion of two companies, grew out of the 19th-century passenger steamers and now has a near-monopoly on west coast routes. Its 30 vessels call at 53 ports, on the mainland and on 23 islands.

The ferries are great. On long routes like the five hours Oban to Barra ferry there are car decks, cabins, comfortable chairs, a restaurant and self-service. On others such as the seven-hour round trip to the tiny island of Eigg, Muck, Rhum and Canna, ferries are basic with wooden seats and minimal refreshments. These working boats, carrying goods and mail as well as passengers, are mainly used by islanders, with some bird-watchers and occasionally curious visitors who take the chilling round trip for interest. For, unless you specify beforehand, disembarking for sightseeing is not allowed. Other companies run pleasure trips that allow time ashore. Caledonian Mac-Brayne runs mini cruises from Oban, one of the key mainland ports for the west coast islands (the other is

Mallaig). It sells island hop-scotch tickets and, best value for visitors with cars, rover tickets for driver and one passenger giving eight or 15 days' unlimited travel on most routes. There is plenty of small private enterprise on the west coast. There are cruises from Arisaig on the mainland to Skye and Mull as well as to Eigg, Muck, Rhum and Canna. Day trips to the National Trust island of Staffa with Fingal's Cave, to the bird island of Lunga and the uninhabited Treshnish islands, start from the Ulva ferry on the west of Mull. There is a virtual 10-minute shuttle service from Fionnphort on the southwest tip of Mull to Iona.

There is no difficulty in finding out about such services when you arrive. Tourist information centres and many hotels have brochures. For forward planning ferry homework, get the Caledonian MacBrayne brochure and timetable from the company at the Ferry Terminal, Gournock, PA19 1QP, Scotland (0475 33755).

In northern Scotland, the ferries to Orkney and Shetland are a great deal easier to grasp than those to the Western Isles; for one thing, there are only two major islands and only two ferry companies. Once again summer booking is essential.

Orkney: There is just one vessel for cars to Orkney, the comfortable roll-on/roll-off St Ola run by P&O which takes two hours to cross from Scrabster on the mainland to Stromness on Orkney. There is one sailing a day except Sunday with extra services

during high summer. The Thomas & Bews passenger only ferry runs from mid May to mid September from John 0' Groats. There is a good car park here and plenty of hire cars, buses and coaches on Orkney if you don't want the expense of taking a car across. There are two daily departures, including Sunday, the crossing takes around 40 minutes. Once on Orkney you can visit the dozen or so smaller islands by local ferries. The tourist office at Kirkwall has more details.

Shetland: During the summer the P&O service, which takes 14 hours between Aberdeen and Lerwick, Shetland's main port, is doubled from one boat to two. Both ferries are modern roll-on/roll-off vessels with cabins, shops, restaurants and cafeterias. The second ferry makes the round trip, calling at Orkney on both the outward and the return journey. Once again local ferries ply between the mainland of Shetland and the tiny islands of Yell, Unst and Fetlar. The P&O Ferries brochure comes from them at PO Box 5, P&O Ferries Terminal, Jamieson's Quay, Aberdeen AB9 8DL (0224 572615). Thomas & Bewis Ferry Office, John O' Groats, Caithness. (095 581 353). Summer only.

Pleasure steamers: In Glasgow, steamer services on the Clyde are run by Waverley Excursions (New Waverley Terminal, Anderston Quay. Tel: 041-221 8152). The "Waverley", built in 1946, is the last sea-going paddle steamer in the world.

On Loch Katrine, which has supplied Glasgow with water since 1859, the SS *Sir Walter Scott*, Scotland's only screw steamer in regular passenger service, makes the 105-minute trip between Trossachs and Stornachlachar piers twice daily in summer. Enquiries to Water Department, Strathclyde Regional Council, 419 Balmore Road, Glasgow G22 6NU (041-336 5333) or to Callander Tourist Information Office, Leny Road, Callander (Callander 30342).

Trains: British Rail is happy to quote the Scottish novelist Robert Louis Stevenson, no stranger to trains in Victorian times: "I travel not to go anywhere, but to go. I travel for travel's sake: the great affair is to move." Certainly, the purpose is splendidly achieved in Scotland, where you can watch spectacular scenery—lochs, glens and forests—from the comfort of a train.

A few possibilities: Glasgow to Fort William and Mallaig (164m/265km). Train enthusiasts head for the West Highland line, which operates steam locomotives throughout the summer from Fort William to the fishing port of Mallaig, from which a ferry departs for Skye. The route passes through hillsides dotted with deer, across the wild Rannoch Moor and over the majestic Glenfinnan Viaduct. For more details: ScotRail West Highland Transport Centre, Fort William PH33 6AN.

Glasgow to Oban (101m/163km). Branches off the Fort William route at Crianlarich and heads past ruined Kilchurn Castle and the fjord-like scenery of the Pass of Bander to Oban, "gateway to the Inner Hebrides".

Perth to Inverness (118m/190km). The route, through forested glens and across the roof of Scotland, takes in Pitlochry, Blair Atholl and Aviemore. As well as being a ski centre, Aviemore is the departure point for steam trains on the five-mile Strathspey Railway.

Inverness to Kyle of Lochalsh (82m/132km). Twisting line taking in lochs, glens and mountains from the North Sea to the Atlantic Ocean. The route passes Dingwall and Duncraig Castles and ends at Kyle of Lochalsh, by the Sound of Sleat, from which ferries depart for Skye.

Inverness to Wick or Thurso (161m/260km). Passes by more castles, across wild moorland and on to Britain's most northerly rail terminals.

Railway preservation societies, which enable fanatics all over Britain to dirty their hands on steam locomotives, are alive and thriving in Scotland. Apart from the popular West Highland line, half a dozen other lines operate steam trains of one sort or another:

The Caledonian Railway (Brechin), Angus. Holds several steam days during the summer and Brechin station is open most weekends. Enquiries to Brechin Station, 2 Park Road, Brechin, Angus DD9 7AF.

The Bo'ness & Kinneil Railway, West Lothian. Steam trains run on summer weekends. A particular attraction is the Scandinavian Vintage Train hauled by a huge Swedish B class engine. Enquiries to Bo'ness Station, Tel: 050682-2298.

Strathspey Railway runs during the summer for five miles (eight km) from Aviemore (Speyside) to Boat of Garten, providing good views of Cairngorm Mountains. Enquiries to Boat of Garten Station, Inverness-shire PH24 3BH.h

West Buchan Railway Company. A 15-inch narrow gauge line mixes steam and diesels and provides public transport as well as sightseeing excursions between Banff Harbour and Swordanes. Enquiries to West Buchan Railway Co., 12 Station Place, Cruden Bay, Peterhead, Grampian AB4 7NF. Tel 077981-2410.

The Mull & West Highland Railway. Volunteers man steam and diesel trains for one and a quarter miles across the Isle of Mull, saving a tiring walk from Craignure to Torosay Castle. Enquiries to 06803-389.

The Lochty Private Railway, Fife. Run by the Fife Railway Preservation Group and open to visitors on Sunday afternoons in summer. Enquiries to FRPG Secretary, 48 Hendry Road, Kirkcaldy, Fife KY2 5JN.

For the traveller in a hurry, British Rail's InterCity division runs long-weekend "land cruises" from London through the Highlands and back. They are not especially luxurious but they're good value: two nights on the train with one at a hotel will cost between £200 and £300.

At the top end of the market, the Royal Scotsman, the local answer to the Orient Express, mixes castles with caviar, carrying no more than 28 pampered passengers, mostly Americans, through the Highlands in wood-panelled but very pricey splendour. Six days in a state cabin costs from £2,500. The train is marketed through the tour operators Abercrombie & Kent.

For more mundane travel, British Rail has a wide range of deals, including seven-day and 14-day Freedom of Scotland tickets for between £40 and £70. Cheaper "Rover" tickets are issued for the North Highlands, West Highlands and Central Scotland. Details from ScotRail information offices in these cities:

Aberdeen   0224-594222
Dundee   0382-28046
Edinburgh   031-556 2451
Glasgow   041-204 2844
Inverness   0463-238924
Perth   0738-37117
Stirling   0786-64754

Buses: Major towns have their own bus services. In addition there are bus services serving rural communities and linking the various towns. These are fairly good and the visitor who intends to make much use of buses should investigate the various tickets which allow unlimited use of buses for specific periods. Details are available from bus stations and tourist offices.

Taxis: The major cities all have taxi services with a reasonable number of stands. Outside the cities it will usually be necessary to telephone for a taxi.

Driving: Scotland has an excellent network of roads which, away from the central belt, are usually not congested. Driving on the left is the rule and front-seat passengers must wear seat belts. In urban areas the speed limit is either 30 or 40 mph, the limit on country roads is 60 mph and on motorways and dual carriageways 70 mph.

In some parts of the Highlands and on many of the islands roads are single track with passing places. The behaviour of drivers on these roads tends to show that good old-fashioned courtesy is not dead.

In the Highlands and on the islands it is wise to fill up on Saturday if you are planning to drive on Sunday. In some places strict Sunday observance means that filling stations will be closed.

Some tourists whose cars will run only on unleaded petrol have found difficulty in finding it in some areas. There is no need to curtail your travels as the Scottish Tourist Board has a leaflet showing where supplies can be obtained.

At the time of writing, the price of a gallon of four-star petrol is about £1.75, although it may be a bit more expensive in remote areas.

A list of car rental companies appears below.

Car Rentals: Self-drive rental costs from £20 to £30 a day, depending on the type of car and the duration of the rental. Reductions apply in the October to April off-season. For more detailed information, apply directly to the car rental companies.

Aberdeen

Avis Rent-a-Car
Aberdeen Agency
Kingsley Car Hire
16 Broomhill Road
Tel: 0224 57452

Budget Rent-a Car
Clark Commercials Ltd
283 King Street
Tel: 0224 639922

Godfrey Davis Europcar Ltd
121 Causewayend
Tel: 0224 631199

Hertz Rent-a-Car
Bucksburn Moat House
Old Mildrum Road
Bucksburn
Tel: 0224 714835

Kenning Car Hire
238-240 Market Street
Tel: 0224 571445

Mitchells Self Drive
35 Chapel Street
Tel: 0224 642642

Valentine Chauffeur Drive
80 Bonnymuir Place
Tel: 0224 630456

Aberdeen Airport

Avis Rent-a-Car
Dyce
Tel: 0224 630456

Godfrey Davis Europcar Ltd
Terminal Building
Tel: 0224 770770

Hertz Rent-a-Car
Terminal Building Dyce
Tel: 0224 722373

Aringagour, Isle of Coll
Isle of Coll Hotel
Tel: 08793 334

Auchterarder

Godfrey Davis Europcar Ltd
Gleneagles Hotel
Tel: 0738 31322

Avoch

Daimler Chauffeur Hire
Avoch Filling Station
Tel: 0381 20247

Ayr

Budget Rent-a-Car
Rosefield Motors (Ayr)
196 Prestwick Road
Tel: 0292 264087

Dalblair of Ayr

127 Prestwick Road
Tel: 0292 269123

Brechin

Ritchie's Self Drive
Car & Van Rentals
2 Montrose street
Tel: 03562 3558

Broxburn

Broxburn Chauffeur Drive
112 Forrest Walk
Uphall
Tel: 0506 855496

Dingwall

Budget Rent-a-Car
MacRae & Dick Ltd
Station Road

Dornoch

Gordon's Coaches
Masonic Buildings
Tel: 0862 810503

Dundee

Budget Rent-a-Car
Tayford Motor Co
Balfield Road
Tel: 0382 644644

Godfrey Davis Europcar Ltd
St Roques Auto Co Ltd 64
Ward Road
Tel: 0382 21281

Hertz Rent-a-Car
19 Roseangle
Tel: 0382 23711

Mitchell's Self Drive
90 Marketgait
Tel: 0382 23484

Practical Used Car Rental
102/108 Logie Street
Tel: 0382 645124

Dunfermline

Laidlaw (Dunfermline) Ltd
Halbeath Road
Tel: 0383 721536

Edinburgh

Avis Rent-a-Car
100 Dalry Road
Tel: 031 3376363

Budget Rent-a-Car
116 Polwarth Gardens
Tel: 031 228 6088

Ghillie Personal Travel
64 Silverknowes Road East
Tel: 031 336 3120

Godfrey Davis Europcar Ltd
24 East London Street
Tel: 031 661 11252

Hertz Rent-a-Car
10 Picardy Place
Tel: 031 556 8311

Kenning Car Hire
Circle Garage

Crewe Toll
Tel: 031 343 3377

Mitchell's Self Drive
32 Torphicen Street
Tel: 031 229 5384

Guy Salmon
Caledonian Hotel
Princes Street
Tel: 031 226 7257

SMT Self Drive Hire
88-91 Haymarket Terrace
Tel: 031 337 2441

Swan National Car Rental
Shrub Service Station
Leith Walk
Tel: 031 556 8187
and
19-21 Glasgow Road
Tel: 031 334 9244

W L Sleigh Ltd
Shandwick Place
Tel: 031 226 3080

Town and Country
Car Rentals
Crest Hotel
Queensferry Road
Tel: 031 332 0580

Wards Car Rentals
16 Ammamdale street
Tel: 031 556 3124
and
51 West Harbour Road
Tel: 031 551 1017

Edinburgh Airport

Avis Rent-a-Car
Tel: 031 333 1866

Godfrey Davis Europcar Ltd
Tel: 031 333 2588

Hertz Rent-a-Car
Tel: 031 333 1010

Swan National Car Rental
Tel: 031 3331922

Elgin

Budget Rent-a-Car
East Road
Tel: 0343 45281

Fort William

Budget Rent-a-Car
MacRae & Dick Ltd
Gordon Square
Tel: 0397 2500

Galashiels

Chalmers McQueen Ltd
Albert Place
Tel: 0896 3304

Glasgow

Alex M Ritchie (Car Hire)
43 Nithsdale street
041 423 3961

British Car Rental
Haldanes of Cathcart
152/180 Clarkston Road
Tel: 041 637 2366
and
215 Queensborough
Gardens
Tel: 041 357 1234

Budget Rent-a-Car
Waterloo Street Service
Station
101 Waterloo Street
Tel: 041 226 4141
and
John P McGee Ltd
Ravenswood Road
Baillieston
Tel: 041 773 2203

Godfrey Davis Europcar Ltd
Queen Street
Tel: 041 332 7635
and
556 Pollokshaws Road
Tel: 041 423 5661

Jim Neary Car and
Van Hire Ltd

15 Faily Street
Tel: 041 427 5457

Little's Chauffeur Drive
1282 Paisley Road West
Tel: 041 883 2111

Milngavie Motors Ltd
Abbiesland Industrial Estate
Tel: 041 954 1500

Mitchell's Self Drive
Multi-Storey Car Park
Mitchell Street
Tel: 041 221 8461

Swan National Rentals Ltd
Broomilaw Autopoint
222 Broomilaw Road
Tel: 041 204 1051

Glasgow Airport

Avis Rent-a-Car
Terminal Building
Tel: 041 887 2264

Budget Rent-a-Car
Phoenix House
Inchinnan Road
Paisley
Tel: 041 887 0501

Hertz Rent-a-Car
Terminal Building
Tel: 041 887 2451

Swan National Rentals Ltd
Terminal Building
Tel: 041 887 7915

Gullane

Fairway Tours
8 Roseberry Place
Tel: 0620 842349

Hamilton

Swan National Rentals Ltd
Wellhall Grove
Wellhall Road
Tel: 0698 286644

Mitchell's Self Drive
Miller Street
Tel: 0698 285744

Hawick

Guthrie of Hawick
(Motors) Ltd
61 High Street
Tel: 0450 72287

Inverness

Budget Rent-a-Car
MacRae and Dick Ltd
Burns Cottage,
Railway Terrace
Tel: 0463 239877

Cordiner's Self Drive
Harbour Road
Tel: 0463 224466

H W Jack (Car Hire) Ltd
17 Adrconnel Terrace
Tel: 0463 236571

Hertz Rent-a-Car
Mercury Hotel
Nairn Road
Tel: 0463 254475

Peugeot Talbot Rental
James Ferries Ltd
Harbour Road
Tel: 0463 231536

SMT Sales and
Service Co Ltd
112 Academy Street
Tel: 0463 234311

Inverness Airport

Avis Rent-a-Car
Dalcross
Tel: 0667 62787

Kilmarnock

Mitchell's Self Drive
52 Beansburn
Tel: 0563 33211

Kirkcaldy

Godfrey Davis Europcar Ltd
Drummond Motor Co
Ferrard Road
Tel: 0592 268497

Kirkwall

Godfrey Davis Europcar Ltd
Scarth Hire Ltd
Great Western Road
Tel: 0856 2601

Kirkwall Airport

Godfrey Davis Europcar Ltd
Terminal Building
Tel: 0856 2125

Lerwick

Bilt's Car Hire
26 North Road
Tel: 0595 2855

Godfrey Davis Europcar Ltd
Terminal Building
Tel: 0595 2855
and
Ferry Terminal
Tel: 0595 2855
and
Bolt's Car Hire
26 North Road
Tel: 0595-2855

John Leask & Son
Esplanade
Tel: 0595 3162

McLeod & McLean
Commercial Road
Tel: 0595 3313

Motherwell

Godfrey Davis Europcar Ltd
477 Windhill Street
Knowetop
Tel: 0698 66354

Paisley

Budget Rent-a-Car
Phoenix House
Tel:041 887 0501

GMT Taxis
Abbey Mill Centre
Tel: 041 889 1155

Godfrey Davis Europcar Ltd
Inchinnan Road
Tel: 041 339 1414
and
Clanford Motors Ltd
Lonend
Tel: 041 889 0504

Mitchell's Self Drive
54 Glasgow Road
Tel: 041 887 7866

Perth

Godfrey Davis Europcar Ltd
26 Glasgow Road
Tel: 0738 36888

Peterhead

Budget Rent-a-Car
MacRae and Dick Ltd
43-45 Windmill Street
Tel: 0779 79191

Pitlochry

Oakfield Self Drive
Hire Cars
12 Higher Oakfield
Rosemount Hotel
Tel: 0796 2302

Prestwick

Godfrey Davis Europcar Ltd
14 Kirk Street
Tel: 0292 77218

Prestwick Airport

Avis Rent-a-Car
Terminal Building
Tel: 0292 77218

Budget Rent-a-Car
Rosefields Motors (Ayr)
106 Prestwick Road
Tel: 0292 264087

Godfrey Davis Europcar Ltd
Tel: 0292 70566

Swan National Rentals Ltd
Tel: 0292 76517

Scatsa Airport, Shetland

Bolt's Car Hire
Terminal Building
Tel: 080622 311

Stirling

Godfrey Davis Europcar Ltd
Mogil Motors Ltd
Drip Road
Tel: 0786 2164

Swan National Rentals Ltd
Williamfield Service Station
22 Randolph Terrace
Tel: 0786 70123

T M Templeton
(Vehicle Hire) Ltd
14 Whitehouse Road
Springkerse Industrial
Estate
Tel: 0786 63137

Stonehaven

Mitchell's Garage
72 Barclay Street
Tel: 0569 62077

Stornoway

Lewis Car Rentals
52 Bayhead Street
Tel: 0851 3760

Western Isles

Mackinnon Self Drive
18 Inaclate
Tel: 0851 2984

Stranraer

E&W Lithgow
(Transport) Ltd
Car Hire
Aird Filling Station
London Road
Tel:0776 2833

Rosefield Motors (Ayr) Ltd
West End Garage
Leswalt Road
Tel: 0776 3636

Sumburgh Airport, Shetland

A J Eunson
Virkie
Tel: 0950 60209

Tingwall Airport, Shetland

Godfrey Davis
Europcar Ltd

Terminal Building
Tel: 0595 2855

Bolt's Car Hire
Terminal Building
Tel: 0595 2855

Wick

Richard's Garage
Francis street
Tel: 0955 4123

FOOD DIGEST

WHERE TO EAT

Scotland is no gastronomic paradise, but the range and standard of eating facilities has been improving. There are various dishes that are distinctively Scottish such as haggis—which is probably more enjoyable if you don't know what should be in it (the heart lungs and liver of a sheep, suet, oatmeal and onion). Fish is something of a Scottish speciality with salmon being particularly good. Kippers and Arbroath Smokies (haddock smoked over wood) are delicious too.

Dr. Johnson remarked that "If an epicure could remove by a wish, in quest of sensual gratifications, wherever he had supped he would breakfast in Scotland." No doubt he would say the same today. There is surely no better way to start the day than porridge, Loch Fyne kippers and Scottish oatcakes.

On a more mundane level, there is no shortage of fast-food outlets of one sort or another throughout Scotland. For a cheap and enjoyable takeaway meal, you could do a lot worse than try the humble "chipper" (fish and chip shop).

The symbols at the end of each entry provide a rough guide to prices, based on the average cost of a three-course evening meal, excluding wine. £ = under £7; ££ = £7 - £17 per head; and £££ = over £17 per head. Lunch is usually cheaper.

Edinburgh

Aye
80 Queen Street
Tel. (031) 226 5467
Japanese and European.

City Art Gallery Café
Open from 9:30 a.m. - 4:30 p.m. Mon.- Sat.
Close to Waverley station. £

Hendersons' Hanover Street
Excellent vegetarian cookery. Tends to be busy at lunchtime. £

Helios Fountain
Grassmarket
Casual restaurant.

Kalpna
2-3 St Patrick Square
Tel. (031) 667 9890
Indian vegetarian. £

Negociant's
45-47 Lothian Street
Tel. (031) 225 6313
Bistro, near University of Edinburgh. £

Champany Grill
2 Bridge Road
Colinton
Tel. (031) 441 2587
Specialises in steak. ££

Pompadour Room
Caledonian Hotel
Princes Street
Tel. (031) 225 2433
Traditional Scottish as well as French cooking. £££

Ferri's Pizzeria
1 Antigua Street
Tel. (031) 556 5592
Italian. £

Glasgow

The city has long enjoyed a reputation for good Indian and Chinese restaurants (the Koh-in-Noor, the Shish Mahal, the Amber Royale, the Loon Fung), but it has been slow to compete with Edinburgh's rapid growth in more general eating places. But it's now catching up and has a wide selection of good, characterful or plain wholesome restaurants and cafés which are patronised by Glaswegians themselves.

PJ's Pastaria
Ruthven Lane
Tel. (041) 339 0932
Specialties include freshly made pasta and home made pizzas. £

La Bavarde
9 New Kirk Road
Bearsden
Tel. (041) 942 2202
Lunch is very good value. ££

Le Provencal
21 Royal Exchange Street
Tel. (041) 221 0798
French cuisine. ££

Baby Grand
3 Elmbank Gardens
Charing Cross
Tel. (041) 248 4942. £

Shish Mahal
45-47 Gibson Street
Tel. (041) 339 8256
Indian. £

Ubiquitous Chip
12 Ashton Lane
Tel. (041) 334 5007
Modern British cooking. ££

Borders

Sunlaws House Heiton
Kelso

Tel. (0573) 5331
Three miles south of Kelso on the A698. ££

Hoebridge Inn
Gattonside
near Melrose
Tel. (089 682) 3082
Italian cooking. ££

Philipburn House Hotel
Selkirk
Tel. (0750) 20747. ££

Burns Country

Kirroughtree Hotel
Newtonstewart
Tel. (0671) 2141. ££

Cringlitie House Hotel
Eddleston, Peebles
Tel. (072 13) 233. ££

Firth of Clyde

Ardenslate Hotel
James Street
Hunters Quay, Dunoon
Tel. (0369) 2068. £

West of the Clyde

West Loch Hotel
Tarbet
Tel. (088 02) 283. ££

Portsonachan Hotel
Portsonachan
Tel. (086 63) 224
Dining room has marvellous view of Loch Awe. ££

Taychreggan Hotel
Kilchrenan
Tel. (086 63) 211. ££

Knipoch Hotel
Oban
Tel. (08256) 208. ££

Isle of Eriska Hotel
Eriska, Ledaig

Tel. (063 172) 371
12 miles from Oban. ££

Airds Hotel
Port Appin
Tel. (063) 173 236

Inner Hebrides

The Captains Table
Tobermory, Mull
Tel. (0688) 2313. ££

Kinloch Lodge Hotel
Isle of Oronsay
Tel. (04713) 214. ££

Skeabost House Hotel
Skeabost Bridge
Isle of Skye
Tel. (047 032) 202. ££

Central Scotland

The Arches
35 Upper Craigs, Stirling
Tel. (0786) 70972. £

Cromlix House
Dunblane
Tel. (0786) 822125. £££

Roman Camp Hotel
Main Street
Callender
Tel. (0877) 30003. ££

The Cross
25/27 High Street
Kingussie
Tel. (054 02) 762. £

Ostlers Close Restaurant
Ostlers Close, Cupar
Tel. (0334) 55574
Uses local produce as far as possible. ££

The Hollies
Low Road
Auchtermuchty, Fife.
Tel. (0337) 28279
Pleasant atmosphere and a chance to discover that

Auchtermuchty is a real location. ££

Timothy's
24 John Street, Perth
Tel. (0738) 26641. ££

The Old Monastery Restaurant
Buckie
Tel. (0542) 32660
A converted chapel, renowned for its food. ££

The Clifton Hotel
Nairn
Tel. (0667) 53119
The food is often excellent and never dull. ££

Pepitas
11 Crails Lane, St. Andrews
Tel. (0334) 74084
Good for snacks during the day and serves dinner in the evening. £

Brambles
5 College Street,
St. Andrews
Tel. (0334) 75380
Open 1 a.m. -4:30 p.m. Good for snacks.

Peat Inn
Peat Inn, Fife
Tel. (033 484) 206
International reputation. £££

The East Coast

The Anarkalie
34 Gray Street

Broughty Ferry, Dundee
Tel. (0382) 737733
Indian. £

The Cornerstone Café
Nethergate, Dundee. Plain cooking with no pretensions. Clean, pleasant cafe where a square meal can be had for under 3. Open 10 a.m.-4 p.m. Monday - Saturday.

Mr. G's
74 Chapel Street, Aberdeen
Tel. (0224) 62411
Wine bar with restaurant. ££

Raffles Café Restaurant
18 Perth Road, Dundee
Tel. (0382) 26344
Provides in a relaxed atmosphere coffee to dinner.

The Old Mansion House Hotel
Auchterhouse, near Dundee
Tel. (082 626) 266. £

Poldinos
7 Little Belmont Street
Aberdeen
Tel. (0224) 647777

Repertory Theatre Restaurant
Tay Street, Dundee
Tel. (0382) 27684
Casual place to have a drink, a snack or a meal. £

Northern Highlands

Altanharrie Inn
Ullapool

Tel. (085 483) 230
You have to be taken by boat from Ullapool and free accommodation is guaranteed should conditions not permit a return crossing. Closed October to Easter. ££

Bayview Hotel
Russell Street,
Lybster
Tel. (059 32) 346
Very friendly. ££

Dornoch Castle
Dornoch
Tel. (0862) 810216
Specialises in good Scottish food. ££

Summer Isles Hotel
Achiltibuie
Tel. (085 482) 282
Uses local products as far as possible. ££

Orkney

Hamnavoe
35 Graham Place
Stromness,
Orkney
Tel. (0856) 850606. ££

Shetland

Burrastow House
Walls,
Shetland.
Tel. (059 571) 307. £££

IN TRANSIT

WHERE TO STAY

A wide range of accommodation is available in Scotland, from hotels of international standard to simple bed and breakfast accommodation. Prices vary as well, from under £10 a night for b&b to around £100 at the most expensive hotel.

How does one select a suitable place to stay? The Scottish Tourist Board has a somewhat complicated assessment scheme. Their approved accommodation will display an oval sign with the Tourist Board logo. This will tell you two things about the hotel. First, how extensive its facilities are; this is indicated by the word "listed" for the most basic facilities to five crowns for those with the most facilities. In addition, the accommodation is graded for quality into three categories to include: "Approved", "Commended" or "Highly Commended".

The intention is to give an idea not just of the quantity of facilities but of the quality of the place. It would be possible for a hotel to have five crowns indicating an excellent range of facilities, but to be awarded only the "Approved" quality grade because the Tourist Board's inspectors didn't think much of the ambience.

If planning a caravan holiday, look out for the Thistle logo. The "Thistle Commendation" is awarded by the industry and the Tourist Board to parks who meet the highest standards of excellence in environment, facilities and the caravans.

If you decide to go for a self-catering holiday, the Association of Scotland's Self Caterers has a quality scheme indicated by their triangular logo.

Staying in b&b accommodation is not only economical; it is also a flexible and, potentially, interesting way to see the country. Local tourist offices operate booking schemes and, except at the height of the tourist season in July and August, it is not necessary to book in advance. B&Bs in the Scottish Tourist Board scheme will, at a minimum, be clean and comfortable. With luck you may find the proprietor friendly and a mine of local information with suggestions about the route to take or the things to see and do.

Particularly good value are Campus Hotels, the name given to b&b or self-catering facilities offered by the Scottish Universities in Aberdeen, St. Andrews, Dundee, Edinburgh, Glasgow and Stirling. These are available during vacations, in addition to accommodation, offer the use of university facilities like tennis courts and swimming pools.

There are about 80 youth hostels, many of them in the Highlands. These hostels provide very cheap accommodation, usually with dormitory-type bedrooms. It costs from £1 to £4 to join the Youth Hostels Association and accommodation costs from £1.80 to £3.50 a night depending on the facilities at the hostel. For details contact the Scottish Youth Hostels Association, 7 Glebe Crescent, Stirling, FK8 2JA (tel. 0786-2821).

Information on all types of accommodation is available at the Scottish Tourist Board and local tourist offices.

Prices quoted below, which are approximate, are for two persons sharing a room, and breakfast is included. A single room will normally cost more and, in most places, the price will vary according to the season.

Edinburgh

Caledonian Hotel
Princes Street.
Tel. (031) 225 2433,
254 rooms and right in the middle of the city. Expensive but you get what you pay for and the staff are genuinely pleasant and friendly. £70.

Campus Hotel Booking Office
Pollock Hotels, University of Edinburgh, 18 Holyrood Park Road, Edinburgh. Tel. (031) 667 1971. Very reasonable rates for B & B or self-catering in student accommodation at Easter and in the summer. From £10.
Heriot Watt University, Riccarton, Edinburgh Tel. (031) 449 5111. Very reasonable rates for B & B or self-catering in student accommodation at Easter and in the summer. From £10.

Kildonan Lodge Hotel
27 Craigmaillar Park.
Tel. (031) 667 2793.
Small, friendly and cheap.
£12.50
Thistle Hotel, 59 Manor Place. Tel. (031) 225 6144. A few minutes, walk from Princes Street. £20.

Borders

Beechwood Country House Hotel
Moffat.
Tel. (0683) 20210.
Good food, excellent wine list and a most comfortable house with many thoughtful touches.

Sunlaws House
Heiton, Kelso
(Tel. 0573 5331).
An opportunity to say that you stayed with the nobility—the proprietors are the

Duke and Duchess of Roxburgh. 21 rooms. £42.

Philipburn House Hotel
Selkirk
(Tel. 0750 20747).

Craiglethie House Hotel
Edleston, Peebles
(Tel. 07213 233).

Firth of Clyde

Ardenslate Hotel
James Street
Hunters Quay, Dunoon.
Tel. (0369) 2068. £20.

Firth of Clyde Islands

Auchrannie Hotel
Brodick, Isle of Arran.
Tel. (0770) 2234.

Royal Hotel
Rothesay.
Tel. (0700) 2500.

South-West

Antrim View
Sea Front
Ballantrae.
Tel. (046 583) 376.
Good value. £10.

Bruce Hotel
Queen Street
Newton Stewart.
Tel. (0671) 2294. £20.

Fordbank Country House Hotel
by Wigtown.
Tel. (09844) 2346.
Family-run hotel. £14.

Selkirk Arms Hotel
Kirkcudbright.
(Tel. 0557 30402).
Robbie Burns wrote the Selkirk Grace here. £20 - £30.

King's Arms Hotel
St Andrews Street
Castle Douglas
Tel. (0556) 2097. £15

Gigha Hotel
Isle of Gigha.
Tel. (005835) 254
20 minutes by car ferry from Kintyre. Modernised building, comfortable.

Sands Hotel
20 Louisa Drive, Girvan.
Tel. (0465) 2178. £11.

Turnberry Hotel
Turnberry
Tel. (06553) 202.
Large hotel on one the finest seaside golf courses in Britain. £45.

The Pickwick Hotel
19 Racecourse Road, Ayr
Tel. (0292) 60111. £25.

Westcliffe Hotel
Lousia Drive, Girvan.
Tel. (0465) 2128. £15.

Elderslie Hotel
Broomfields, Largs.
Tel. (0475) 686460. £22.

Glasgow

Greater Glasgow Tourist Board will send lists of hotels and guest houses on request. The city has a growing range of international hotels (Holiday Inn, Hospitality Inn) and their local equivalents such as the Stakis Ingram Hotel. Other comfortable central hotels are the Copthorne, the Central and the Crest. The Scottish Tourist Board's grading system is by no means infallible: we found uninhabitable one modest city centre hotel awarded two "crowns" by the Board. Some other choices:

The Albany
Bothwell Street
Tel: 041-248 2656. £50

Burbank Hotel
67-85 West Princes Street.
Tel: 041-332 4400. £18

Glynhill Hotel
169 Paisley Road, Renfrew
Tel: 041-886 5555
80 rooms but still in private ownership; this gives it a personal touch lacking often in the hotel chains. Convenient both for the airport and the city centre.

McLays Guest House
268 Renfrew Street
Tel: 041-332 4796.
£13-£20.

Campus Hotel Booking Office
University of Glasgow, 52 Hillhead Street. Tel: 041-330 5385. Very reasonable rates for B & B or self-catering in student accommodation at Easter and in the summer.

Campus Hotel Booking Office
University of Strathclyde (Dept GVL), 73 Rotten Row East. Tel: 041-552 4400 exts. 3560/3565. Student accommodation which is simple but clean and comfortable and good value; available only at Easter and during the summer.

West of the Clyde

Aird's Hotel
Port Appin
Tel. 063 173 236

Ardentinny Hotel
Tel. 036 981 2090.
Open March to October.
Was once favourite watering
hole of comedian Harry
Lauder.

Clifton House Hotel
Nairn
Tel. (0667) 53119
Interesting decor and owner,
very relaxing, good food.

Cozac Lodge
Glen Cannich by Beauly,
Inverness
(25 miles S.W. of Beauly)
Tel. (045 65) 263
Remote, spacious hotel in
magnificent scenery.

Culloden House
Tel. (0463) 790461
Bonnie Prince stayed here
the night before Culloden.

Polmailly House
Tel. (045 62) 343

Creggans Inn
Strachur
Tel. 036 986 279
Lovely setting on Sir Fitzroy
Maclean's estate on the
shores of Loch Fyne. £40

Crinan Hotel
Crinan
Tel. 0054 683 235

West Loch Hotel
Tarbet
Tel. 08802 283

Knipoch Hotel
Knipoch
Tel. 085 26 251.
Inverlochy Castle, Fort William. Tel. (0397) 2177. Won
the Good Hotel Guide 1984
award for its "incomparable
grandeur". £60-£95.

Inner Hebrides
Tiroran House

Tiroran, Mull
Tel. (06815) 232
Closed from mid-October to
May 1. £40.

Western Isles Hotel
Tobermory, Mull
Tel. (0688) 2012
Marvellous views over To-
bermory Bay.

Outer Hebrides

Broadford Hotel
Broadford, Isle of Skye
Tel. (047 12) 204. £20

Isle of Raasay Hotel
Raasay
Tel. (047862) 222. £18

Cross Inn
Ness, Isle of Lewis
Tel. (0851 181). £14

Scarista House
Scarista, Isle of Harris
Tel. (0859) 85 238
Former manse overlooking
beach.

Lochmaddy Hotel
Lochmaddy
North Uist
Tel. (08763) 285

Castlebay Hotel
Castlebay
Isle of Barra
Tel. (08714) 383

Royal Hotel
Portree
Tel. (0478) 2525
Associations with Bonnie
Prince Charlie.

Skeabost House Hotel
Skeabost Bridge, Skye
Tel. (047 032) 202

Central Scotland

Roman Camp Hotel
Main Street, Callender
Tel. (0877) 30003. £35

Arden House Guest House
Bracklinn Road,
Callendar
Tel. (0877) 30235
Used for location shots in
Doctor Finlay's Casebook
TV series, friendly with
good food. £12

Argyle House Hotel
127 North Street
St. Andrews
Tel. (0334) 73387

Old Course Hotel
St Andrews
Tel. (0334) 74371

Campus Holidays, Resi-
dences Office, University of
St Andrews, 79 North St. St
Andrews, Tel. (0334) 76161
ext. 544. Very reasonable
rates for B & B or self-catering in student accommoda-
tion at Easter and in the
summer.

**Campus Hotel Booking
Office**, University of Stirling, Stirling. Tel. (0786)
73171. Student-style ac-
commodation available in
January, June, July and
August on one of the loveliest campuses in Britain.
From £10

Four Seasons Hotel
St Fillans,
Perthshire
Tel. (076 485) 333
At east end of Loch Earn,
good for water sports.

Cromlix House
Dunblane
Tel. (0786) 822125

Killiecrankie Hotel
Killiecrankie
Pitlochry
Tel. (0796) 3220

Dunkeld House Hotel
Dunkeld
Tel. (035 02) 243

The Log Cabin Hotel
Kirkmichael
Perthshire
Tel. (025 081) 288
Scandinavian-style hotel four miles from Pitlochry.

Rufflets Hotel
Strathkinness Low Road
St Andrews
Tel. (0334) 72594
Attractive country house hotel.

Royal Jubilee Arms Hotel
Cortachy
Kirriemuir
Tel. (057 54) 381
Close to the Angus glens.

Salutation Hotel
34 South Street
Perth
Tel. (0738) 22166

Invereshie House Hotel
Kincraig
Tel. (054 04) 332

Ard na Coile Hotel
Newtonmore
Tel. (054 03) 214

The Cross
25/27 High Street
Kingussie
Tel. (054 02) 762
Primarily a small restaurant but has some delightful rooms. The proprietor is an interesting experience.

Northern Highlands

Altanharrie Inn
Ullapool
Tel. (085 483) 230
Only four rooms and the only hotel to which you have to be taken by boat. Closed October to Easter. £30

Bayview Hotel
Lybster
Tel. (05932) 346

The Ceilidh Place
Ullapool
Tel. (00854) 2103
Has conventional hotel accommodation and the Bunk House which is more spartan but ideal for families.

East Coast

Caledonian Thistle Hotel
Union Terrace
Aberdeen
Tel. (0224) 323 505
City centre hotel, 80 rooms.

Campus Hotel Booking Office, Conference and Vacation Letting Office, Kings College, Aberdeen. Tel. (0224) 480241. Very reasonable rates for B & B or self-catering in student accommodation at Easter and in the summer. From £10.

Fife Arms Hotel
Mar Road, Braemar
Tel. (03383) 644
80 rooms.

Forbes Arms
Bridge of Alford
Alford
Tel. (0336) 2108
Cheap and cheerful. £12

Kildrummy Castle Hotel
Kildrummy
36 miles west of Aberdeen
Tel. (03365) 288. £30

Marine Hotel
Shorehead
Stonehaven
Tel. (0569) 62936. £15

Old Mansion House Hotel
Auchterhouse
Dundee
Tel. (082 626) 366
Five miles from Dundee, this 17th-century house is set in attractive grounds. £32.50

Seymour House Hotel
Newport on Tay
Fife
Tel. (0382) 543122
Views of Dundee and the River Tay. Good value at £12.50

Letham Grange
Gowanbank, near Arbroath
Tel. (024189) 373
Has a curling rink and a golf course. £32.50

Tullich Lodge
Ballater
Tel. (0338) 55406
In baronial mansion with own character.

University of Dundee
Tel. (0382) 23181 Ext. 4040. Student accommodation is used out-of-term time and visitors have the use of university sports facilities such as tennis courts and swimming pool. £11.

Shetland

Burrastow House
Walls, Shetland
Tel. (059) 571 307. £28

Lerwick Thistle Hotel
South Road
Lerwick
Tel. (0595) 2166. £30

Orkney

Ayre Hotel
Kirkwall
Tel. (0856 79) 2197

Barony Hotel Birsay Tel. (0856 72) 327. £12	**Burnmouth Hotel** Hoy Tel. (0856 79) 297. £8	**Royal Hotel** Kirkwall Tel. (0856) 3477

ACTIVITIES

THINGS TO DO

Museums

Edinburgh

The National Gallery of Scotland (free) (open 10 a.m.-5 p.m. Mon.-Sat. and 2-5 p.m. on Saturdays) At the foot of the Mound.

The Royal Scottish Academy, Princes Street. Adults £1.20, children 50p. open 10 a.m.-7 p.m. (Sun. 2-5 p.m.).

Gallery of Modern Art, Belford Road, free, (open 10 a.m.-5 p.m. Mon.-Sat. and 2-5 p.m. on Saturdays).

The National Museum of Antiquities, Queen Street. Admission free.

Museum of Childhood, 38 High Street, free.

The Georgian House, 7 Charlotte Square, Admission for adult £1.20, children 60p. Town house furnished as a New Town House would have been in the period 1760-1820. Admission includes a video of Georgian Edinburgh.

Camera Obscura, Outlook Tower, Castlehill, 10 a.m.-5 p.m. adult £1.25, children 60p. Fascinating 19th-century version of TV projects a moving picture on to a screen. Very popular with children.

Gladstone's Land, 447b Lawnmarket 10 a.m.-5 p.m. Sun 2-5 p.m. adult £1 children 50p. 17th-century tenement with one floor furnished as as the home of a merchant and the ground floor reconstructed as a 17th-century shop.

Royal Museum of Scotland, Chambers Street 10 a.m.-5p.m. Sun 2-5 p.m. Free National collection of decorative arts, ethnography, natural sciences and technology. Often has special exhibitions and lectures.

Lothian Region

Scottish Agricultural Museum, Ingliston, near Edinburgh. Free. Open May-September (except Saturdays) Mon.-Fri. 10 a.m.-4p.m. Sun. 12-5 p.m.

House of the Binns, Linlithgow. National Trust for Scotland. Open Easter weekend (excluding Friday) and May-September 2-5 p.m. Admission is £1.40 for adult and 70 p for children . Earliest part of the house dates from 1478 with major 17th-century additions.

Linlithgow Palace, Linlithgow. Open all year. adults £1, children 50p. The ruined palace where Mary Queen of Scots was born.

Scottish Mining Museum, Lady Victoria Colliery, Newtongrange. Open all year (except Mondays) Tue-Fri. 10 a.m.-4:30 p.m. Saturdays and Sundays 12-5 p.m. Adult £1, children 50p.

Hopetoun House, South Queensferry. Open Easter and May-Sept. Adult £2, child £1. Home of the Hope family since 1703, this Adam house is set in magnificent parkland.

Glasgow

Burrell Collection. Open all year Mon-Sat. 10 a.m.-5 p.m. Sun 2-5 p.m. Free. Magnificent collection of paintings and artefacts of the ancient world and the Orient collected by a Glasgow shipowner, a Scottish version of William Randolph Hearst. A fitting gallery has been constructed in Pollok Country Park.

Charles Rennie Mackintosh Society, Queen's Cross, 870 Garscube Road. Open Tues., Thurs. and Fri. 12-5:30 p.m. and Sun. 2:30-5 p.m. Free. Exhibitions and library in a church designed by Mackintosh, an architect who went largely unrecognised in his own land.

Hunterian Museum and Hunterian Art Gallery, University of Glasgow, Hillhead Street, Free. Open all year Mon-Fri 9:30-5 p.m. Sat 9:30-1 p.m.

Third Eye Centre, 350 Sauchiehall Centre, Free. Open all year (not Mondays) Tues-Sat. 10 a.m.-5:30 p.m. Sat 10 a.m.-5:30p.m. Sun. 2-5:30 p.m. Multi-purpose arts centre promoting the visual arts through a programme of regular exhibitions.

The Tenement House, 145 Buccleuch Street. Open Easter-Oct 2-5p.m., Sun 2-4 p.m. and Nov-Mar Sat and Sun 2-4 p.m. Adult 90p. child 35p. 1892 house furnished as it was in its heyday.

The Borders

Abbotsford House, Melrose. Open Mar-Oct Mon-Sat 10 a.m.-5 p.m. Sun 2-5 p.m. Adult £1.50, child 75p. The 19th-century mansion built by Sir Walter Scott has many relics associated with famous characters in Scotland's history as well as Scott's library.

John Buchan Centre, Broughton, Biggar. Open Easter-Oct daily 2-5 p.m. Adult 50p. child 20p.

Galashiels Museum and Exhibition, Nether Mill, Huddersfield Street, Galashiels. Open Apr-Oct Mon-Sat 9 a.m.-5 p.m. and June-Sept Sun 1-5 p.m. Free.

Hawick Museum and the Scott Gallery. Wilton Lodge Park, Hawick. Open all year Apr-Sept Mon-Sat 10 a.m.-12 and 1-5 p.m. Sunday 2-5 p.m. Oct-Mar closed Saturdays Mon-Fri 1-4 p.m. Sun 2-4 p.m. Adult 45p child 25p.

Traquair House, Innerleithen, Peeblesshire. Open Easter-Oct daily 1:30-5:30 p.m. July, Aug and early Sept 10:30 a.m.-5:30 p.m. Adult £1.90, child 50p.

Central Region

Bannockburn Heritage Centre, Bannockburn, near Stirling. Open all year Adult

30p. child 30p.

Bo'ness and Kinneil Railway, Union Street, Bo'ness. Steam trains run on Easter weekend and during May-Sept on Sat and Sun.

Doune Motor Museum, Doune, Perthshire. Open Apr-Oct 10 a.m.-5. p.m. Adult £1.50, child 75p.

Dunblane Cathedral Museum, Dunblane, Perthshire.

South-West Scotland

Burns Cottage and Museuem, Alloway, near Ayr. Open all year Mon-Sat 10 a.m.-5 p.m. Sun (not winter) 2-5 p.m. Adult £1, child 50p.

Land O'Burns Centre, Murdoch's Lane, Alloway, near Ayr. Open all year 10 a.m.-5 p.m. and June-Sept 10 a.m.-9 p.m. Free.

Burns House, Burns Street, Dumfries. Open all year (closed Sun and Mon Oct-Mar) Mon-Sat 10 a.m.-1 p.m. and 2-5 p.m., Sun 2-5 p.m. The house where Burns spent the last years of his life.

Gladstone Court Museum, Biggar. Open Easter-Oct Mon-Sat 10 a.m.-12:30 and 2-5 p.m. Sun 2-5 p.m. Adult 80p, child 40p. Interesting recreation of 19th/early 20th-century street.

Scottish Maritime Museum, Laird Forge, Gottries Road, Irvine. Open occasionally. Admission fee for adult 50p, child 20p.

Souter Johnnie's Cottage, Main Street, Kirkoswald. Open Easter-Sept. daily 12-5 p.m. Adult 60p, child 30p.

Old Blacksmith's Shop, Gretna Green. Open all year Mar-Oct 9-8 rest of year 10 a.m.-5 p.m. Reminder of the

days when young couples eloped from England to take advantage of Scotland's marriage laws.

Carlyle's Birthplace, Ecclefechan, Dumfriesshire. Open Easter Oct. (closed Sun.) Mon-Sat. 10 a.m. -6 p.m. Adult 60p, child 30p.

Fife

Andrew Carnegie Birthplace Museum, Moodie Street, Dunfermline. Open all year Apr-Oct Mon-Sat 11a.m.-5 p.m., Wed 11 a.m.-8 p.m., Sun 2-5 p.m., Nov-Mar daily 2-4 p.m. Free.

Crawford Centre for the Arts, 93 North Street, St. Andrews. Open all year Mon-Sat 10 a.m.-5 p.m. Sun 2-5 p.m. Free. University arts centre with various exhibitions and performances, including some excellent children's shows.

Fife Folk Museum, The Weigh House, Ceres, near Cupar. Open Apr-Oct (closed Tues) Mon-Sat 2-5 p.m., Sun 2:30-5:30 p.m. Adult 50p, child 20p.

North Fife Light Vessel, the Harbour, Anstruther. Open May-Sep. 10 a.m.-6 p.m. Adult 40p, child 25p.

Scottish Fisheries Museum, Harbourhead, Anstruther. Open all year Apr-Oct Mon-Sat 10 a.m.-5:30 p.m. Sun 2-5 p.m., Nov-Mar (closed Tues) 2-5 p.m. Sat 10 a.m.-5:30 p.m. Adult 85p, child 40p.

Grampian

Aberdeen Art Gallery. Schoolhill, Aberdeen. Open all year Mon-Sat 10a.m.-5 p.m., Thurs 10 a.m.-8 p.m. Sundays 2-5 p.m.

Arbuthnot Museum, St Peter Street, Peterhead. Open all year (closed Sun) Mon-Sat 10 a.m.-12 p.m. and 2-5 p.m. Free.

Brander Museum, The Square, Huntly. Open all year Tue-Sat 10 a.m.-12 p.m. and 2-4 p.m. Free.

Buckie Maritime Museum, Townhouse, West Cluny Place, Buckie. Open all year Mon-Fri 10 a.m.-8 p.m. Sat 10 a.m.-12. Free.

Carnegie Museum, Town Hall, The Square, Inverurie. Open all year Mon-Fri 2-5 p.m. Sat 10 a.m.-12. Free.

Crathes Castle, Banchory. Open Easter and May-Sept Mon-Sat 11 a.m.-6 p.m. Sun 2-6 p.m. Adult £1.40p, child 70p. 16th-century home of the Burnetts of Leys, it has remarkable painted ceilings and some original Scottish vernacular furniture.

Fochabers Folk Museum, Pringle Antiques, High Stret, Fochabers. Open all year Mon-Fri 9:30 a.m.-5:30 p.m. Adult 40p, child 20p.

Grampian Transport Museum and **Railway Museum**, Alford, Aberdeenshire. Open Apr-Sept daily 10:30 a.m.-5 p.m. Adult £1, child 50p.

North East of Scotland Agricultural Heritage Centre, Aden Country Park, Mintlaw near Peterhead. Open Easter and May-Sept daily 12-6 p.m. Free.

Tomintoul Visitor Centre, The Square, Tomintoul. Open Apr-Oct Mon-Sat 9 a.m.-6 p.m. Sundays 11 a.m.-7 p.m.

Highland Region

Culloden Visitor Centre, Culloden Moor, near Inverness. Easter-Oct 9:30 a.m.-5:30 p.m., Jun-Sept 9 a.m.-7:30 p.m. Adult £1.10, child 55p. Excellent displays and multi-lingual audio visual programmes on the site of the Battle of Culloden (1746).

Dingwall Museum, Town Hall, Dingwall. Open Apr.-Sept. Free.

Eden Court Gallery, Eden Court Theatre, Inverness. Open all year Mon-Sat and some Suns 10:30 a.m.-10 p.m. Free to exhibitions.

Gairloch Heritage Museum, Gairloch, Ross-shire. Open Easter-Sept (closed Sun) 10 a.m.-6 p.m. Adult 30p, child 10p.

Glenfinnan Monument and **Visitor Centre**, Glenfinnan, Inverness-shire. Open Easter-Jun and Sept-Oct daily 10 a.m.-5:30 p.m., July-Aug daily 9 a.m.-6:30 p.m. Adult 55p, child 25p. Commemorates the day, August 19, 1745, when on this spot Bonnie Prince Charlie raised his standard.

Highland Folk Museum, Duke Street, Kingussie. Open all year Nov-Mar Mon-Fri 10 a.m.-3 p.m., Apr-Oct Mon-Sat 10 a.m.-6 p.m. Sun 2-6 p.m. Adult £1, child 50p.

Landmark Visitor Centre, Carrbridge. Open all year winter 9:30 a.m.-5:30 p.m. summer 9:30 a.m.-9:30 p.m. Adult £1.95, child £1.10.

Loch Ness Monster Exhibition, Drumnadrochit, Invernesshire. Open all year 10 a.m.-4 p.m. July and Aug 9 a.m.-9:30 p.m. Adult £1.35, child 45p. Strathnaver Museum, Bettyhill, near Thurso. Open Jun-Sept Mon-Sat 2-5 p.m.

Queen's Own Highlanders Regimental Museum, Fort George, Ardersier, Inverness-shire. Free. Open all year Apr-Sept Mon-Fri 10 a.m.-6:30 p.m. Sun 2-6:30 p.m., Oct-Mar Mon-Fri 10 a.m.-4 p.m.

Strathclyde

David Livingstone Centre, Blantyre. Open all year Mon-Sat 10 a.m.-6 p.m. Sundays 2-6 p.m. Adult £1.25, child 50p.

Esadale Island Folk Museum, Easdale Island, off Seil Island, by Oban. Open Apr-Oct daily 10:30 a.m.-5:30 p.m. Adult 50p, child 20p.

New Lanark, The Counting House, New Lanark, Lanark Village. Open at all times; exhibitions in mills usually open summer daily 10 a.m.-5 p.m. Free. Reconstruction of the mill associated with the social reformer Robert Owen.

Tayside

Angus Folk Museum, Glamis. Open Easter and May-Sept daily 12-5 p.m. Adult 90p, child 40p.

Arbroath Abbey, Arbroath. Open Jan-Mar and Oct-Dec Mon-Sat 9:30 a.m.-4 p.m. Sun 2-4 p.m., Apr-Sept Mon-Sat 9:30 a.m.-7 p.m. Sun 2-7 p.m.. Adult 50p, child 25p.

Barrie's Birthplace, 9 Brechin Road, Kirriemuir, Angus. Open Easter and May-Sept Mon-Sat 11 a.m.-5:30 p.m. Sun 2-4:30 p.m. Adult 60p, child 30p. Museum devoted to the creator of Peter Pan.

Blair Castle, Blair Atholl, Pitlochry. Open Easter and Apr-Oct Mon-Sat 10 a.m.-6 p.m. Sun 2-6 p.m. Adult £2, child £1.20.
Scottish Tartans Museum, Davidson House, Drummond Street, Comrie. Open all year Apr-Oct Mon-Sat 10 a.m.-5 p.m. Sun 2-4 p.m., Nov-Mar Mon-Fri 2-5 p.m. Sat 10 a.m.-1 p.m.
Barrack Street Museum, Dundee. Open all year Mon-Sat 10 a.m.-5 p.m. Free.
Broughty Castle Museum, Dundee. Open all year Mon-Thurs and Sat 10 a.m.-1 p.m. and 2-5 p.m. July-Sept, also Sun 2-5 p.m. Particularly interesting on whaling.
Frigate Unicorn, Victoria Dock, Dundee. Open Apr-Sept (closed Tues) 11 a.m.-1 p.m. and 2-5 p.m. Sun 2-5 p.m. Adult 50p, child 25p.
Glamis Castle, Glamis. Open Easter and May-Sept (closed Sat) daily 1-5 p.m. Adult £2 child £1.
McManus Galleries, Albert Square, Dundee. Open all year Mon-Sat 10 a.m.-5. p.m Free.
Meigle Museum, Meigle, Perthshire. Open all year (not Sundays) Adult 50p, child 25p. Remarkable collection of sculptured monuments of the Celtic church said to be one of the most notable in Western Europe.
RRS Discovery, Victoria Dock, Dundee. Open Apr-Sept. Adult £1, child 60p. The ship, built in Dundee, which took Captain Scott on his ill-fated voyage to the Antarctic is now being renovated and is the centre of an exhibition.
Scone Palace, near Perth. Open Easter-Sept Mon-Sat

10 a.m.-5:30 p.m. Sun 2-5:30 p.m. Adult £1.90, child £1.50.

Firth of Clyde Islands

Bute Museum, Stuart Street, Rothesay, Isle of Bute.
Museum of Islay Life, Port Charlotte, Isle of Islay.
Isle of Arran Heritage Centre, Rosaburn, Brodick, Isle of Arran.

Orkney

Skara Brae. Adult £1, child 50p. Dwellings dating from 1400 to 1600 BC.
Stromness Museum, 52 Alfred Street, Stromness.

Shetland

Jarlshof, Sumburgh Head. Adult 50p, child 25p. One of the most remarkable archaeological sites in Britain, containing the remains of three villages occupied from Bronze Age to Viking times. Shetland Museum, Lower Hillhead, Lerwick. Free.

Outer Hebrides

Black House, Arnol, Isle of Lewis. South Uist Folk Museum, Bualadhubh, Eochar, South Uist.

Inner Hebrides

Iona Abbey, Isle of Iona.
Colbost Museum, Colbost, Isle of Skye.
Dunvegan Castle, Dunvegan, Isle of Skye. Home of the clan Macleod.
Skye Cottage Museum, Portree, Isle of Skye.

Theatre: Edinburgh has the Lyceum Theatre and the

more experimental Traverse Theatre, while Glasgow's Citizens' Theatre has a deservedly high reputation. There are repertory theatres in Dundee, Perth and St. Andrews and during the summer the Pitlochry Festival Theatre provides professional performances.

Sports: Hill-walking, climbing, skiing, golf and fishing are only some of the most obvious sports available, and are the subject of organised special interest holidays. The Scottish Tourist Board has a useful free booklet, *Adventure and Special Interest Holidays in Scotland*. This includes details of various holidays including not only the activities already mentioned, but also such diverse pursuits as leathercraft courses near Loch Ness, summer painting holidays in Perthshire and sub aqua diving.

Golf: Scotland is the home of golf and the game can claim to be the national sport. There are hundreds of courses, most of them open to the public. Even the most famous courses like St. Andrews or Carnoustie are public courses and anyone prepared to pay the appropriate fee is entitled to play at these courses.

Climbing and Walking: Scotland has more than 500 mountains over 3,000 feet (900 metres) and provides a wide range of climbs and walks. The importance of proper equipment and dress cannot be over-emphasised. The Scottish Tourist Board publishes *Scotland for Hill-Walking* and the Countryside Commission has a free leaflet on the West Highland Way, one of the best walks in Scotland. The British Mountaineering Council (Crawford House, Precinct Centre, Booth Street East, Manchester M13 9RZ, tel: 061-273 5835) can provide more information about mountaineering clubs.

Fishing: Some of Britain's best fishing is to be found in Scotland. Local permits must be obtained; details of where to get these are available from tourist offices. The trout season is from mid-March to early October.

Skiing: Skiing has become increasingly popular as facilities have improved. The main centres are at Aviemore, Glencoe, Glenshee and the Lecht. There is also the largest artificial ski slope in Britain at Hillend in the Pentland hills just south of Edinburgh.

DIPLOMATIC MISSIONS

EMBASSIES

United States
3 Regent Terrace
Edinburgh EH7
Tel: 031 556 8315

Australia
Hobart House
Hanover Street
Edinburgh EH2
Tel: 031 226 6271

Austria
33/34 Charlotte Square
Edinburgh EH2
Tel: 031 225 1516

Belgium
89 Constitution Street
Edinburgh EH6
Tel: 031 554 3333

Canada
Canadian Trade Office
Tel: 041 204 1373

Denmark
50 East Fettes Avenue
Edinburgh EH4
Tel: 031 552 7101
49 Meadowside
Dundee
Tel: 0382 23044

Finland
50 East Fettes Avenue
Edinburgh EH4
Tel: 031 552 7101
26 East Dock Street
Dundee
Tel: 0382 23111

France
7 Weymss Place
Edinburgh EH3
Tel: 031 225 7954
30 Whitehall Street
Dundee
Tel: 0382 29311

German Federal Republic
116 Eglinton Crescent
Edinburgh EH12
Tel: 031 337 2323

Greece
9 Regent Terrace
Edinburgh EH7
Tel: 031 556 1701

Iceland
50 Grange Road
Edinburgh EH9
Tel: 031 667 2166

Italy
6 Melville Crescent
Edinburgh EH3
Tel: 031 226 3631
16 Kelso Street
Dundee
Tel: 0382 65222

Monaco
39 Castle Street
Edinburgh EH2
Tel: 031 225 1200

Netherlands
8/12 George street
Edinburgh EH2
Tel: 031 225 8494
26 East Dock Stret
Dundee
Tel: 0382 23111

Norway
50 East Fettes Avenue
Edinburgh EH4
Tel: 031 552 7101
49 Meadowside
Dundee
Tel: 0382 23044

Portugal
Gogar Park House
167 Glasgow Park
Edinburgh EH12
Tel: 031 3395345

South Africa
Stock Exchange House
69 West George Street
Glasgow G2 1BX
Tel: 041 221 3114

Spain
51 Lauderdale street
Edinburgh EH9
Tel: 031 447 1113

Sweden
6 St John's Place
Edinburgh EH6
Tel: 031 554 6631

Switzerland
6 Moston Terrace
Edinburgh EH9
Tel: 031 667 2386

The following countries do not have consulates in Scotland. Below are listed the telephone numbers of their London embassies. In all cases it is necessary to dial 01 if dialling from outside London.

Algeria
221 7800
Argentina consular matters are dealt with by the Brazillian Embassy (see list)

Bahrain
370 5132
Brazil
499 0877
Burma
499 8841
Chile
580 6392
China
636 9375
Iran
584 8101
Iraq
584 7141
Ireland
235 2171
Israel
937 8050
Japan
493 6030
Jordan
937 3685
Kuwait
589 4533

Lebanon
229 7265
Mexico
235 6393
Netherlands
584 5040
Pakistan
235 2044
Panama
353 4792
Peru
235 1917
Philippines
937 1600
Poland
580 4324
Saudia Arabia
235 0831
Syria
245 9012
USSR
229 3628

LITERATURE

FURTHER READING

History
Fraser, A: *Mary Queen of Scots.*

Prebble, John: *Culloden* and *The Highland Clearances.*

Smout, T.C: *A History of the Scottish People 1560-1830.* Fontana

Smout, T.C: *A Century of the Scottish People 1830-1950.* Fontana

Poetry
Robert Burns: many editions available

William McGonagall: *Last Poetic Gems.* Winter/ Duckworths. Scotland's (and perhaps the world's) worst poet, who has become something of a cult.

Miscellaneous
Allan, John R: *The Northeast Lowlands of Scotland.* Robert Hale.

Berry, Simon and Whyte, Hamish: *Glasgow Observed.* John Donald Publishers.

Brogden, W.A: *Aberdeen, An Illustrated Architectural Guide.* Scottish Academic Press.

Daiches, David: *A Companion to Scottish Culture.* Arnold.

Daiches, David (ed.): *Edinburgh: A Travellers' Companion.*

Daiches, David: *Glasgow.* Andre Deutsch.

Graham, Cuthbert: *Portrait of Aberdeen and Deeside.* Robert Hale.

House, Jack: *The Heart of Glasgow.* Richard Drew Publishing.

Johnson, Dr. Samuel: *A Journey to the Western Isles*; and Boswell, James: *Journal of a Tour to the Hebrides.* These are two accounts of the same trip made in the late 18th century by the great lexicographer and his biographer. A combined volume is published by Oxford University Paperbacks.

Munro, Michael: *The Patter, A Guide to Current Glasgow Usage.* Glasgow District Libraries.

Exploring Scotland's Heritage. Excellent series published by Her Majesty's Stationery Office.

ART/PHOTO
CREDITS

142-143	Douglas Corrance	197	Dymphna Byrne	254	Topham Picture Library
144	Douglas Corrance	198-199	Douglas Corrance		
145	Douglas Corrance	200	Douglas Corrance	255	Douglas Corrance
148	Douglas Corrance	201	Douglas Corrance	256	Tony Stone Worldwide
149	Douglas Corrance	203	Marius Alexander		
150	Tony Stone Worldwide	204	Douglas Corrance	258	Topham Picture Library
		205	Douglas Corrance		
151	Douglas Corrance	206	Douglas Corrance	259	Douglas Corrance
152	Marcus Brooke	207	Douglas Corrance	261	Topham Picture Library
153	Marcus Brooke	208-209	Douglas Corrance		
154	Marcus Brooke	210	Douglas Corrance	262-263	National Galleries of Scotland
155	Douglas Corrance	212	Douglas Corrance		
156	Marcus Brooke	213	Douglas Corrance	264	National Galleries of Scotland
157(L)	Douglas Corrance	214(L)	Marcus Brooke		
157(R)	Douglas Corrance	214(R)	Marcus Brooke	265	Tony Stone Worldwide
158	Marcus Brooke				
159(L)	Douglas Corrance	215	Eric Ellington	266	National Galleries of Scotland
159(R)	Douglas Corrance	216	Marcus Brooke		
160	Douglas Corrance	217	Marcus Brooke	267	National Galleries of Scotland
161	Douglas Corrance	218	Eric Ellington		
162-163	Denis Waugh	219	Douglas Corrance	268	National Galleries of Scotland
164	Alain Le Garsmeur	220	Eric Ellington		
166	Marcus Brooke	221	Eric Ellington	269	National Galleries of Scotland
167D	Douglas Corrance	223	Tony Stone Worldwide		
168-169	Douglas Corrance			270	Marcus Brooke
170	Alain Le Garsmeur	224(L)	Douglas Corrance	271	Eric Ellington
171	Marcus Brooke	224(R)	Douglas Corrance	272	Kenneth Griffiths/ Topham
172	Douglas Corrance	225	Alain Le Garsmeur		
173	Eric Ellington	226-227	Douglas Corrance	274-275	Denis Waugh
174	Eric Ellington	228	Douglas Corrance	276	Douglas Corrance
175	Tony Stone Worldwide	230	Douglas Corrance	277	Douglas Corrance
		231	Eric Ellington	278	Marcus Brooke
176	Alain Le Garsmeur	232	Hans Hoefer	279	Topham Picture Library
178-179	Landscape Only	233	Topham Picture Library		
180-181	Topham Picture Library			280	Douglas Corrance
		234	Alain Le Garsmeur	281	Douglas Corrance
182	Douglas Corrance	235	Douglas Corrance	284-285	Douglas Corrance
184(L)	Marcus Brooke	236	Douglas Corrance	287	Douglas Corrance
184(R)	Dymphna Byrne	237	Douglas Corrance	288-289	Denis Waugh
185	Douglas Corrance	238-239	Topham Picture Library	290	Topham Picture Library
186	Douglas Corrance				
187	Douglas Corrance	240	Marcus Brooke	291	Tony Stone Worldwide
188	Tony Stone Worldwide	242	Tony Stone Worldwide		
				292	Douglas Corrance
189	Tony Stone Worldwide	243	Douglas Corrance	294-295	Eric Ellington
		244	Tony Stone Worldwide	296	Eric Ellington
190	Douglas Corrance				
191	Eric Ellington	245	Douglas Corrance		
192	Topham Picture Library	246	Denis Waugh		
		248	Douglas Corrance		
195	Marius Alexander	250-251	Denis Waugh		
196	Denis Waugh	252-253	Douglas Corrance		

INDEX